*Saint James School
of Maryland*

Saint James School of Maryland

175 Years

Edited by
W. L. Prehn

Foreword by David Hein

WIPF & STOCK · Eugene, Oregon

SAINT JAMES SCHOOL OF MARYLAND
175 Years

Copyright © 2021 Wipf and Stock. All rights reserved. Except for brief quotations in critical publications or reviews, no part of this book may be reproduced in any manner without prior written permission from the publisher. Write: Permissions, Wipf and Stock Publishers, 199 W. 8th Ave., Suite 3, Eugene, OR 97401.

Wipf & Stock
An Imprint of Wipf and Stock Publishers
199 W. 8th Ave., Suite 3
Eugene, OR 97401

www.wipfandstock.com

PAPERBACK ISBN: 978-1-5326-5259-2
HARDCOVER ISBN: 978-1-5326-5260-8
EBOOK ISBN: 978-1-5326-5261-5

04/01/21

Scriptural quotations are from the *New Revised Standard Version* Copyright © 1989 by the National Council of the Churches of Christ in the USA

Contents

Foreword by David Hein | vii
Editor's Preface | ix
Contributors | xv

1. "Cadets of the Church": A Prologue to the History of Saint James | 1
   Frederick Jordan

2. The "Soul of the Thing": Saint James
   in the Beginning, 1842–61 | 13
   W. L. Prehn

3. Slavery, War, and Destruction:
   The College of St. James, 1861–64 | 51
   Emilie Amt

4. Reconstruction of a Vision: The Onderdonk Era Begins,
   Saint James School, 1869–95 | 86
   John McCardell

5. Adrian Onderdonk's Memoir: Saint James School, 1903–39 | 107
   Annotated by W. L. Prehn

6. Father Owens, Eighth Headmaster of Saint James, 1955–84 | 137
   Stuart Dunnan

7. Dunnan of Saint James, 1992–2017 | 154
   W. L. Prehn

Bibliography | 181
Index of Names | 191

Foreword

ALL SCHOOLS ARE HISTORICAL, because all have histories, but few are historic. Saint James School manages to be both, for it has played a distinctive role not only in the lives of its own students and masters but also in the history of American education at large. The corps of able writer-researchers assembled here set forth in accurate detail and in lively prose the course of that influential history. Thus their work should be of interest and value not only to Saint James parents, faculty, and alumni but also to any reader curious about the origins and history of independent schools in America.

That Saint James is a historic and highly regarded foundation does not mean that it has been spared the challenges that have confronted other small schools across the land. During this school's history, some economic eras have proved more propitious than others, some social conditions more hospitable, some headmasters more visionary and capable. In this book, readers will traverse the changing topography of that historical course: the ups and downs of a unique institution south of Hagerstown, Maryland. They will discover that institutional history is embedded in the social, economic, and political history of three centuries. Although geographically isolated, Saint James has never been able to get away from it all. Wars, financial depressions, changing mores: in the chapters that follow, these factors and others are vividly present, as they must be.

If there is one feature above all others which has enabled Saint James to survive—indeed, it's a *sine qua non* of any estimable enterprise that endures through good times and bad—it is that Saint James has stood fast to its core traditions concerning true belief and right conduct. In this way, the school has represented something valuable in its own right. Its chief aim has not been to offer a commercial package appealing only to the present day, in blind conformity with contemporary standards. For this reason, it has succeeded: by consistently embodying and making available a strong, clear, and beneficial alternative within the marketplace of secondary education. In the changing winds of time, Saint James has smacked more of the oak than of the willow.

Affiliated with the Episcopal Church in the United States, Saint James has nevertheless been successful in preserving an independent stance. Holding fast to a traditional Christian ethos, Saint James could never be accused of trying to be trendier than thou. Thus it has avoided some of the vicissitudes that have afflicted liberal Protestantism in the United States since at least the turn of the twenty-first century. Partly because American Episcopal schools do offer a clear alternative to mainstream culture—to secular state schools in particular—their history, largely a story of institutional building and flourishing, has not tracked the history of Episcopal congregations, for the most part a story of decline.

Although social context and national events are important for readers to keep in mind, the richest features of the history revealed in these pages are those that are local, specific, concrete, and personal. These telling details are displayed in abundance. In teaching and learning, no innovative programs, no dazzling assessment plans, can even approach the significance of the interaction between each student and his or her teacher, coach, headmaster, or dorm parent. Nor can an outstanding curriculum, coupled with demonstrated excellence in interscholastic sports, suffice: Saint James unabashedly keeps faith with the view that truth is transcendent, that values are eternal, that participation in the sacrificial life of Jesus Christ is indeed the Way, the noblest path to human flourishing. Thus at Saint James the center of school life is the chapel.

Keeping up with but not surrendering to the times, Saint James has proved itself over its long history to be conservative but not hidebound, happy but not self-satisfied. Resilient and timely because grounded in timeless principles, this little school provides not only an outpost of sound teaching and learning but also a stimulating example for others on the American educational scene.

David Hein
Senior Fellow
George C. Marshall Foundation
Lexington, Virginia

Editor's Preface

THE FOLLOWING SEVEN CHAPTERS offer the reader a history of Saint James School from its founding in 1842 through the twenty-sixth year of Stuart Dunnan's headship, which coincided with the one hundred and seventy-fifth anniversary of the school. This book covers the history by focusing on the long headships of Kerfoot, Onderdonk, Onderdonk *fils*, Owens, and Dunnan. No less than 140 years of Saint James history are accounted for in these five headships. When we survey the history of the school, we see that these were defining executive tenures. Although the headships of Dr. Vernon B. Kellett (1942–55) and the Reverend Richard H. Baker, Jr. (1984–91) were significant indeed, by concentrating on the five very long reigns, we are able to publish a manageable history of the school.

In our enjoyment of and commitment to the latter-day school at Fountain Rock, we sometimes forget that Saint James School is important in the history of American education itself. Saint James is not only one of the oldest Episcopal boarding schools in the United States created as a boarding school; Saint James was the second iteration of the scholastic vision of William Augustus Muhlenberg (1796–1877) whose work gave rise to some of the best college preparatory schools in the United States.

Saint James and other church schools such as St. Paul's, Concord, New Hampshire, and St. Mark's, Southborough, Massachusetts, were closely related by their philosophy, practice, and exchanges of personnel. They were more than a national network extending from New Hampshire to California. As the history of Saint James reveals, these educators were a scholastic brotherhood and a merry fellowship of teachers who felt the freedom to pursue excellence in all it means to be a human being. Close relationships and an inspiring common purpose made these academic institutions successful. It was the rare alumnus who did not sense that he was gaining something very special indeed during his schooldays. Because they continuously got good results with all sorts of young men, Kerfoot and the other headmasters of these private schools were often asked for their advice by common-school boosters and public high school promoters.[1]

The writers who bring you *Saint James School of Maryland: 175 Years* are historians. They used primary and secondary sources to fashion their reflections upon the spiritual, economic, political, and social forces which shaped the school in certain eras. They offer interpretations of the school and of key players. They are not concerned so much with timelines and chronologies as with the way people and ideas shaped the future. The reader will be treated here to good scholarship and excellent writing. I thank the chapter authors for their contributions. Professor David Hein, Senior Fellow at the George C. Marshall Foundation, knows as much about our historic Episcopal schools as anyone alive. I am grateful to him for his generous foreword, for his steady interest in this project, and for his skillful guidance of the editor. His good taste and wisdom are manifest in many other parts of the book.

Frederick Jordan of Woodberry Forest School gives us a great orientation to the subject at hand. Dr. Jordan is an expert on the history of the rise of the boarding school in America. He began his teaching career at Saint James, where he served from 1977–80. He is also a scholar sensitive and candid about the changes our boarding schools have lived through and the secularization many have experienced. Emilie Amt of Hood College is a respected scholar of uncommon commitment to forgotten people and events in our American story. The scholarship Dr. Amt offers in this book is no less than groundbreaking.

Dr. McCardell, lately the vice chancellor of Sewanee, had the most difficult assignment. When he cheerfully accepted the request to write about Henry Onderdonk's twenty-six-year headship, extending from 1869 to 1895, Dr. McCardell was faced with the challenge that he would

---

1. According to James McLachlan (1970), there were fewer than five hundred high schools in America in 1870. Moreover, many of the old academies in New England—including Andover and Exeter—were not the academic flagships they became after the Civil War. The schools founded by Muhlenberg, Breck, Kerfoot, Van Bokkelen, the Coit brothers, and their ilk during the antebellum period got such impressive results that they were the admired models for founders of many public high schools. Endicott Peabody founded a Muhlenberg-type prep school in Groton, Massachusetts, in 1884. So quickly did Groton become admired for the work it was doing with boys that public-school boosters came to Peabody for advice.

have fewer primary sources than any other contributor. Dr. McCardell would appreciate the remark of an eminent historian and Saint James alumnus who noted in the preface of one of his own books that "the chief problem in writing this work was not the overabundance of unsubstantiated rumors but a scarcity of materials about key figures."[2] John McCardell has shown his scholarly mettle! With the help of Mary Klein of the Maryland Diocesan Archives; Mr. Camp, Senior Master at Fountain Rock; and the sweat of his own brow, Dr. McCardell presents us with an excellent short history of the school in the first Onderdonk era.[3] It is a most important chapter, because Henry Onderdonk *refounded* an institution the Civil War destroyed.

We treat the reader to the interesting four-decade headship of Henry's son Adrian "as told by himself." We made the decision to allow Mr. O. to speak of his beloved Saint James by way of his quite revealing *Memoir*. The chapter offers both insight into the essence of Saint James and plenty of comic relief. In that curious autobiography, the younger Onderdonk shows himself a true school man who understood what Thomas Arnold called "boy nature." That he was elected to the original Headmaster's Association should be a matter of pride for those who love Saint James School.

The current rector and headmaster has provided the chapter on Father Owens, who led the school from 1955 to 1984. Dunnan's is a perceptive and heartfelt portrait of a great man. The chapter reveals that Owens was far more than a preserver of the traditions of the school. He was an innovator even as he dared the Vandals to tamper with his inheritance in terms of churchmanship and piety.

---

2. Bertram Wyatt-Brown, SJS Class of 1949, Preface to his *House of Percy* (New York: Oxford, 1994), viii.

3. Kemp Hall burned down in 1857. There was a fire in Claggett in 1910 and the building was destroyed by fire in 1926. J. B. Kerfoot's papers were incinerated after his death, when a fire burned the headquarters of the Episcopal Diocese of Pittsburgh. On top of these calamities for the historian, Dr. Muhlenberg ordered his executive assistant and official biographer, Miss Ayres, to destroy his letters and papers after his death. Unfortunately, she obeyed him. Surely Muhlenberg's papers were full of priceless correspondence between him, Kerfoot, and many others associated with the church school movement. The Maryland Diocesan Archives and the Maryland Historical Society are full of Saint-James-related primary sources. Mr. Ted Camp has done an exemplary job of organizing and cataloguing the school archives, and there are plans for such an expansion of these resources that Saint James will soon become a center of scholarly studies of the history of the nineteenth-century church-school movement on both sides of the Atlantic.

Last among chapters is the sketch of the headship of Stuart Dunnan. As we go to press, Father Dunnan is in his twenty-ninth year as headmaster. Assessing the work of a sitting head is a tricky business. I have only attempted a kind of bas relief carved into the backdrop of his numerous achievements. I hope that readers will see in chapter 7 reasons why Saint James School has once again a national reputation.

Father Dunnan wanted a history of the school prepared for the 175th Anniversary in the 2017–2018 session. We now have something to offer, even if it was not on the dais for the festivities. I hasten to say that the history is not a coffee-table book. The alumna or alumnus looking for a detailed account of his or her years at the school—in each case these were the "glory days" and "best years" of the school, of course!—will be disappointed. Current and past faculty and staff who expected to find long accounts of the curricular, instructional, and extracurricular programs which they rightly cherish will not find those inspiring stories here. Father Dunnan wants the book to be the beginning of a Saint James history project directed by Mr. Ted Camp. The project will produce ongoing articles and, eventually, a much more comprehensive history of the school. We are all grateful for the beautiful historical displays we were treated to during the 175th Anniversary celebrations. These splendid exhibits were the joint work of Mr. Camp, Mrs. Margaret McGuigan and her Development Office staff, trusted students, and enthusiastic parents.

One hundred and seventy-five years is a considerable amount of history. If reckoned in boarding-school time, it is thirty-five generations. The events that ought to be recounted, the stories that must be told, and the hundreds of personal biographies upon which we would do well to meditate if we would understand professional quality, expertise, vocation, and commitment in the complex life of a beloved boarding school: Only a fraction of these have made it into this particular effort. We intend in this history of a great and historic American school to come to a better understanding of "the soul of the thing," in Dr. Muhlenberg's words. We have wanted to know as much about the *why* of Saint James as the *how* and the *who*. We pray that the following chapters will suffice for the purpose.

I wish to heartily thank the people at Wipf & Stock for their optimism about the project, their great professional competence, and their general gregariousness throughout the process. Matthew Wimer and Daniel Lanning got the ball rolling. George Callihan built the momentum. Caleb

Editor's Preface

Shupe, copy editor, and Rachel Saunders, typesetter, did many tedious chores with grace and dispatch. Mike Surber designed the cover and Joshua Little nursed the book all along to completion.

W. L. Prehn
"Stone Branch,"
Augusta County, Virginia
Autumn 2020

Contributors

Emilie Amt, DPhil (Oxford) is the Hildegarde Pilgram Professor of History at Hood College in Frederick, Maryland. Educated at Swarthmore and Oxford, she has published numerous books and articles on medieval English history. Since 2010, her historical work has focused on African Americans in western Maryland in the era of slavery. She was awarded the 2017 Nelson R. Burr Prize by the Historical Society of the Episcopal Church.

D. Stuart Dunnan, DPhil (Oxford), received AB and AM degrees in history from Harvard University in 1981. In 1983, he received the BA in Theology from Oxford University, proceeded to the MA in 1990, and was awarded the DPhil degree in Historical Theology in 1991. He was elected headmaster of Saint James in 1992. Dunnan is an Episcopal priest and a head of school with uncommon scholarly credentials. He is a much sought after speaker, preacher, and teacher, and he has published two volumes of writings and addresses to date.

David Hein, PhD (Virginia), is a senior fellow at the George C. Marshall Foundation, in Lexington, Virginia. He is also an affiliated scholar of the John Jay Institute and a trustee of Saint James School. He was educated at St. Paul's School (Brooklandville, Maryland), the University of Virginia, and the University of Chicago. He began his teaching career as an English master and coach at Blue Ridge School, a historic boarding school in the mountains of Virginia. Professor Hein's publications include ten books and more than sixty articles in the *Journal of Military History*, the *Intercollegiate Review*, *Army* magazine, the *Mississippi Quarterly*, *Modern Age*, and other professional journals. Dr. Hein is a Fellow of the Royal Historical Society and a member of the Raven Society.

Frederick W. Jordan, PhD (Notre Dame), is the chairman of the History Department at Woodberry Forest School in Virginia. Jordan was prepared at Andover and earned a BA degree from Swarthmore, an MA degree from the State University of New York, Stony Brook, and he studied with George Marsden at Notre Dame, where he wrote his dissertation on the changing role of Protestant Christianity at six historic boarding schools. For many years he read Advanced Placement United States History exams and served as the Assistant Chief Reader from 2009–13.

John M. McCardell, Jr., PhD (Harvard), was the vice chancellor and president of Sewanee: The University of the South until June 30th, 2020. An Americanist specializing in antebellum, Southern political, and Civil War history, McCardell won the Allan Nevins Prize awarded by the Society of American Historians for his dissertation which became a standard book, *The Idea of a Southern Nation* (1977). McCardell taught American history at Middlebury College in Vermont from 1976 to 2010 and served as president of the college from 1992 to 2004. McCardell is a native of Frederick, MD.

Adrian Onderdonk (1878–1956) was headmaster of Saint James School from 1903 to 1939. He was a founding member of the Headmasters Association. Adrian grew up at St. James, Maryland, where his father Henry Onderdonk (1816–95) reestablished Saint James School in 1869.

W. L. Prehn, PhD (Virginia), an Episcopal priest, has served Episcopal schools as a headmaster, chaplain, teacher, and coach. He is a partner of Dudley & Prehn Educational Consultants. He is a trustee director of the Living Church Foundation, publisher of *The Living Church* magazine since 1878. Prehn's scholarly specialty is indicated by the title of his dissertation: "Social Vision, Character, and Academic Excellence in Nineteenth-Century America: William Augustus Muhlenberg and the Church School Movement, 1828–1877." Prehn writes poetry, fiction, and journalism, and is working on a book about the application of Muhlenberg's principles for twenty-first-century schools.

1

"Cadets of the Church"
A Prologue to the History of Saint James

Frederick Jordan

THE DEEP ROOTS OF the history of Saint James School lie in the English planting of the Anglican Church in North America more than two centuries before the school was founded. When the Virginia Company of London's expedition settled the Jamestown colony in 1607, their primary purpose was to make money. But they were clearly concerned with both God and gold, for among their company was the Reverend Robert Hunt, an Anglican cleric whom Captain John Smith described as "an honest, religious, and courageous Divine."[1] It is also worth noting that within that first colony was an Anglican school.[2] Thus when the expedition survived its hazardous first decades, the church gained a foothold on the continent.

Over time, English monarchs authorized additional colonies. Two were established in Massachusetts in the 1620s. Maryland attained legal status in 1634 when King Charles I awarded a grant of land to George Calvert, Lord Baltimore, noteworthy in that the Protestant king had made the award to a Roman Catholic. The civil war that broke out in England shortly afterward delayed but did not halt further colonization. By the

---

1. Noll, *History of Christianity*, 36.
2. Prehn, "Episcopal Schools," 1.

end of the seventeenth century, thirteen separate colonies had sprung up on the eastern coastline from Maine to Georgia.

As these colonies grew, so did the Anglican Church. Largely through the efforts of the Society for the Propagation of the Gospel (SPG), the missionary wing of the Church of England, there were some 43,000 Anglican church members in British North America by 1701. An estimated twenty thousand of these were in Maryland, where—notwithstanding the Roman Catholic origins of the colony—they comprised about three-quarters of its residents. There were another twenty thousand in Virginia, about one-third of the population.[3] This strength was legal as well as numerical: in both colonies the church enjoyed an "established" status, which meant that the parishes were the beneficiaries of their government's financial support. Practically speaking, this entitled a Maryland clergyman to receive forty pounds of tobacco from each person in his parish and to be paid five shillings for every marriage, thus benefitting from both vice and virtue.[4]

In spite of these advantages, not all was well for the church. The fact of the matter is that the colonies were on the periphery of the growing British empire—"the very edges of the civilized world," historian Gordon Wood has called it, of little concern to either monarchs or bishops.[5] The colonial Anglicans had no bishop of their own and the one headquartered in London always seemed to have other priorities. One unfortunate result of this was a chronic lack of clergy as few candidates for the ministry, it seemed, wanted to come to America.[6]

But the colonial faithful were also complicit in the situation as parish vestries, eager to strengthen and preserve their own power in both church and local affairs, habitually evaded their legal obligation to provide support for their ministers. As a result, throughout the colonial period only half the parishes in the two colonies had a rector. Some historians have seen a link between the power exercised by these vestries and the coming of the American Revolution—their control of parish matters was the seedbed of a desire to have a greater say in political matters as well.[7]

3. Ahlstrom, *Religious History*, 217.
4. Manross, *History*, 74.
5. Wood, *Radicalism*, 6.
6. Finke and Stark, *Churching of America*, 36. It did not help, as one colonist put it, that some of the clergy who did come to America were suspected of fleeing "debts or wives or onerous duties."
7. Bonomi, *Under the Cope of Heaven*, especially chapter 7. See also Isaac,

While the subsequent revolution did secure political independence, it proved to be an utter disaster for what was now called the Protestant Episcopal Church in the United States of America. The Episcopal Church suffered more than other denominations because so many of its members, particularly in the southern colonies, supported the British during the war, were held suspect, and then fled during or at the end of the conflict. Tainted by disloyalty and hampered by declining membership, by the end of the war many—perhaps a majority—of the Anglican parishes were defunct. In Virginia the number of clergy declined from ninety-one to twenty-eight.[8]

If that were not enough, powerful egalitarian forces had been loosed by the Revolution and in the years following the conflict many forms of "aristocratical privilege" came under attack.[9] State-supported churches were an obvious target. After independence was declared Maryland acted quickly, revoking the Episcopal Church's established status in late 1776.[10] Virginia followed suit in 1785 with its Statute of Religious Freedom, a law which Thomas Jefferson came to regard as one of his three greatest achievements.[11]

Disestablishment removed the church's state-sponsored monopoly and threw it into a religious open market. In the generations following the Revolution, that market was roiled by the growing popularity of what some historians have called "the upstart sects," the Baptists and Methodists. Baptists emerged from the dissenting churches of the English Reformation which opposed the Anglican Church. Methodism was a closer cousin, an offshoot of Anglicanism which emphasized a Christian believer's personal, often emotional, encounter with God. Together the two denominations catalyzed rapid changes in the American religious landscape in the opening decades of the nineteenth century, a movement known as the Second Great Awakening.

Transformation of Virginia.

8. Finke and Stark, *Churching of America*, 74. It was even worse in other states: Rhode Island reported only two Episcopal ministers and Delaware, three. See Holmes, *Brief History*, 60.

9. See Wood, *Radicalism*.

10. See "Disestablishment," in Hill et al., *Encyclopedia of Religion in the South*.

11. Jefferson ordered the Statute of Religious Freedom to be recorded on the headstone of his grave; the other two accomplishments were his authorship of the Declaration of Independence and his role in founding the University of Virginia.

This powerful movement spanned most of the period from the end of the Revolution until after the Civil War. Historians have debated whether it was a single coherent movement or a series of related ones, but there is no question that its results were far-reaching. The Second Great Awakening unleashed powerful leveling forces in society, redefined the role of women in the churches, fueled the emergence of the middle class (and its bourgeois family structure), furthered settlement of the trans-Appalachian West, and significantly reordered Americans' denominational loyalties. Many of the movement's adherents called themselves "Evangelicals," from the Greek *evangel* ("good news"), which reflected their emphasis on a dramatic conversion experience. These new believers not only joined churches (especially the Baptist and Methodist) but also created a vast "benevolent empire" of transdenominational organizations which promoted Sunday Schools, spread the Bible across the country, and sought to eradicate such social evils as alcohol, dueling, flogging in the navy, and abuse of the incarcerated and insane. They also worked for the preservation of the Sabbath, voting rights for women, and freedom for slaves.[12] The Awakening accelerated the democratization of the nation as ordinary men and women who had undergone powerful religious experiences claimed and then exercised greater authority, both ecclesiastical and secular. Many of the same impulses were spreading across the British Isles, forging a transatlantic movement which began to restore lost ties between the United States and Great Britain.[13]

Much of the Evangelicals' success was due to their use of "new means," innovative ways of securing new converts. These included the use of emotional preaching, less formal worship services (sometimes held in the evening), Sunday schools, and extemporaneous prayer meetings. The new means were pioneered by evangelist Charles Finney. Finney left his law practice in 1821, reputedly telling a client, "I have a retainer from the Lord to plead his case, and cannot plead yours."[14] He regarded his preaching merely as a change in venue and not method, arguing for conversions the way he had once argued for judicial conviction or exoneration. He

---

12. Noll, *History of Christianity*, chapters 7 and 9; Ahlstrom, *Religious History*, chapters 26–29. For good overviews that treat the social reform movements sympathetically, see Smith, *Revivalism and Social Reform*, and Dayton, *Rediscovering an Evangelical Heritage*.

13. See the essays by David Hempton, John Wolfe, Michael Gauvreau, and Richard Carwardine in Noll et al., *Evangelicalism*.

14. Hambrick-Stowe, *Charles G. Finney*, 19.

began preaching in the 1820s in the economically transforming "burnt-over district" of upstate New York. As Finney traveled widely, pioneering the new measures which included extemporaneous group prayer and the "anxious bench," an area near the pulpit in which those close to conversion might ponder their sinfulness. He was at the forefront of Evangelicals' concern with social reform, urging new converts give themselves to work which would end the social ills of the nation.[15]

The most significant innovation was the emergence of the camp meeting. The first one in the United States occurred at Cane Ridge, Kentucky, in 1803, but historian Paul Conkin has demonstrated that it in fact appropriated an older form of worship brought to America from the highlands of Scotland.[16] Intensely emotional gatherings, these meetings attracted hundreds or even thousands of people who gathered over a period of several days to hear preaching, conduct prayer meetings, banish evil spirits ("treeing the devil") and convert the unbelievers in their midst. Camp meetings proved highly effective, bringing enormous numbers of converts into Methodist and Baptist churches as well as into newer denominations such as the Disciples of Christ. Tamer versions of the meetings soon began appearing in the East, less emotional and therefore more palatable to the proper business classes prospering from the rising economy.

The Methodists pioneered another important innovation called "circuit riders," ministers who traveled across the newly-settled Ohio and Mississippi Valleys to serve widely dispersed congregations. Defying the idea that clergy should be "settled," Methodist Bishop Francis Asbury set the standard by traveling more than three hundred thousand miles in his lifetime of ministry.[17]

All of these developments—wartime Anglican support for the British, disestablishment of the church, and the increased competition from the upstart sects—roiled the Episcopal Church of America for more than a generation. In 1776, nearly one in six Americans had been an Anglican-Episcopalian. By 1850, that figure had dropped to fewer than four in a hundred.[18] In Virginia, only seven parish priests showed up for the

---

15. Hambrick-Stowe, *Charles G. Finney*; Cross, *Burned-Over District*, chapter 10; Ahlstrom, *Religious History*, 625; Dayton, *Rediscovering*, chapter 8.

16. Conkin, *Cane Ridge*, 36.

17. Noll, *History of Christianity*, 171.

18. Finke and Stark, *Churching*, 55.

Episcopal Church state convention in 1813.[19] Clearly the church had to do something to meet the demands of the new era, but a precise strategy was unclear. Many Episcopalians opposed use of the new means as antithetical to a church whose old means—ecclesiastical authority, attachment to tradition, and sacramental worship—had worked quite well for almost two millennia. At the heart of these reservations lay a fundamentally different outlook about the question of Christian spiritual growth, which the Bible calls sanctification.

For Evangelicals such as Finney, spiritual growth was the product of an emotional encounter with God and a dramatic conversion, something akin to the cloudburst of a summer thundershower. However, in the Episcopal Church's sacramental tradition, Christian maturation was a longer-term process, more like growth resulting from the gentle sprinkling of the daily morning dew.[20] But the latter seemed wholly out of place in the emotion-laden atmosphere of the Second Great Awakening.

That the Episcopal Church in America didn't die out entirely was largely due to the efforts of two men. John Henry Hobart and Alexander Viets Griswold were both consecrated as bishops in 1811, Hobart in New York and Griswold in the large "Eastern Diocese" later divided into six New England dioceses.[21] Together the two men revitalized the Episcopal Church but did so in entirely different ways. In the bigger picture, they represented two emerging strains in American (and English) Anglicanism, differences which seemed complementary at the time but which ultimately led to the emergence of two distinct parties within the Anglo-American communion. In a way, the two men also represented both a reaction to and an accommodation with the Second Great Awakening.

John Henry Hobart's theology and practices were grounded in the Anglican High Church tradition as translated into the American situation. In England, both Hobartian High Churchmen and the later adherents of the Tractarian or Oxford Movement valued the doctrines and practices of the historic church, prized the writings of the church fathers, and assumed

---

19. Ahlstrom, *Religious History*, 624.

20. Butler, *Whirlwind*, chapter 2.

21. Manross, *History*, 213. Griswold's diocese was referred to as the Eastern Diocese, which comprised all of New England except Connecticut. His efforts bore so much fruit that upon his death it was deemed necessary to divide the region into five dioceses. See Don S. Armentrout's entry "Griswold, Alexander Viets," in Reid et al., *Dictionary of Christianity in America*, 500–501; Butler, *Whirlwind*, 11.

that the Anglican Church had moved too far away from pre-Reformation Christianity. In their view of history, the Reformation had been necessary as the means to preserve and advance the "one, holy, catholic, and apostolic Church" of the Creed. But they worried that, since the Reformation, the "protesting" (Protestant) churches had taken things too far and that the Church of England had followed too closely. The High Churchmen therefore saw themselves, in the memorable words on one historian, as "standing midway between Protestant errors and Roman corruptions."[22] They therefore sought to affirm "the essential catholicity" of the church, particularly by emphasizing the doctrine of apostolic succession, the importance of dogma, and the need for holy living.[23]

These beliefs led Hobart to active opposition to some practices of the Great Awakening. When Evangelicals formed the American Bible Society to spread the Scriptures across the republic, Hobart responded by founding the New York Bible and Common Prayer Book Society, whose very name implied that the efforts of the ABS were deficient.[24] Hobart also actively opposed the American Sunday School Union for much the same reason. For High Churchmen, spiritual growth based only on the Bible was incomplete without an understanding of the grace of the sacraments and the tradition and authority of the church—or, as Hobart put it, holding "evangelical truth and Apostolic order" in equal balance. Hobart's convictions would endure and, as we shall see, profoundly shaped a segment of Anglicanism which ultimately influenced the founding of Saint James School.

If Hobart was a High Churchman, Alexander Viets Griswold was decidedly Low Church, a self-styled Evangelical Episcopalian. As such, he was quite sympathetic to much of what the Second Great Awakening had to offer, particularly in the revivalists' insistence on the necessity of an identifiable conversion experience which led to an active, personal faith in Christ. This process, Griswold believed, would prevent a believer's faith from descending into mere formalism, one of the primary shortcomings Evangelicals saw in the High Church movement.[25] Unlike Hobart, he saw no real conflict between the new means and the manner in

---

22. Manross, *History*, 218.

23. See R. Bruce Mullin's entries "Anglo-Catholicism" and "Tractarianism," in Reid et al., *Dictionary of Christianity in America*, 66–67, 1183.

24. Butler, *Whirlwind*, 44, 46; Mullin, *Episcopal Vision*, 50–59; Tiffany, *History*, 412.

25. Butler, *Whirlwind*, 15, 27–28, 33.

which Episcopalians practiced their faith. The Bible could coexist nicely with the *Book of Common Prayer*, with no inherent conflict between the two.[26] As a parish priest, Griswold led his flock in Bristol, Rhode Island, in a series of revivals which embraced the new means, particularly the use of evening meetings and extemporaneous prayer meetings.[27]

The rivalry between the two groups intensified in the 1830s and 1840s as the Episcopal Church's overall numbers declined, each side blaming the other for the problem. One of the primary battlegrounds was the state of Maryland where High Church "Formalists" battled Evangelicals for control of parishes, appointment of bishops, and command of popular loyalty.[28] But there was a small bit of common ground in this struggle: both sides could agree on the importance of education. In fact, schools represented a decidedly Episcopalian response to the challenge of the revivalists and their "awakening." Properly understood, education involved instilling Christian faith in young people over time, developing a faith which was neither spontaneous nor emotional. Belief grew in the soil of consistent devotion, disciplined development of habits, and time on task. It involved the study of the Scriptures, sacramental piety, and an appreciation of the church as the body of Christ. For both Evangelicals and High Churchmen, education was an affirmation of their approach to the Christian faith. It was also everything that their common opponent, the revivalists, appeared to be lacking.[29]

Griswold and Hobart had influential and energetic allies in three other bishops: Richard Channing Moore, Jackson Kemper, and Philander Chase. Moore sounded the claxon in 1810, calling for the establishment of seminaries for formal theological education and colleges to prepare the clergy for seminaries and to educate the laity. As a result, the General Theological Seminary was founded in New York in 1817, largely due to Hobart's efforts.[30] As bishop of Virginia, Moore helped establish the Virginia Theological Seminary in Alexandra, Virginia, in 1823.[31]

26. Manross, *History*, 215.
27. Butler, *Whirlwind*, 39.
28. Butler, *Whirlwind*, 12–16.
29. For a groundbreaking discussion of the reasons why so many outstanding schools were founded and presided over by High Church Episcopalians, see Hein, "High Church Origins of the American Boarding School," 577–95.
30. Perry, *American Episcopal Church*, 506.
31. Brewer, *Religious Education*, 228, 233–35.

Seminaries were the top tier of schools; colleges were the next. Western land proved to be most fertile for planting them. The reformers had their most noteworthy successes in Bishop Chase's large Western Diocese, which until 1835 covered the vast area between the Appalachian Mountains and the Mississippi River.[32] Consecrated as the first Missionary Bishop of the Episcopal Church in 1835, Kemper helped to found schools in four states, including Kemper College in Missouri (1838); Nashotah House and Racine College in Wisconsin (1842 and 1852); and the Shattuck School and Seabury Theological Seminary in Minnesota (1858). The bishops also oversaw the establishment of a number of other colleges: Geneva College (renamed Hobart College in 1852, testimony to the bishop's influence), Washington College (now Trinity College, Connecticut), Kenyon and Worthington colleges (Ohio), and Bristol College (Pennsylvania).[33]

They also envisioned a third tier of schools, designed to prepare, or "prep," students for these colleges and seminaries. As early as 1814, Hobart had attempted to set up what he called a "theological grammar school" in New York City, but it failed for lack of adequate funding.[34] Chase's college in Kenyon, Ohio, actually housed all three tiers, combining a seminary, a college, and a preparatory school.[35] The bishops also established preparatory schools in Pittsburgh, North Carolina, New Jersey, Vermont, South Carolina, Missouri, and New York State. However, most of them failed to survive the economic depression that struck in 1837.[36]

In retrospect, one failed school had an impact far beyond its short-lived existence. In 1828, the Reverend William Augustus Muhlenburg, an Episcopal priest in Hobart's diocese, founded a school at Flushing in Queens County on Long Island, New York.[37] The Institute at Flushing and its successor, St. Paul's College and Grammar School (1836), marked a new era in American education. They were a new kind of educational institution which Muhlenberg called the "church school."

---

32. Brewer, *Religious Education*, 236–42.
33. Brewer, *Religious Education*, 247–55.
34. McVicar and Hook, *Hobart*, 338–39.
35. Brewer, *Religious Education*, 255–56.
36. Brewer, *Religious Education*, 262–67; McLachlan, *American Boarding Schools*, 131. Among the schools that did survive were Ravenscroft School in Raleigh, North Carolina; Cheshire Academy in Connecticut; and Troy Female Seminary in Troy, New York. Troy Female Seminary (now Emma Willard School) was the first girls boarding school in America. See Prehn, "Episcopal Schools," 8; Brewer, *Religious Education*, 265.
37. Brewer, *Religious Education*, 258–62.

Like Hobart, Muhlenburg stood in the middle of the High Church-evangelical division in America. He called himself an "Evangelical Catholic" who blended what he saw as the best of both. "Catholicism, unchecked, leads to consolidated churchism and superstition," he wrote, "[and] Evangelicalism to individualism and rationalism."[38] But he leaned toward the former, heavily influenced by John Henry Newman, an Englishman who was the primary force in the Oxford Movement before converting to Roman Catholicism in 1845. Though influenced by his writings beforehand, Muhlenburg did not meet Newman until he visited Littlemore, Oxford, in 1843. The meeting evidently made a deep impression on Muhlenburg, as he compared Newman to Christ.[39]

Both Newman and Muhlenberg were educational reformers who saw schools as the key to the future of the church.[40] Muhlenburg once wrote that "a church without schools may be fitly compared to a mother who neglects or abandons the nurture of her offspring."[41] But that education must be comprehensive in scope, developing *all* areas of a student. He was critical of the nation's growing academy movement as too oriented toward intellectual development, with a little religion thrown in on the side. "The head should not be furnished at the expense of the heart," was his oft-quoted aphorism.[42] Schools, he believed, were like the Christian family. Christ was head over all; the headmaster, akin to a parent; and the teachers played the role of older brothers.[43] Inherent in this model was the idea that the headmaster must be an ordained cleric, for such a comprehensive ministry to mind, body, and soul should—and could—only be undertaken by the church.[44] The schools were the key to reviving the church, but they must reflect the body of Christ in every aspect. Such a

---

38. William A. Muhlenburg to the Rev. John Kerfoot, Nov. 26, 1852, in Harrison, *Life of Kerfoot*, 1:140–41. See also Tiffany, *History*, 484.

39. Prehn, "Episcopal Schools," 12. Muhlenberg would read Newman's sermons to his boys at Sunday afternoon Vespers. Kerfoot of Saint James did likewise until Newman's conversion to the Roman Church in 1845.

40. Dr. Paul Shrimpton of the Magdalene College School in Oxford has addressed the poverty of scholarship regarding Newman's keen interest in education. See *A Catholic Eton?* and *'The Making of Men': The Idea and Reality of Newman's University in Oxford and Dublin*. For an introduction to Muhlenberg's "theology of education," see Prehn, "Episcopal Schools," 2012.

41. Prehn, "Episcopal Schools," 11.

42. Prehn, "Episcopal Schools," 15.

43. Prehn, "Episcopal Schools," 19; Brewer, *Religious Education*, 259–60.

44. Prehn, "Episcopal Schools," 13.

comprehensive education could not fail to produce men who would enter the ministry, thus solving the clergy-shortage problem.

Historian James McLachlan has rightly seen in Muhlenberg's concept of holistic education the seeds of the American boarding school which emerged in the nineteenth century.[45] Rather than locating the roots of such schools in England, as many Anglophilic historians have done,[46] McLachlan maintained that schools such as Muhlenberg's were quintessentially American, rooted in a mix of democratic egalitarianism, middle-class values, and, increasingly over time, preparation for a competitive economy and social accomplishment. The English schools sought to perpetuate a hereditary aristocracy, whereas American schools sought to, in McLachlan's words, "*prevent* the development of aristocratic attitudes." English schools were hierarchical; American schools, democratic. English schools sought to educate pre-made aristocrats; American schools sought to form bourgeois gentlemen.[47] It was in Flushing, Long Island—and not in Eton or Harrow, England—that American boarding schools were planted. But those roots would not grow deep in Queens County. Muhlenberg's St. Paul's College and Grammar School was unable to withstand the Panic of 1837 and financial depression which followed. By 1845, St. Paul's was no more.[48]

All of this would be of little relevance to the history of Saint James School if it were not for an incident that occurred before the final demise of St. Paul's. In 1840 a group of Episcopal laymen in Hagerstown, Maryland, together with the bishop of Maryland, William R. Whittingham, decided to start a school. They made an offer to Muhlenberg to come and run their new enterprise. Would he entertain the possibility of coming south? Perhaps still hoping his institution on Long Island would survive, Muhlenberg declined their offer. But he did give the undertaking his blessing. In a letter to Bishop Whittingham, he wrote that the goal of the undertaking must be "to get the Church to endow an Institution which shall do the same service for the Church that West Point is doing for the

---

45. McLachlan, *Boarding Schools*, 105–35. McLachlan was not entirely sympathetic to the endeavor, at one point describing the comprehensive daily schedule for the "inmates" (126).

46. For a classic example of this approach see Mann, *Yankee Reformers*.

47. McLachlan, *Boarding Schools*, 10–11. McLachlan, however, envisioned a secular process that gravely underestimated the need for the religious component that Muhlenberg believed was essential to such schools.

48. McLachlan, *Boarding Schools*, 130–31.

army." The "Cadets of the Church" would go forth, latter-day Jesuits, to further the fortunes of the Episcopal Church in America.[49]

Muhlenberg not only endorsed the project but recommended his right-hand man to run it. John Barrett Kerfoot agreed to serve as the first Rector of "the College and Grammar School of St. James." Kerfoot shared Muhlenberg's broad educational outlook and was intimately acquainted with the operation and challenges of the Flushing Institute and St. Paul's College and Grammar School. He would, wrote Muhlenberg, be an ideal headmaster. The Maryland Episcopalians were amenable to the suggestion and engaged Kerfoot as the first headmaster of the yet-unborn enterprise.

And so in the spring of 1841, John Barrett Kerfoot traveled south to Fountain Rock, an old estate in Western Maryland, where he would open a school.[50]

---

49. The Rev. Wm. Augustus Muhlenberg to "the Bishop [of] Maryland," August 24, 1841, in Harrison, *Life of Kerfoot*, 1:35–36.

50. Kerfoot's diary entry for May 8, 1841, in Harrison, *Life of Kerfoot*, 1:30. See also McLachlan, *Boarding Schools*, 131–32.

2

The "Soul of the Thing"
Saint James in the Beginning, 1842–61

W. L. PREHN

SAINT JAMES SCHOOL WAS founded in 1841 as "St. James's Hall." By 1843 the name was "The College and Grammar School of St. James."[1] The evolution of the name reflects the growth of the founders in their understanding of their mission. Their first purpose was to prepare able boys for the Bachelor of Arts program and then matriculate young men into that more advanced program as each was prepared for higher education. The institution would be at once a strong Christian brotherhood and academically superlative. This was their main object: to establish the best academic institution in America upon strongly Christian principles. The founders were thus ambitious.

Saint James was and was not a typical denominational college in antebellum America. While the college was certainly founded by committed members of a particular ecclesial organization, the Protestant Episcopal Church in the United States of America, and the institution

---

1. The latter-day name spelled out as *Saint James* will be used throughout this chapter, even though it is technically anachronistic. The founders of Saint James called the fledgling institution "St. James's Hall," likely in emulation of an English usage, for example at Oxford University, where an endowed academic foundation was called a "college" and a less well-endowed institution was called a "hall."

reflected that religious subculture, Saint James was the second iteration of what the founders believed was an altogether new kind of educational institution in America which they called a "church school." Students rose gradually through the Grammar School into the College. In 1862, the founding Rector of the College, John Barrett Kerfoot (1816–81), noted in his correspondence that the college had conferred only a few "Bachelor in Arts" degrees. This was not unusual at the time. Until after the Civil War, the great majority of college students in America were in fact boy-members of the "preparatory departments" of the various colleges. Fewer than we might expect actually entered the BA track at all. Thus, in large measure, most antebellum colleges in the United States were prep schools with every trait and characteristic of same.[2]

Kerfoot was an ardent disciple of William Augustus Muhlenberg (1796–1877). The latter was the pioneer of the novel scholastic concept mentioned above. The prototype school was founded at Flushing, Long Island, New York, in 1828. Muhlenberg's Church Institute was unique and challenged the status quo in American secondary education. In his study of American schools, James McLachlan discovered that Muhlenberg's schools were rather original and not mere copies of the English public school model.[3] By 1836, Muhlenberg's Institute at Flushing had evolved into the more ambitious St. Paul's College and Grammar School situated a mile north of Flushing at College Point overlooking Long Island Sound. By 1842, Muhlenberg's schools had earned an excellent national reputation for preparing boys of impressive learning, noticeable virtue, and inspiring faith for the third-year course at older colleges such as Columbia, Penn, Harvard, Yale, Princeton, and the University of Virginia.

Most of Muhlenberg's students were Episcopalians. The rector of St. Paul's was dedicated to the Anglican Christian tradition he freely chose as a boy of Lutheran origins. Personal experience with adolescent boys taught him that "there can be no such thing as Christianity in the abstract."[4] Yet Muhlenberg was a true Philadelphian who abhorred narrow sectarian religion and party spirit. He was one of the most ecumenically minded Episcopal priests of his generation. As he conceptualized what a school should be, this remarkable man was adamant that Christianity is neither

---

2. Rudolph, *American College*, 435n. Rudolph notes that as late as 1870 only twenty-six colleges in the United States operated *without* preparatory departments.

3. McLachlan, *Boarding Schools*, chapter 3.

4. Muhlenberg, *Application*, 4.

a fond idealism nor a mere philosophy of life. The Christian faith is a live practice in the real world.

The church-school movement founded by Muhlenberg and his younger protégés in six states was one aspect of the nineteenth-century Anglican church revival on both sides of the Atlantic. Inspired by the leaders of the Oxford Movement in England (1833–45), Muhlenberg and his disciples assumed that the *church* in the church school denotes a living body with Christ as the Head. The head or principal of such a school should be no mere administrator of a small bureaucracy but the head of the academic family. It was for the sake of the students that these educators insisted that none else but the head of the school should have total authority over the school. In spite of nuances between their respective theological views, the leaders of the church school movement in the United States recognized the radical relationship between the reality of the "one, holy, catholic, and apostolic church" of the Creed and the daily business of curriculum, instruction, and the common life of the school. They assumed that they could set high standards because God's grace (or divine help) would be available to each member of the community. As a little image of the church, members of the school body are likewise nourished by God in mysterious ways but chiefly by consuming the word of God in Holy Scripture and the Sacraments. This is one reason why Muhlenberg and his disciples were adamant about daily chapel. As in the church, so in the school: The standards are high and lowered for no one, but God's grace is available to each member of the scholastic brotherhood in order to help him make the grade. In this sort of school, Christ is not only the Model of school ideals but the Means to realizing those ideals. This was Muhlenberg's beau ideal of a school.

Fountain Rock

William Rollinson Whittingham (1805–79), Bishop of Maryland since 1840, invited the pioneer of the American church school to come to his diocese and found a new school. Muhlenberg declined the invitation but sent his right-hand man. Kerfoot had known "the Doctor" since boyhood and worked with him on Long Island. Kerfoot was Muhlenberg's understudy for thirteen years and knew the secrets of his success. Since Bishop Whittingham's 1841 prospectus is clear that "St. James's Hall is designed to be in every respect modeled after St. Paul's College and Grammar

School," the Bishop found the offer of Kerfoot highly acceptable. For his part, Kerfoot wrote in his 1841 prospectus for Saint James that "the course of studies, the mode of religious instruction, the discipline and, as far as possible, the arrangements of [St. Paul's, College Point] will be copied. Those who are desirous of more detailed information than can here be given of the plan proposed for the Hall, are referred to the published statements of "The studies and discipline of St. Paul's College and Grammar School."[5] The bishop informed his diocese that "the Rev. Dr. Muhlenberg, whose praise as a teacher needs not my tribute . . . consented to the removal hither of his tried associate as pupil and assistant from the commencement of the school at Flushing, the Rev. Mr. Kerfoot, acting as Principal, under the constant advice of Dr. Muhlenberg."[6]

Once the decision was made to send Kerfoot to Maryland instead of going himself, Muhlenberg wrote to the eager bishop.

> Right Rev. and Dear Sir,
> The more I think of the proposed branch of our institution in your diocese, the more disposed I feel to attempt to realize it . . . I believe it would operate favorably on the cause of education in various ways, and not the least by showing the true way of *beginning* a Church School. I have often wished for an opportunity of starting *de novo*, with a few select men and with perfect independence as to patronage. This, it appears to me, we could do at "Fountain Rock." We would send out a colony of pious, intelligent, respectable young fellows, with Kerfoot at their head, who would care nothing about their support, and enter upon their work *con amore*. They would be the soul of the thing and gradually they would generate the body around them. I have the whole arranged in my mind, and I believe we would realize the very beau ideal of a Catholic School,—something of a kind which has not been realized in this part of the world. You smile, I dare say, but I know what can be done. I mean a genuine Church School, not a great literary institution . . . Our entire independence will be indispensable to our success, at least to that kind of success which will be permanently and really desirable. We must appear rather indifferent to patronage and popularity, while we leave nothing undone to deserve it . . . .While I look forward to the undertaking with peculiar pleasure, I would not wish on any account that you should lose an opportunity of

---

5. Kerfoot, "Prospectus for St. James's Hall," 1.

6. Whittingham, "Bishop's Address," *Journal of the Proceedings of the Council of the Episcopal Diocese of Maryland, 1841,* 48.

opening the school by waiting for us. There are more ways than one of doing a thing; other men might do as well in their way as we in ours; only we are sure of our way and we naturally think it the best.[7]

With characteristic confidence, the bishop addressed the clergy and delegates of the diocesan council in 1841.

It is no experiment that our school is to undertake, at the risk of injury to the first subjects. A system, the growth of years of study, labor, and experience, is to be transplanted in the full vigor of adult perfection, by those who have grown with its growth, and have been thoroughly molded into its character and trained in all its workings. I have had full opportunity of observing the result of that system of training upon the youth who have shared its benefits, and can confidently testify that it is equaled by none within my knowledge.[8]

The other person key to the founding of Saint James was the Reverend Theodore B. Lyman (1815–93), Rector of St. John's Church, Hagerstown, and later Bishop of North Carolina. Lyman was thrilled the college would be in Washington County. Whittingham authorized Lyman to act as agent for the Diocese of Maryland to purchase an old estate located on beautiful land between Hagerstown and Sharpsburg. The outstanding feature of the property was an artesian well pouring pure, cold water into a beautiful basin. The Native Americans called the place *Bai-Yuka*, which is translated "Fountain Rock." The estate of twenty acres, including the manor house, was purchased from the Ringgold family. Whittingham and Lyman arranged to buy Fountain Rock when it became available at a bargain price. The owners had not lived in the mansion since 1819. The original lord of the manor was General Samuel Ringgold (1762–1829), a close friend of George Washington. Whittingham got the mansion—a handsome federal-style building designed by Benjamin Latrobe—and acreage for $5000.

---

7. Muhlenberg to Whittingham, 19 March 1841, in Harrison, *Life of Kerfoot*, 1:33–34.

8. Whittingham, "Bishop's Address," *Journal of the Proceedings of the Council of the Episcopal Diocese of Maryland, 1841*, 48. General Ringgold owned 17,000 acres at one time. The school purchased additional acreage from the family and other neighbors as it became available. Father Dunnan has ensured that the estate is now over 800 acres. There is ample evidence that African American slaves who belonged to the Ringgold family remained at Fountain Rock. See Professor Amt's chapter.

The bishop took a keen personal interest in every single aspect of the work and considered the College of St. James the greatest achievement of his episcopate. He supported Kerfoot in every way and put a considerable amount of his own resources into the college until his "pride and joy" was destroyed by the Civil War in 1864. In the latter year, Whittingham wrote, "What your bishop lost in all this process . . . I shall not attempt to tell. For him, it makes a large part of the work of a quarter of a century a blank. No future on earth holds out any promises of compensation. There can be no replacement, for him, of the bonds of almost life-long growth that have been broken."[9] Lyman worked effectively to attract benefactors to the cause and was a warm friend and supporter of the new rector of the college.[10]

The inaugural session of the College and Grammar School of St. James began on October 3, 1842. Muhlenberg's vision of a national movement in academically serious Christian education was a reality. In the same year, the scholastic brotherhood at Nashotah, Wisconsin, was founded by James Lloyd Breck (1818–76), another Episcopal priest carefully mentored by Muhlenberg at Flushing and College Point. In September 1842, Muhlenberg stood in the chapel pulpit of St. Paul's College and formally bid adieu to Kerfoot, just as he had done with Lloyd Breck the year before. Kerfoot's send-off from Long Island was no less than a solemn commissioning of a missionary educator, Muhlenberg's beloved school son and protégé.

> The feelings I experience at the departure of one of our Brothers, who has so long been a faithful and beloved assistant in my duties, are greatly modified by the interest which the occasion possesses in another's point of view. It is the commencement of a mission in Christian education. It is not indeed the immediate act of the Church—I wish it were—but as the act of an institution recognized by the ecclesiastical authority, it is a good beginning, and a step towards that which I believe to be the especial duty of our Church in this country.[11]

---

9. Whittingham, bishop's address, *Journal of the Diocese of Maryland, 1864*, 19. See chapter 3 of this book for more details about Saint James during the Civil War.

10. Theodore Benedict Lyman (1815–93), of the Massachusetts Lymans, served as rector in Hagerstown from 1841 to 1850, when he accepted a call to a parish in Pittsburgh. Lyman later served as the Fourth Bishop of North Carolina (1881–93).

11. Harrison, *Life of Kerfoot*, 1:49.

Kerfoot wrote in his journal in 1841, "Dr. Muhlenberg gives me up to carry on *his* work in a new field."[12] Kerfoot was certainly saturated with Muhlenberg's philosophy and practice of education when he arrived in Maryland. Muhlenberg wrote to Kerfoot six years later, "I thank God most devoutly that St. James's is an offspring of St. Paul's."[13] It was all part of a plan. Both Kerfoot and Breck held an inspiring sense of vocation and mission firmly rooted in the ancient faith. From Wisconsin, Breck sent letters home to the East comparing his work on the frontier to the sixth-century initiative of St. Columba and his Irish companions who founded a missionary center on the island of Iona in western Scotland. Bishop Whittingham imagined the new initiatives in much the same way.[14] Kerfoot was cut from the same cloth.

Kerfoot wrote in his *Statement of the Studies, Discipline, Order, &c., of St. James's Hall, Near Hagers-Town, MD* (December 1842) that "St. James's Hall is the offspring of St. Paul's College, and is intended, as far as possible, to resemble the parent Institution in its character and discipline."[15] The blueprint Muhlenberg provided Kerfoot for his scholastic endeavor allowed for much freedom to adjust the plan according to the situation he found on the ground. The liberty given Kerfoot is a positive

12. Kerfoot's diary, Easter Day, 1841; quoted in Harrison, *Life of Kerfoot*, 1:30 (emphasis in original).

13. Muhlenberg to Kerfoot, 15 May 1848; quoted in Harrison, *Life of Kerfoot*, 1:131. By this year, the first St. Paul's was no more and Muhlenberg had been living in New York City for two years.

14. St. Columba (A.D. 521–97) is known to the Irish as Colum Cille, "dove of the Church." His own teacher was a great one, St. Finnian. It is not often appreciated that Columba and his disciples founded *schools* in the hope that the church would grow out of the ministry of teaching and learning. From Iona these missionary educators established churches, schools, and monasteries among the Scots. The commitment to the teaching ministry was instrumental to the conversion of the Scots. See "Columba, St," Oxford Dictionary of the Christian Church, 379.

15. Kerfoot, *Statement*, 2. Asked by Miss Ayres to name schools directly descended from Muhlenberg's schools on Long Island, one of Muhlenberg's "school sons," Libertus van Bokkelen (1815–89), named the Raleigh, North Carolina, Episcopal Institute (1834); St. Mary's on the Delaware (1836); the Episcopal High School in Alexandria, Virginia (1839); St. James School in Lancaster, Pennsylvania (1840s); and "the schools of Bishops Kemper and Otey in their respective dioceses [of Minnesota, Missouri, and Wisconsin, and of Otey's Tennessee]." Van Bokkelen included the schools of Bishops Chase and McIlvaine in Ohio and Illinois (e.g. Kenyon and Jubilee Colleges), but Muhlenberg's influence in the latter schools was quite indirect. Muhlenberg likewise had little influence at the EHS in Virginia once his former pupil Milo Mahan departed Alexandria. See Ayres, *Life of Muhlenberg*, 176n.

reflection on the character of both Dr. Muhlenberg and the Bishop, especially since the latter had strong opinions of his own on the subject of education. In the *Statement* of 1842, the new Rector demonstrates that a torch had been passed to a younger generation of school-makers. The description he offers is taken in large measure from the brochure he and the rector of St. Paul's assembled for the New York school earlier in the same year.

According to Kerfoot's *Statement* of 1842, the college was to be one "household" made of the Rector and his assistants "devoting their whole care to the Institution." This ensures not only that all staff are working for the same ends but that the spirit of authentic Christian brotherhood may affect the entire school.[16] The offices of instruction and supervision were not to be separated. The instructors were seen as the older, more accomplished brothers who were still growing in grace and wisdom right alongside their students.[17] The instructors mingled with pupils, taught them, worked the garden with them, and joined them for exercise and recreation.[18] The wisdom of Kerfoot's idea that "the vexations of the class are forgiven and forgotten in the merriment of the game" cannot be denied. All returned from the outdoor recreation to the afternoon "study" where lessons were prepared for the recitations. On most days, there were four hours of study and recitations before lunch and four hours after. Teachers and students spent a lot of time together. By this humanized if demanding routine,

> the asperities of discipline everywhere are thus rubbed off, whilst its efficiency is increased. Experience has proved that no one qualified to have the government of boys can be impeded at

---

16. Kerfoot soon jiggled the model a bit. He was married to Miss Eliza Anderson in 1843.

17. It was remarked of Thomas Arnold (1795–1842) that one reason for his great success as headmaster of Rugby was the way he gave the boys the idea that he too was still learning, struggling, growing, and working hard to improve morally and intellectually. The ideals of Rugby School were not for the students alone but for the entire fellowship. Arnold's influence on the Muhlenbergian school men grew in the 1830s and especially after Stanley's two-volume biography became available in 1844. Muhlenberg, Kerfoot, and their fellow school men were cut from the same cloth in some important respects, especially the belief that religion is integral to the deepest kind of learning.

18. Organized sports as we know them were just over the horizon in 1842. Rowing was pursued with great gusto on Long Island Sound by the students and masters of St. Paul's, College Point. At both College Point and Fountain Rock, members of the community took long walks, rode their horses, and swam.

all in the discharge of his duty by a becoming familiarity; and the Instructor who does not take pleasure in such a familiarity, has wholly mistaken his calling.[19]

The growth of expertise in education shows that Muhlenberg, Kerfoot, Breck, and their school-making companions were right to see that close relationships between pupil and teacher enhance the learning experience. Few other schools in America at the time approached education this way. Kerfoot might not have given "child-centered" learning the same meaning we do, but he and the other teachers at Fountain Rock did take the needs of each individual student seriously in working out his course of study at the college.

In the beginning, the College of St. James was divided into seven "classes" of students. The two highest classes were roughly equivalent to the freshman and sophomore years at colleges such as Columbia and Yale. A student would be assigned to a class not always according to his age but according to the level of his academic prowess. Achievement of solid attainments at one level resulted in immediate promotion to the next. By the 1850s, this approach evolved into the British-style six "form" concept but the way the forms were used by Kerfoot was congruent with his original idea: A student was not necessarily *bound* by his age to a certain one of the forms but could, if qualified in a subject area, jump into a higher form.

Kerfoot's High Aim

Kerfoot aimed high in every way. Education for him concerns the forming and maturation of persons in all aspects of human nature. Reason was highly valued but human nature was not reduced to the rational faculty alone. The moral sense must be educated, and the aesthetic sensibility requires good examples and exercise. The will and the affections must be inspired and nurtured. As at College Point, the standards of excellence for which the community was aiming at Fountain Rock were fixed and made known to every member of the brotherhood; they were not fleeting. The students knew both the targets for which they aimed and the recommended means to hit the targets. The teachers were there to show the way and took their modeling role seriously. Every student was

---

19. Kerfoot, *Statement*, 3. The quotations above and below are from the same source and page.

encouraged to pursue the standards and was taught that hard work is of greater value than native intellectual power. Diligence was complemented by the helping community. The long day was organized round the stated ideals of the institution. There was ample time for a student to prepare for his recitations in the study and to develop the habits of good scholarship under the direction of the teaching masters.

At first glance, the curriculum of the college was a traditional classical course of study. But visitors to Fountain Rock recognized immediately that the way lectures and studies were prosecuted was innovative. The teachers gave classic texts life and made them relevant to the students.[20] Kerfoot knew the importance of carefully recruiting only the most learned, accomplished, and morally good men for his teaching staff. True to the time, the feminine influence was minimal but never neglected. As on Long Island, so at Fountain Rock: There was always a "matron" on the staff who took care of maternal chores and expectations. Some of the instructors were married; most were not.

The idea was to inspire the younger generation to reach for high ideals. Each student was given the liberty to derive his own best means to achieve the agreed upon standards of the institution. Crucial to the philosophy of the college was the doctrine that the student could succeed or fail according to his own willpower and diligence; yet every student knew the entire brotherhood was expecting him to succeed and would help him do so. In the Muhlenberg-type church school, high standards form the moral person. Muhlenberg, Kerfoot, and their fellow teachers would

---

20. Kerfoot favored a method exemplified by one of the most gifted teachers in the church-school network, the Reverend Dr. Milo Mahan (1819–70), who was able to bring the classics to life by allegorizing classic texts. Mahan sometimes read the *Odyssey* in such a way that the boys saw in Homer's hero moral lessons for themselves. Mahan was a native Virginian whom Muhlenberg prepared at Flushing (1833–36), earned the BA degree from the University of Virginia in just two years (1838), then returned to teach classics at College Point. Muhlenberg wrote that Mahan was "the first, intellectually, of all my pupils" (Hopkins, *Milo Mahan*, 3). Bishop William Meade of Virginia wanted Muhlenberg to start a school in his diocese. Muhlenberg declined the offer but sent Mahan to be the kingpin of the small faculty at the Episcopal High School in Alexandria (1839). When the Low Church/Evangelical Meade learned that Mahan was greatly influenced by "Oxfordism," which the bishop took for a disease in the Episcopal Church, Mahan was invited to move on. Except for a short tenure at the General Theological Seminary in New York City, Mahan spent the rest of his life as the rector of parish churches. He offered public lectures and wrote books on biblical and theological themes. It is ironic that Mahan was as adamant *contra* the Roman Church as Bishop Meade and (unlike the bishop) wrote a brilliant monograph in which he systematically addressed what he took to be the Roman Catholic errors.

have heartily agreed with Bishop Westcott in "the moral value of exact scholarship."[21] Educators who care about truth and the formation of the human mind and heart upon truth do not see the value in making school easy. The boys were not pampered. The idea was to gain strength so that they could make a difference in the world. But assistance was there if required. Visitors saw that the brotherhood valued mutual encouragement and that teachers were there for the students and not for themselves.[22] Thus the difficulty of both the academic and extracurricular work was taken for granted. Shortcuts were discouraged.

As they asked their students to translate Vergil or Xenophon, the faculty of Saint James were not afraid to distinguish excellent, good, and average work. The college was characterized by much honesty and truth-telling. The highest grade in any subject or pursuit in the college—including conduct, manners, and decorum—was declared a 9. One student's mother wrote him that she took a 5 to be a low mark.[23] The following passage from Kerfoot's 1842 *Statement* is worth quoting at length. It is full of the wisdom accrued over many years by Kerfoot and his scholastic ilk.

> Diligence in study is sought to be promoted only by motives and incentives of the purest kind. Prizes seldom are offered, or any of the ordinary methods adopted of exciting the spirit of rivalry. The degrees of the scale by which standing in scholarship is marked are fixed and have no reference to the merits of the pupils as compared to one another . . . Arbitrary rewards as well as punishments are excluded; the chief inducements proposed to industry and good conduct being the gratification

---

21. Quoted in Honey, *Tom Brown's Universe*, and see Collini, *Public Moralists*, 105. Brooke Foss Westcott (1825–1901) taught classics at Harrow for almost twenty years before he moved to Cambridge to become one of the great New Testament scholars of his generation. He was later Bishop of Durham. A school wherein a rich and challenging course of study is used as one of the means to virtue or character is very different from a school where character is used as the means to academic excellence. In the one school, the goal is virtue; in the other, the goal is less than transcendent. It is the former goal that Kerfoot and his colleagues pursued.

22. Later in the nineteenth century, the daily life of certain schools in this scholastic family was called "Spartan." The word was used by biographer Frank Ashburn to describe Endicott Peabody's Groton School (founded 1884). The adjective has its power as long as we remember that the sources show that the teaching masters at Groton, St. Paul's, St. Mark's, Pomfret, St. George's, and other newer church schools were both compassionate and unselfish, and dedicated to their students.

23. Hester Ann Davis to W. Wilkins Davis (November 28, 1857), in Hein, *Religion and Politics*, 61.

of parents, the prospect of future respectability, and above all, the approbation of conscience. With a view to this, marks for *industry* are given, which must often, of course, differ widely from those which indicate only *success*. Duty, with all the secondary motives that can be properly called to its support, is the consideration continually enforced.

Hence, whatever amount of application is secured, the process by which it is gained is also a salutary discipline. This is a great point in education, though not always considered. Whether a lesson is mastered in obedience to conscience or from a dread of punishment—from filial affection, or determination to beat a rival—is a question of little moment . . . in respect of the stock of knowledge acquired, but of incalculable importance in respect to the bearing of the moral character. It may suit the pedagogue, who aims at nothing but lodging so much Latin or Greek in a boy's brains, equally well whether he does it by flagellation or pitting one scholar against another, or by any other expedient. Not so the Christian teacher. His zeal to make scholars will not outstrip his zeal for better things. He will not wish to furnish the head at the expense of the heart. He knows that it is at most exchanging fine gold for silver when the culture of gracious affection and holy principle is neglected for any attainments of intellect, however brilliant or varied. Not that Christian discipline is unfavorable to intellectual superiority—on the contrary, the purer the motives to such superiority, the more efficient and lasting will be their operation.

Indeed, the highest inducements to the cultivation of our rational nature are peculiar to Christianity. Literature and science have won their highest honors in the production of minds mostly deeply imbued with its spirit. However, it must be acknowledged that the effect of Christian discipline in a seminary of learning is not to produce a few prodigies which shall be the boast of the master, but to increase the average amount of application among the whole; to raise the standard of proficiency among the many of moderate abilities rather than to multiply the opportunities of distinction for the gifted few; [and] to give to all whatever polish they are capable of receiving, not merely to set diamonds.[24]

As already indicated, students were assessed in the most comprehensive way and never assumed that a good education is about the cultivation of the intellect alone.

---

24. Kerfoot, *Statement*, 11.

The carefulness of Kerfoot's approach is astonishing. Since the College and Grammar School of St. James was a church school and would reflect somewhat the variety of personalities in the church as found in the real world, the rector expected that the student body would have a variety of natural gifts and powers. The college did not welcome the best and the brightest only. The diligence of less naturally gifted students was also celebrated. The members of the fellowship pursued the many ideals of the college on a level playing field because the objective that the whole person be educated to excellence was as difficult for the person of great intellectual gifts as for the person of average academic ability. Kerfoot and company understood that natural advantages and powers are not synonymous with virtue and character. One sometimes gets the impression about education in our own time that intellectual brilliance and academic prowess, high test scores and selective college admissions, are regarded as ends in themselves; hence the clever student often finds his vices overlooked and the acquisition of virtue and character not particularly required. Muhlenberg, Kerfoot, and company would find such a situation intolerable.

Fellows and Friends

Kerfoot believed that all members of a household have responsibilities and duties to the whole. To the rector of the College of St. James fell the responsibility of governance, discipline, and the religious and moral training of the students. It has been suggested above that the way Muhlenberg and his companions at College Point treated their students was a revolution in American education because these educators realized that loving, firm, and steady admonishment worked better than fear and violence. These instructors encouraged goodness. Their expectations were high, and this made all the difference in terms of both the quality of the college life and the impressive outcomes of their program. This does not mean that Kerfoot failed to exercise his authority. The rector's authority was definite and undisputed, even as it was warm and loving. While they believed that the relationships should be fraternal or at least avuncular, and neither threatening nor antagonistic, it was clear that at the helm of the ship was a person of power and strength. Kerfoot wrote in his *Statement*:

> Corporal punishment will be so rarely resorted to that it should not be mentioned as a part of the ordinary discipline. It is not objected to on principle but as it is peculiarly the duty of the parent, it is judged on the whole inexpedient in a school which relies chiefly for its power on the affections and conscience... The error of the School is, perhaps, likely to be too much lenity, from a dread of increasing the temptations to falsehood and deceit by a system of terror. The Christian educator desires above all things to keep the heart of his pupil open to such considerations as belong to his peculiar province. He will deal with him as much as possible in private. He will admonish, reprove, and persuade with all patience and long-suffering. His field of culture is the heart, and he will be cautious how, in the pursuit of a minor gain, he crushes any germ of goodness there.[25]

In assuming that a teacher's "field of culture is the heart," Kerfoot and his staff were almost unique on either side of the Atlantic during their time.

The staff awarded "disorder marks" which showed up in the monthly report sent home to parents. The major punishment was that privileges were taken away for varying periods of time, depending on the offense. For one infraction, a boy's refectory fare might be simplified or he might find himself eating alone. More serious offenses not corrected would result in something like on-campus suspension or "grounding." While Kerfoot was not afraid to expel a boy, he did not want to do so for fear that such an act would scar the victim too early in his life. He would discreetly ask parents to withdraw incorrigible and recalcitrant boys. It stands to reason that older boys whom Kerfoot began to call "prefects" took care of a great deal of business in the dormitory.[26]

Some students were not allowed to stay in Fountain Rock. Kerfoot wrote, "The Christian Instructor cannot lose sight of the individual... It is indeed extreme delicacy towards one parent, and injustice to the children of all the others, to keep a boy whose company is injurious or who has committed offences that can be punished only by demission; but to be considerate and kind in the manner of dismissing him is a Christian

---

25. Kerfoot, *Statement*, 12. Muhlenberg allowed that corporal punishment was an option a student could choose among other options. Depending on the student's plans for his leisure, a flogging might be more convenient than a grounding.

26. Muhlenberg had older students or teaching masters responsible for twelve students, but it has been difficult to ascertain how many boys were under delegated authority at Saint James while Kerfoot was Rector.

duty."[27] Kerfoot understood that his Christian commitment must inform his attitude toward and behaviors with the students. He must do his best to model the gospel. It was impressed upon scholars and masters that membership in this scholastic fellowship was a privilege. Most of the boys realized the fact and were grateful for the opportunity their parents afforded them. The positive, delightful ethos of the college soon gained it a fine reputation. Christianity, high academic standards, and high moral civilization can and do go together.

Godliness and Good Learning[28]

The objective at Fountain Rock was to educate the whole person to excellence. Kerfoot and the staff were committed to forming minds and souls in community. In the minds of these educators, a "church school" would offer a superlative academic program wherein growth in holiness was expected. The whole program relied on good and learned human beings working with boys and young men willing to improve themselves. Only persons who could adequately model the ideals were selected for the work of the teaching masters.

Good schools are built on good teaching. Good teaching is a two-way process—always a relationship—and the best schools will expect that teachers and pupils spend a lot of time together. That such an education was residential was taken for granted. The built-in advantage of Muhlenberg's scholastic philosophy developed by Kerfoot was the strong and authentic relationship the teachers expected to have with their students. Kerfoot had been shaped by this standard and was as successful replicating it in Fountain Rock as circumstances permitted. A most perceptive alumnus of Muhlenberg's school on Long Island observed that

> Muhlenberg knew that what is wanted first and always is a teacher. And the true teacher will find his own method, which will infallibly be the right one for him. The real teaching force resides in the individuality of the teacher, which the Lord has

---

27. Kerfoot, *Statement*, 1. That Kerfoot got to discipline so quickly in this pamphlet indicates that the subject was very much on the minds of educators and parents at the time.

28. The phrase "godliness and good learning" has been used often over the centuries but appears to originate in the prayer Bishop William of Wykeham (1320–1404) wrote to be prayed regularly for the benefactors of New College School in Oxford and Winchester College, founded in 1379 and 1382, respectively.

made and not man, and which is worth more than all the man-made methods in the books . . . The only stimulating force in the realm of spirit is spirit; the one creative and inspiring agency in the domain of character is character; just as the indispensable condition prerequisite to the development of mind is the presence of other minds . . . Having the perfection of character as the ideal end of education, he perceived with the intuitive glance of the seer that character could not be formed by precept, rule, and dogma, but only by its exemplification in the daily and hourly relation of the teacher with the taught; in other words, by incarnating and transfusing the spirit of love by means of all manners, tempers, words, and actions of the teacher's life.[29]

When Kerfoot began his work at Fountain Rock, his reputation as a classroom teacher was already made.[30] Kerfoot's mentor in New York naturally trained him for effective administration but it was the qualities he possessed as a master teacher that made his reputation as a celebrated educator.[31] The following excerpts are taken from the reminiscences of one of Kerfoot's students. The man who writes was looking back on his first week at Fountain Rock.

> The ideals of St. James's were, of course, far better than the results attained, but I early perceived that the ideals were always vividly present in Dr. Kerfoot's mind. He was ever aiming at them—modifying them, indeed, by experience, but never losing sight of them as incentives to progress. These ideals, moreover, grew out of the principle, which was the ground both of his theory and practice—viz. that education comprehended in its training and work the three parts of man's nature—body, soul, and spirit.
>
> If I were to sum up in one word the most characteristic mark left by Dr. Kerfoot's methods and spirit of teaching, I should use the term sincerity or genuineness . . . Our intellectual handling had also other definite moral effects, which I clearly recognize now, and there was an atmosphere of vigorous positiveness,

---

29. Newton, *Muhlenberg*, 49, 69.

30. This is indicated by the fact that, in 1841, Kerfoot was unanimously elected (*in absentia*) president of a college founded by Bishop Jackson Kemper near St. Louis, Missouri.

31. Cambridge University awarded Kerfoot the LL.D. degree, *honoris causa*, in 1867. He was in England for the first Lambeth Conference. *Dictionary of American Biography*, 10:354.

strong love of truth, and unaffected frankness pervading Dr. Kerfoot's class-room.[32]

The idea at Fountain Rock was to learn to pursue the right goals through hard work. Noble aspiration and a good work ethic must become a way of life.

Each student was required to give himself to three or four recitations per day, except Thursdays, Saturdays, and holy days when the load was reduced to two or sometimes three. Kerfoot recognized from his long experience with American boys that the "first object of the school in regard to learning is to make the pupils good English scholars."[33] The study of the Greek and Latin classics had pride of place because "they give rich and various matter to a developing mind," but such studies cannot be isolated from the maturing ways and means of an English-speaking person. On the English side of studies, every student at Fountain Rock was required to read aloud daily, learn good penmanship, be adept at the grammars, become skilled at writing from dictation, learn vocabulary and synonyms, and read history (ancient and modern) in its most exemplary English-language authors. Students were taken through their paces in rhetoric, composition, and elocution. The last requirement made every Saint James graduate confident in public associations and requirements. The requirement at College Point and Fountain Rock of more than customary English literature, mathematics, and natural science was characteristic of only the most innovative American schools at the time. Navigation, astronomy, botany, and chemistry were also de rigueur.

At Fountain Rock the assumption was that excellence in English grammar, writing, and speaking only strengthens one's facility with Latin and Greek, and vice versa. Improvement in one will mean improvement in the other. If memory power requires development, let "the best that has been thought and said" be the substance of the memoriter exercises, and let the work include our best English and American poets. The teachers at Fountain Rock wanted and were given the freedom to pragmatically address (with the aid of human reason) the challenges and problems encountered along the route toward their objective: the complete Christian person. The lines a boy memorized from Shakespeare or Vergil gave him a way to think and to reason creatively and in new ways about the world

---

32. Coit's "Recollections," in Harrison, *Life of Kerfoot*, 1:322, 331, 334, 335, 337–38. J. H. Coit succeeded his brother (1895) as Rector of St. Paul's School, Concord, NH.

33. Kerfoot, *Statement*, 13.

in which he lived. The memoriter exercises were not just for the sake of developing brain power.[34]

As at College Point, "the study" was a key tool in the entire scheme.[35] There was and is much to recommend the practice, which prepared each student for the afternoon's or the next day's recitations. A student prepared to recite to his peers and not only to his instructors. Preparing for then delivering the recitations involved the student in many operations—moral as well as intellectual—simultaneously. For instance, the student may have been asked to stand beside his desk to recite thirty lines of Vergil from memory. This was called the "memoriter exercise." In addition to the simple recitation of lines, the instructor might ask the student to explain to the class the meaning of the lines in terms of the history of the Roman Empire, or the young man might be asked to discuss a central moral idea introduced by the poet. And it was customary to ask the student to take the thirty Latin lines and translate them into comprehensible eloquent English. Some young men were more gifted than others but every student benefited by the requirement.

It is worth noting that for all their academic reputation, teachers at Fountain Rock seldom used straight and protracted lectures to educate students. The teacher would listen to the recitations, perhaps break in to correct the student caught in a solecism (verbal or mental), then very likely speak to the boys about an important point related to the subject. The teachers were invariably learned. They were happy to share their knowledge of a subject. But it was the daily expectation of both students and teachers that the student would take responsibility for his education and was being trained to acquit himself impressively, correctly, and without any superficial knowledge, false learning, or affected manner. Such a goal requires plenty of practice, which means that teachers dedicated a lot

---

34. The quotation is from Matthew Arnold's preface to *Culture and Anarchy*, viii. In the original context, Arnold is defining culture as "the pursuit of our total perfection by means of getting to know, on all matters which most concern us, the best which has been thought and said in the world; and through this knowledge, turning a stream of fresh and free thought upon our stock notions and habits, which we now follow staunchly but mechanically, vainly imagining that there is a virtue in following them staunchly, which makes up for the mischief of following them mechanically." That for Arnold culture is "the study of perfection" (xi), and thus becomes something like a tool in hand—but more powerfully one part of a *method*—enabling us to think clearly about the world around us, or to help the younger generation so to think, is a hope very similar to the vision which possessed Muhlenberg and his disciples.

35. After the Civil War, the study became "study hall" at Saint James and most other independent schools.

of time to their students and not to the preparation of their own lectures. While this practice in the recitation rooms cannot be described as casual, it was nonetheless more relaxed (and we may say caring) than obtained in many American schools at the time. From most extant accounts of this sort of pedagogy, we can see how extraordinary were the results. As was the case at College Point, so at Fountain Rock: Visitors who attended the public examinations in June were astonished by the attainments of the young scholars.[36]

Instructors shared the duty in the study on mornings, afternoons, and at night.[37] Instructors would also follow their students out of doors for recreation and sports. The younger students were seldom left alone. The ever-presence of the teachers made their discipline and admonishment natural, constant, discreet, and gentle. This approach is the source of bona fide rigor. True rigor requires a relationship between teacher and student. The teacher has convinced the student that he really does care about the student and wants the best for him; hence the teacher does not have to relax the high expectations or standards of the school and the student knows he will get help to meet the unwavering demands. Some subjects are undoubtedly more difficult than others, but rigor is more of an atmosphere than a practice or a standard. Rigor is based on *interaction* between two conscientious human beings.

John Kerfoot set the tone at Fountain Rock. One former student, Joseph H. Coit (later the second rector of St. Paul's, Concord), left a memoir of his days at Fountain Rock. His observations of the rector's teaching practice are worth including in this chapter. Coit remembered that the

---

36. There is some evidence that a shift in English education did influence the instructors at Saint James. An important innovation came to classical studies in England about this time. William Whewell (1794–1866) of Trinity College, Cambridge (Master from 1841), was a scientist who strongly believed that Latin and Greek are necessary to liberal knowledge and the complete education; but as one who had served as a college tutor and not only a university lecturer, Whewell, when he became Master of Trinity, was quick to relax the requirement that *every* student must produce eloquent English translations of the Greek and Latin. Knowing for a fact that talented students yet have different and various aptitudes, Whewell was satisfied with an accurate translation of the original language into workable English, even as he never changed his mind that the cultivated intellect will have gained a good grounding in Latin, Greek, and mathematics. See Whewell, *On the Principles of English University Education*, beginning on page 34.

37. Boys in the grammar school who were sixteen years of age and older could use the college study instead of the grammar school study. To be invited "up" was considered a privilege. W. Wilkins Davis to Hester Ann Davis (January 3, 1862), in Hein, *Religion and Politics*, 62.

memoriter exercises "were rigidly exacted and usually required considerable effort to do satisfactorily, but they amply repaid one for the labor and time expended. They not only strengthened the memory, but they enlarged one's vocabulary, and cultivated the taste." The "frequent writing of translations and abstracts" was also a key part of the daily tuition. These "were carefully reviewed" and the best were "read before the class and commented upon" by teachers and peers.[38]

> The whole body of teachers caught in greater or less degree the tone and method of their head. His skill in questioning and explaining, inspiring, and, so to speak, invigorating a class, were the models admired and followed by all . . . I noticed that he took great pains to make us catch the meaning of the author; that he had a great dislike of verbiage and inaccuracy, and that the simpler and clearer the language used in translating, the better he was pleased. His habit was a terse and almost epigrammatic conciseness . . . And one reflex result of such teaching was the formation of the habit of saying what was in one's mind directly and simply, and stating facts in clear and definite language.[39]

Coit admired above all in the rector the "strong love of truth," "unaffected frankness," and thoroughness with every single boy created a school spirit that "invigorated all who breathed it and aided the growth of kindred tempers and qualities."[40] This was no system; it was a way of life and the rector's full-time job was showing the other members of the community how to do it.

The Annual Session and Daily Schedule

The school year at the college was a ten-month session running through the feast of St. James on July 25th.[41] College bulletins reveal that the cost of tuition per session remained about $225 per student for a number of years. The daily regimen of prayer, study, recitations, recreation, and common meals in a close-knit family presided over by a strong moral leader was patently Muhlenbergian. Kerfoot introduced more frequent formal examinations which were held three times per session, but the

---

38. Coit's "Recollections," in Harrison, *Life of Kerfoot*, 1:332.
39. Coit's "Recollections," in Harrison, *Life of Kerfoot*, 1:333.
40. Coit's "Recollections," in Harrison, *Life of Kerfoot*, 1:334.
41. By the late 1850s, the session was finished by mid-July.

shape of the academic year was roughly the same as at Flushing and College Point. In the early 1840s, students were required to submit to public examinations each month, but by 1850 the public examinations were held less frequently: one before Christmas, one during Lent, and one at the end of the annual session in July. These were in effect trimester exams but a student would not be advanced unless he proved himself worthy of promotion during the final examinations in July.[42]

A simple daily schedule fit a no-frills plant and facilities. Had Kerfoot and the brethren desired nicer accommodations, there was no money to make good their intention. While the Ringgold mansion was large and exquisite on the inside, the two other buildings—divided in three floors into lavatory, study, and dormitory (considering them from basement to top story)—were merely functional and Spartan. The chapel was set up on the second floor of the main building and was kept a sacred and lovely space until the late 1840s, when a separate building was erected for it on the north side of the manor house.

To achieve the academic and moral objectives of the college, a very long day was required. Excepting Sundays, the daily schedule was as follows:

```
5:45 A.M.   Waking Bell (earlier in June and July)
6:08 A.M.   Roll Call
6:10 A.M.   Washing Room time (tubs for bathing)
6:20 A.M.   "On Line" for inspection
7:00 A.M.   Breakfast in the Refectory
7:30 A.M.   Chapel then Free Time
8:00 A.M.   Elocution with the Rector (in the Study-Hall)
8:15 A.M.   Study & Recitations (times two)
12:00 P.M.  Washroom
12:10 P.M.  Chapel Bell (call to prayer) for Noons
12:35 P.M.  Dinner Bell
12:55 P.M.  Reports
1:00 P.M.   Outdoor Recreation
2:00 P.M.   Study and Recitations
4:00 P.M.   Outdoor Recreation
6:00 P.M.   On Line for inspection
6:15 P.M.   Tea (Supper)
6:45 P.M.   Chapel
7:00 P.M.   The Evening Study
```

42. *Register of the College of St. James, 1858*, 20; quoted in Hein, *Religion and Politics*, 79.

8:30 P.M.   Scripture Reading
8:40 P.M.   Chapel (Late-Evening Prayers)
9:00 P.M.   To Dormitories
9:30 P.M.   Lights Out[43]

The twin objects of the daily schedule were to make good use of daylight and to get much work done. When the wake-up bell sounded at 5:45 A.M. (summer reveille was forty-five minutes earlier), the entire community had eight minutes to get to the "line" for the roll call, after which they headed down to the two basements (grammar school and college, respectively) to use the lavatories.[44] They assembled again for the "inspection line" at 6:20 then went to breakfast. Breakfast was followed by morning prayer in the chapel. The first morning study began at 8:15 A.M. and was followed by the morning recitations. Attendance at "noons" (as Kerfoot called the noonday chapel) was optional but the rector himself led this short office every day of the session at 12:10 P.M. except on Sunday.[45]

Dinner began at half-past noon, followed by "on-line reports," a check-in when chores and disciplinary penalties were assigned. Following the reports, the students were free for a small amount of recreation until the afternoon studies and recitations. Additional recreation time was allotted after the academic day was finished.

At approximately 6:00 P.M., the community assembled "on line" for another inspection. (In the early years, a third cycle of study-and-recitations followed afternoon exercise but this appears to have ceased by 1845.) Each student was assigned his desk in either of the two studies (grammar school or college), and the discipline of the morning, the

---

43. In his *Statement* of 1842, Kerfoot wrote that only on Wednesdays, Fridays, and major Holy days would the full Prayer Book service of morning prayer be used. The noonday bell was the signal for all to stop what they were doing for a moment of silent reflection and prayer. Kerfoot led what he called "Noons" in the chapel at ten minutes past noon. Notice that Kerfoot's intention was to *never wait too long* to give constructive feedback. Let admonishment be gentle but immediate for every boy, every day.

44. Wilkins Davis reported in October 1858 that he was rising at 5:20 A.M. Hein, *Religion and Politics*, 72. In the late 1850s, Davis used the half hour between breakfast and chapel for a brisk walk of over a mile.

45. In letters to Kerfoot, Muhlenberg (*q.v.* in Harrison's *Life of Kerfoot*) warned against any sort of rigor in relation to religious observance and the daily chapel routine. Daily "morning prayers" and other chapel disciplines were required but the leaders executed them in what we would call "developmentally appropriate" ways. Muhlenberg's fame as an educator was first made by his unique and successful approach to religion. Kerfoot more or less followed suit.

afternoon, and the two-hour evening studies was maintained. Kerfoot fully intended to "form habits of personal neatness and habits of punctuality" in every student. The inspection was a means to this end.[46]

The brotherhood moved to "tea" (i.e. supper) following the inspection. Immediately after supper, the community assembled in the chapel on the second floor of the main building for evening prayer read from the *Book of Common Prayer*. Just as at Flushing and College Point, the evening study at Saint James began a little after 7:00 P.M. The first quarter of an hour of this study was reserved for Bible reading. That the students called it the "Bible hour" is worth noting, though Joseph Coit wrote that there was no requirement to open the Bible at all.[47] It was Kerfoot's daily habit to use the first half of an hour of the evening study to roam around and speak quietly to the boys about their progress in all aspects of their lives. It was not idle time for the rector. Like a good shepherd, he was considering his sheep.

At 9:00 P.M. the bell sounded the retreat to the dormitories. The dormitories featured small alcoves of half a dozen beds, each student assigned to his own bed. Some older grammar school boys were given small rooms. The standard size was apparently ten by thirteen feet.[48] Prefects were given even more privacy. In contrast to contemporary English schools and New England academies at the time, a bed per boy was an innovation Muhlenberg and his scholastic heirs brought to the American boarding school.[49] There was never a light not burning in the dormitories. Authority over students in the dormitories was delegated to either teaching masters or student prefects who lived on each floor.

The Sunday schedule at Saint James was much the same as at Flushing and College Point. The sacredness of the day was impressed upon all who lived in the community. Sunday hinged on two major chapel celebrations, one mid-morning service and the more worshipful vespers in the late afternoon. The vespers sermon was often a text read to the assembled

---

46. Coit, "Recollections," in Harrison, *Kerfoot*, 1:331.

47. Coit, "Recollections," in Harrison, *Kerfoot*, 1:325, 327. "Peer pressure" had its effect.

48. W. Wilkins Davis to Hester Ann Davis (January 27, 1861), in Hein, *Religion and Politics*, 111. Davis's room at "Greenwood," his family home in Montgomery County, MD, was commodious. In the same letter, Davis complained about the food. He believed that "Dr. K." paid so little for food that the local grocers did not bring good food to sell.

49. Later in the century, Peabody of Groton, a great admirer and emulator of Muhlenberg and company, added a cloth door to each alcove for additional privacy.

college by the rector, chaplain, or another master. Until 1845, the sermons of John Henry Newman (1801–90) were popular with Kerfoot.[50] The *Maxims* of Bishop Thomas Wilson (1663–1755) and selections from the doctrinally rich writings of Bishops Jeremy Taylor (1613–67) and George Bull (1634–1710) were also favorites among the Muhlenbergian school men.[51]

At Saint James there was more free time on Sundays than at College Point. Kerfoot and his colleagues developed what became an institution at the church schools they ran: the "Sunday Library." Students were free to check out books from this carefully chosen collection of works of history, theology, poetry, drama, and fiction. The historical novels of

50. Newman's *Parochial and Plain Sermons* was being published individually and was available in the United States beginning in 1839. All the sermons comprising the eventual eight volumes were preached before Newman converted to the Roman Catholic Church in 1845. The first of the sermons was preached in 1825, the last in 1843. Muhlenberg's journal (cited in Miss Ayres's biography on page 166) notes that Kerfoot and Muhlenberg met Newman in person at Littlemore outside of Oxford on September 16, 1843. During the same visit to Oxford, Kerfoot and Muhlenberg heard Newman preach at the University Church of St. Mary the Virgin. The contents of *Parochial and Plain Sermons* are edifying to this day. They are at once Evangelical and Catholic in the truest sense of the words. Dean R. W. Church, who was very close to Newman and heard him preach often during these years, wrote, "No sermons, except those which his great opposite, Dr. Arnold, was preaching at Rugby, had appealed to conscience with such directness and force. A passionate and sustained moral earnestness after a high moral rule, seriously realized in conduct, is the dominant character of these sermons." Church, *Oxford Movement*, 21. When he was an undergraduate, Matthew Arnold was smitten by Newman's sermonic power. When lecturing to an American audience later in the century, Arnold said of his undergraduate experience of Newman, "Who could resist the charm of that spiritual apparition gliding in the dim afternoon light through the aisles of St. Mary's, rising into the pulpit, and then, in the most entrancing of voices, breaking the silence with words and thoughts which were a religious music—subtle, sweet, mournful." Arnold, "Emerson," *Discourses in America*, 139–40. See also Delaura, *Hebrew and Hellene in Victorian England*, 21–26. David Delaura notes that Newman continued to influence Matthew Arnold's thinking and sensibility, even long after the latter lost his orthodox Christian faith. Renouncing him as they did in 1845, Muhlenburg and Kerfoot nonetheless remained deeply shaped by Newman's mind and religion.

51. In 1827, the Clarendon Press, Oxford, brought out an edition of Bull's *Twenty Sermons* (1714) edited by a High Churchman, Edward Burton of Christ Church. The use of Bull at College Point and Fountain Rock is clear evidence of High Church sentiments among the leaders. Bull was a Tory High Churchman who lived through the Commonwealth regime a powerful critic of the saints' regime. An indication of Bull's intellectual courage and moral boldness is the title of the first of his *Twenty Sermons*: "The necessity of works of righteousness in order to salvation," an exposition of the Epistle of James.

Sir Walter Scott were naturally enjoyed, and Charlotte Yonge's romantic "blockbuster" *The Heir of Redclyffe* (1853) was taken up with alacrity.[52] Whereas Muhlenberg was somewhat suspicious of Wordsworth and Coleridge, these poets were held in great esteem at Fountain Rock and romanticism in general was not avoided.

The church year and the academic year were somewhat interchangeable at the College of St. James. As at College Point, great pains were taken to make the high holy days festive and interesting, and feast-days were literally that: special fare was prepared and enjoyed by all. Just as duty and conscience were made the sole motivations for right action in the schoolhouse, so in religious life the Rector was concerned to teach the students that religious commitment must be governed by reliance on "constant training rather than occasional stimulants" in the interest of "seriousness and devout sensibilities" over religious excitements. Discreet conversations and gentle suasion between master and pupil were the means by which much religious and moral instruction were given at both College Point and Fountain Rock. For example, instead of giving general admonitions to the whole school about the use of "profane and corrupt language," which profanity seldom reaches the ears of a faculty anyway, Kerfoot instructed his staff to pull suspect boys aside in order to customize a request that the violator please refrain from the use of profanity. Wise educators indeed, Kerfoot and company discovered that these private, one-on-one approaches often yielded admissions from the student. The teacher then could ask the student to stop the behavior. Another method was more commonly used in most American schools: to embarrass a student publicly. This fast and easy method makes young people angry and resentful instead of making them mindful of their need to reform habits.[53]

---

52. Yonge (1823–1901) published the admired *Heir of Redclyffe* in 1853. It is the story of a more or less orphaned boy who develops virtue and holiness by way of High Church Anglicanism. Ann Douglas saw Yonge's work (especially *The Daisy Chain*, 1856) as part of the "sentimentalization" of North Atlantic culture. Douglas misses what seems obvious in Yonge's fiction: that it was part of the international resistance to modernity of which the Tractarian movement was a part. As for Sir Walter Scott (1771–1832), how can we adequately measure his unexpected influence on nineteenth-century North Atlantic culture? The poetry—e.g. *The Lay of the Last Minstrel* or *Rokeby* (Dr. Pusey's favorite)—and novels such as *Waverly*, *Kenilworth*, *The Talisman*, and *Ivanhoe*, opened up a fascinating Christian world rather ignored for three hundred years in England and America: medieval Europe and England.

53. Kerfoot, *Statement*, 14.

It is interesting that, in the first several years of Saint James, the *Prayer Book* services of morning and evening prayer were read on Wednesdays and Fridays only, though (as mentioned) Kerfoot never failed to lead daily "Noons" in the chapel. By the 1848–49 session, the experiment was finished and the College Point routine of daily morning and evening prayer was resumed. On major saints' days, morning academic work ended one hour early and the community assembled in the chapel for the commemoration which included Ante-Communion and a special sermon on the saint's life and significance. There was no pressure to receive the Holy Communion. Only properly prepared students and teachers were encouraged to do so. Joseph Coit reported that the chapel services were "short, attractive, and had nothing unreal or sentimental about them."[54] The successful approach to daily chapel was continued at St. Paul's School in New Hampshire and at many other church schools across the United States.

Daily chores were required of each boy enrolled. For example, each student had a garden plot and was required to till, weed, and otherwise make fruitful this little farm. While there were persons at Saint James referred to as "servants," most of these African American slaves or freedmen, it was generally the case that the students were not waited on and were expected to pull their own load.[55] Southern aristocrats—of which there were many at Saint James—would have expected black servants to wait on them. It is reasonable to suppose that, in the pursuit of the ideal of a brotherhood of mutual responsibility and shared duties, Kerfoot would have discouraged reliance on others at Saint James. But the question is uncertain. (Professor Amt addresses the topic in the following chapter of this book.)

As for changes in the mechanics of the program and the routines he brought from Long Island, Kerfoot left some practices alone and modified others. While he continued to put trusted older boys—prefects—in charge of a dozen younger boys, he broke with Muhlenberg's rule and began to award prizes at commencement in the 1850s. The sources show that Kerfoot held chapel after meals instead of before. This innovation doubtless introduced novel sounds among the brethren and thus increased the humor of the place. As the years rolled on, Kerfoot tended to standardize punishments where Muhlenberg had adjudicated each case

---

54. Coit, "Recollections," in Harrison, *Kerfoot*, 1:325.

55. Hein, *Religion and Politics*, 100, 97. See Professor Amt's chapter 3 of this book for a groundbreaking account of the servants and slaves at Fountain Rock.

and often allowed the boys to choose their own punishments. On the other hand corporal punishment (rarely used by Muhlenberg) appears to have been dropped altogether by Kerfoot, though (as Professor Hein notes) the possibility was not dropped from the *Register* of the college.[56] If there was more leisure on Sundays, there is plenty of evidence that the ensign ran an even tighter ship than the captain, and the captain was known to be a strict disciplinarian.[57] Another important point is that a large percentage of Saint James students came from south of the Mason and Dixon Line. We can be sure that Kerfoot resolved to tame "the froth and whip-syllabub of Southern character."[58] How successful Kerfoot was in this last objective is difficult to determine.

If this outline of the routine proves that Fountain Rock was prospected from the mother-lode of College Point, Kerfoot's *Statement of Studies* shows that a translation of Muhlenberg's philosophy of education was occurring in the hands of the younger generation. Muhlenberg was the pioneer, and his pupils the perfecters, of the new way of doing school. In fact, this development pleased the founder as he watched his basic principles unfold in different settings in Maryland, Wisconsin, Minnesota, New England, and California. And Kerfoot was as much the pragmatist as his school father. If the scholastic philosophy of the college and grammar school of Saint James was that of College Point, this does not mean that the philosophy was a "system" of education. Muhlenberg, Kerfoot, and their fellows in the movement banished the word. The rectors of College Point and Fountain Rock took it for granted that, if learned masters and willing scholars come together in a vigorous family-like community or brotherhood, beautiful things can happen. The purpose was to form the Christian character and to acquire good habits, republican virtues, and sound learning.

A Worthy Target

In a tournament of longbow archers, the prize goes to the archer who can hit the target set far away in the distance. Not only strength but a

---

56. E.g. for 1858. Hein, *Religion and Politics*, 86.

57. Skardon, *Muhlenberg*, 71.

58. Russell Trevett (an instructor) to Kerfoot, 17 November 1843, in Harrison, *Kerfoot*, 1:102. "Syllabub" is a refreshment of English origin using heavy cream, citrus juice (orange or lemon), and sack or sherry. It was a popular drink among affluent Americans and especially enjoyed in the American South.

high aim is required. Kerfoot's college attained a general academic excellent because the community aimed above academic excellence. In fact, the masters and scholars of the College of Saint James aimed for a target beyond this world. Their vision was of the virtuous man, the person of character, in the Christian sense of the word. Their first purpose was to educate the inner person, and they assumed that boys and young men of rather various aptitudes would gain a first-class academic formation along the way to something more worthy. One motive for their high-aim philosophy and for their pursuit of excellence generally was the need to thoroughly prepare young men for the ministerial priesthood of the Episcopal Church. They wanted these young men to have the foundation to excel in theological studies and already possess the habits of the priest if they were called to the ministry. Hence the program at Saint James was comprehensive in its requirements. In their somewhat clericalist way, they reasoned that, if the course of study was aiming so high as to produce future leaders of the church, then every student in the college would be well served and the quality of the institution guaranteed. The record shows that they were fundamentally correct in their assumption.

At Saint James, academic skills and attainments were a byproduct of a higher aim. The philosophy worked. The more mundane achievement of academic excellence did happen routinely at Fountain Rock. The principle that you'll gain superlative academics if you aim above them is as important to the history of education as the principle of lift was for the history of aviation.

Given the intimate relationship he saw between sound learning and the growth of souls, Kerfoot was sure that he must "watch over the mind and religious growth" of individual students and hope for the best in each.[59] He was pleased to mold character upon "God's revealed will."[60] Kerfoot simply assumed that every youth finds and then fashions a spiritual culture of some kind and will be profoundly shaped by it, whether it be based on a secular or a religious tradition.[61] He told parents, trustees, and others in his first Baccalaureate Address (1846),

> No might of intellect, no mass of knowledge, will do anything without humble faith ... Even were it possible for the proud and

---

59. Harrison, *Life of Kerfoot*, 1:41. The phrase is made in reference to Kerfoot's brother-in-law, Kip Anderson, who was his pupil at College Point and later a colleague at Saint James.

60. Kerfoot, *Faithful Parent*, 9.

61. This fundamental point appears to be confirmed by much modern psychology.

self-sufficient mind to apprehend intellectually every doctrine, it would gain but little. The truth, to work out its full blessing, must first possess the heart, and through that sanctify the head . . . The late excellent Dr. Arnold, of England, strikingly illustrated this. He had a great and, no doubt, an honest dread of his boys adopting opinions on his authority, and yet in the very page on which his admiring biographer tells us this, he also unwittingly adds, that his boys would persist in trusting and following their good teacher in spite of all his warnings. So it must always be. Any man worthy to be an educator will impress himself upon the minds and hearts of his best pupils.[62]

Kerfoot believed that responsible adults must teach the Christian tradition to children and youth and bring them steadily into the faith. Adults can decide the spiritual culture in which the young will grow up. He and his colleagues worked fifteen-hour days for twenty-two years to make the church school a worthy option for American families.

> Each day is too valuable to be lost. [Do not] think of Education as only the giving forth of precepts and doctrines. It is the imbuing of the heart, training and practicing it in holy affections and habits. This is a work of love, of a love influential and inexhaustible as only a parent's can be. None can so mould the whole nature as that one *in* whom and *towards* whom love is the strongest. But any molding must begin early; therefore, must the parents begin it, and none so well as they can carry it to its completion.[63]

Expectations were everything for Kerfoot and his associates at Saint James. The program revolved around a paradoxical hopefulness: Boys were expected to act at all times like mature Christian adults while their teachers made allowances for their age and level of maturity.

> Now, while it is unreasonable to desire in the child the gravity of the man, it is yet, I am persuaded, an error productive of great practical harm to allow, as is too much the fashion, that the law of morality for the youth is to be easier and lower than that for the man . . . Let that brief but precious time be lost in calling sins by gentle names, and *justice* and *judgment* will never be to that child the definite, high, sacred realities they might have been. Hence the virtues of obedience, truth, honesty, purity in word and act, and of reverence to God—to His Fearful Name, and to

---

62. Kerfoot, *Three Addresses*, 30, 31.
63. See Kerfoot's first Baccalaureate Address in *Three Addresses*, 13.

> all that specially belongs to Him—these virtues must be taught to the child as fully and on as high a standard as you allow that the law of God does present to the adult.[64]

The high standards were lowered for no member of the school, but grace and love would enable and inspire each student to stay steady on the quest.

Kerfoot was a good American who believed in republican virtue. He believed that God required human beings to both trust in the Lord and take personal responsibility; to think and to judge for themselves. Anti-intellectualism linked to Christian faith was not encouraged at Saint James.

> Every department of truth demands for its full comprehension much preparatory knowledge and much previous training of mind. Divine truth—that which embraces all we can know of God—His will and dealings with man, our own "fearful and wonderful nature"—this calls at the least for as much preparation of mind as any other study.[65]

In this quotation, Kerfoot shows that the "fearful duty" of independent judgment actually requires faith. Faith is the first step to deeper understanding. Kerfoot's view was, then (like Muhlenberg's), rather Augustinian: Rather than a shortcut to understanding (dispensing with the intellect), faith is the means by which we gain greater understanding. Both religious and academic learning require faith. Kerfoot assumed that "[t]he *chief* preparation needed is that of a believing heart. You must begin by heartily believing, if you would aim hereafter to comprehend."[66] This was the old Augustinian philosophy of *fides quaerens intellectum* or (as Kerfoot put it), *crede ut intelligam*—"believe, that you may understand."

---

64. See Kerfoot's first Baccalaureate Address in *Three Addresses*, 10–11, 20.

65. Kerfoot, "Education Catholic," part 1, 63. Kerfoot's purpose in this 1843 article is to make the connection between authority, faith, and sound learning. The insight is as much Lockean as Catholic or Christian. Locke wrote in *Some Thoughts Concerning Education* (1693) that, unless a pupil accepts "on faith" what the authorized master is teaching, the very beginning of sound learning cannot happen. Kerfoot wanted to make the point that, just as saving faith is the response to the authorized testimony of an other or others, so what he called "first faith" is necessary to begin building knowledge. Just as saving faith depends on the trusting belief in propositions that cannot be proved rationally (e.g. "Jesus is the Son of God" or "on the third day, he ascended into heaven"), so "first faith" in the academic realm puts the student on the path of solid learning. If saving faith requires prevenient grace, then real learning requires a grace-filled academic community wherein trust and obedience are highly valued and expected.

66. Kerfoot, "Education Catholic," 63.

As Kerfoot saw it, truth is a very large thing and cannot be comprehended in the manner of geometric theorems or a bug pinned on a board. In the same manner that understanding religious truth cannot possibly happen in an instant, Kerfoot expected that the truth of anything becomes known gradually over an entire lifetime.[67] For the Muhlenbergians, truth was suspect if discovered apart from the living community wherein it matters and where it is lived out over time in the life of that community. Since each learned truth sheds a new light on other learned truths, a community of learners is required in order to allow the process of learning the truth to continue and the community as a whole to flourish. One commences an authentically reasonable life, then, by first accepting the authorized beliefs of the community (for example, those of the church catholic).

> If faith has saved the soul, then knowledge will build it up, otherwise it can only destroy ... True knowledge of God cannot be without previous faith, while saving faith may readily exist in every mind, for no mind is unable or forbidden to acquire all knowledge needful for salvation. The universal, indispensable gift to the soul, must be faith ... Secure, then, to the soul that which she must have—faith; and to it, by every right method, that other thing which she ought to have—knowledge ... On no principle but the Church teaching with authority can faith be from the first—as for its perfection it must be—inculcated and cherished. Under no other teaching can knowledge be safely communicated.[68]

Kerfoot did believe in the republican virtues, including self-reliance. But he considered it a reckless spirit that would presume that human beings can always judge for themselves the great and deepest questions of life without benefit of community, religious guides, time, and tradition.[69] This is a crucial principle of the Muhlenberg-type church school in the history of American education. While they were seen in their day as rather progressive, they were not rationalists and they did not idolize modern scientific rationality. These educators believed that rationalism is irrational, since, in this context, rationalism is the assumption that

---

67. Kerfoot, "Education Catholic," 63.

68. Kerfoot, "Education Catholic," 65.

69. Like Coleridge and Edmund Burke, Kerfoot saw the value of "prepossessions"—a.k.a. biases or even prejudices—for providing assumptions that are usually, when we are perplexed, sound guides to good actions.

something is true and important *only* if the mind can grasp it *clearly*, quickly, and without much effort.[70]

It follows that Kerfoot believed that all education is inescapably biased; it begins in "the prejudice of the mind in favor of some system of truth,"[71] and to believe otherwise was to him irrational.

> Believe and obey at once, with an honest heart—pray and study for an enlightened mind and a tender conscience; go through faith to knowledge, and thus as you attain knowledge, it will be a blessing confirming your faith, not a curse blighting your soul with infidelity.[72]

Kerfoot had firsthand experience of boys. He was a professional possessed of a knowledge he wished to share with the world. He was not an idealist; for him it was simply a matter of fact that a community of "patience and prayer" can bring remarkable results such as faith, virtue, competence, and public-spiritedness.[73] Professor Hein's careful study of the letters of a former College of Saint James student yielded the conclusion that the institution came quite close to realizing its principles, which were different from either the English public school or the American academies of the time.

---

70. "Rationalism" was an important subject to Muhlenberg, Kerfoot, and their colleagues. While they prized human reason, like all good Anglicans, they took "rationalism" to be an aspect of intellectual pride; for example, "captious reason" and "private judgment" used against the doctrines of the Bible. In this usage, "rationalism" connotes the *inordinate self-reliance* of a rational being. The Muhlenbergian school men would have been familiar with J. H. Newman's Tract 73, *On the Introduction of Rationalistic Principles into Revealed Religion* (1836). Newman's fifteen University Sermons (preached between 1826 and 1843) on the relationship between faith and reason were taken up by Americans in the 1830s and eagerly read. The sermons were published together in 1871.

71. Kerfoot, "Education Catholic," 64. Incidentally, the title of this exceptional essay shows that Kerfoot was not afraid of the word "Catholic" or to conceive of his Anglican Christianity as Catholic.

72. Kerfoot, "Education Catholic," 63. Kerfoot's principle was *crede ut intelligas*, "believe, that you may understand." This clearly harkens back to the formula found in the *Proslogion* of St. Anselm of Canterbury (published A.D. 1077), *fides quarens intellectum*, or "faith seeking understanding." Anselm's principle was derived from Saint Augustine's *credo ut intelligam* ("I believe, that I may understand"), which is introduced in the *Confessions*. One of Francis Bacon's maxims from the *Essays* is, "A little philosophy tendeth the mind to atheism, but depth in philosophy tendeth it to faith."

73. Kerfoot, "Education Catholic," 14.

> [T]he College of Saint James really was a thoroughly different place from Shrewsbury or Eton or Charterhouse in the 1850s. The boys at Saint James's led closely supervised, highly regulated lives in a rural location six miles from the nearest town. They lacked the tradition of rebellion and much of the opportunity for wild behavior available to their British counterparts. They were all younger brothers in a patriarchal household whose *raison d'être* was the training of boys' minds, souls, and bodies according to Christian principles . . . . [T]his controlled environment, reinforced by the family at home, did have an effect. The sort of cynicism that an Etonian or Harrovian of this period would have expressed toward his school's chapel and curriculum is not present in Wilkins's letters, save in regard to the College's food.[74]

Faith and Reason

At the College of Saint James, the faculty took it for granted that it was their duty to "train up a child in the way he should go, and when he is old he will not depart from it."[75] They assumed that the tuition of the mind and the tuition of the soul are pursued together because the growth of the one depends on the growth of the other. In his first baccalaureate address (1846), the Rector promised parents that "there can be no effectual teaching that . . . does not avow its right and purpose to pre-occupy the whole spiritual and moral nature from childhood onwards."[76] Such a holistic formation of young men requires that teachers have confidence that their pedagogy can be concerned with the hidden realities in the heart. In some mysterious way, the growth of the soul makes the mind more capacious. It is as if religious faith, reaching for the knowledge of unseen realities, gives to the rational aspect of human nature an aptitude.

---

74. Hein, *Religion and Politics*, 144. In this superb work of historical scholarship already cited, Hein proves that Saint James was not so much like an English public school, which many have assumed about the whole family of Muhlenberg–type church schools. The best principles and practices of schools such as Winchester, Eton, and Rugby were admired but borrowed with discretion. Henry Coit (1830–95), founding rector of St. Paul's, Concord, and one of Muhlenberg's most devoted disciples, wrote of St. Paul's in 1891: "The school is American in the strictest sense of the word, on American soil, under American institutions, for American needs, and not an imitation, however good, of what cannot be reproduced on this side of the Atlantic—a great English public school." Coit, "American Boys' School," 5.

75. Prov 22:6.

76. See Kerfoot's first Baccalaureate Address in *Three Addresses*, 24.

A former student of Kerfoot's wrote as an old man, "Religion gives power to receive education."[77]

Kerfoot had a favorite marble in his pocket from St. Tully. *Nullum theatrum virtutis conscientia majus est*: "No display of virtue is greater than the conscience."[78] These educators knew they were shaping the very souls of their students. They took on the responsibility with reverence but without hesitation. Since they cut their teeth on the works of Bishop Joseph Butler (1692–1752), especially the *Fifteen Sermons* on morals (1726) and *The Analogy of Religion* (1736), they assumed that "the voice of God" in a boy (his conscience) required fine tuning.

> The truth is, this business of conducting a school of the Church is an art and profession by itself, requiring as much study and training, and involving as deep and distinct principles, and at least as many minute details, as any other art—whether it be Medicine, Law, or Divinity . . . [God's] representative on earth, the Church, receives these children in His name at the hands of their parents, assuming their charge and training the sons of God . . . Here the Church has constituted a household, ruled by her delegated authority, for the education of every department of the children whom through her, you—their parents—have given to God . . . We are here no mere pedagogues; though with the full sense of the title my ambition would be satisfied . . . What we do besides mere teaching in the daily class—*the watchful, ceaseless care and instruction of minister and parent combined*—this is the work we seek. For this we accept no money; we give it freely, over and above the other. This higher part of our work is what we love and labor in for God; the other part we do as well as we can, that we may gather around us young souls to train for the Church on earth and in heaven . . . Education in any kind of good is a slow work, not often very perceptible until months and even years go by.[79]

In the 1840s, Joseph Coit was impressed as a young student at Fountain Rock with the simplicity of every aspect of school life.[80] As the finan-

---

77. Coit, "American Boys' School," 14. When Henry Coit wrote these words in 1891, he had himself been educating boys in a church school in New England for over forty years.

78. See Kerfoot's second Baccalaureate Address in *Three Addresses*, 45. Cicero's maxim may be found in *Tusc.* 2.26.

79. Kerfoot, *Address to Parents*, 9–10.

80. Coit, "Recollections," 330.

cial situation got a little better, improvements were made in the facilities and the food, but relative to the expectations of the social class patronizing the college, life at Fountain Rock remained simple throughout the 1840s and 1850s and became especially simple during the Civil War. As perhaps belabored by now, Kerfoot's idea was that human relationships and the cultivation of authentic intellectual and moral culture were the aims of education; thus most luxuries were religiously avoided. The pressure to add the marks of refinement must have been great in that place, at that time, and with that clientele. Kerfoot and his colleagues were only human, and of course the whole purpose of the brotherhood was improvement, but they did a remarkable job of keeping things simple.[81]

The Flight of the Arrow

One respected student of the American boarding school found Fountain Rock to be so much like College Point that he concluded (if redundantly) that Kerfoot followed Muhlenberg's example "to the literal letter."[82] McLachlan's assessment is only half true, as Kerfoot's Anglophilia proves. Time does not stand still and of course Muhlenberg's program and inclination to romanticism continued to evolve at Saint James. McLachlan is correct to see that Kerfoot's enterprise was a *development* of an existing tradition rather than a fundamental departure from it. The fruit did not fall far from the tree. The program remained much the same in terms of both mechanics and goals. But in Maryland Muhlenberg's philosophy and practice came under the influence of Bishop Whittingham, who was something of a Hobartian High Churchman. Kerfoot had great respect for his bishop, and his bishop had formed in his own right many ideas about high-caliber Christian education. This does not minimize the

---

81. Harrison, *Life of Kerfoot*, 1:42. Kerfoot violated Muhlenbergian simplicity in one important respect: He chose marriage over celibacy. He married Eliza Anderson of New York in early 1842. The wedding was solemnized by Muhlenberg. Eliza was the sister of Kip Anderson, a former pupil at College Point. Anderson was soon a member of the staff at Fountain Rock. While Mrs. Porter was the matron for the boys and young men, Mrs. Kerfoot was a diligent hostess on the college's and her husband's behalf. Harrison wrote that the Andersons "had no inconsiderable influence" on Kerfoot's churchmanship. Harrison meant that the Andersons' Hobartian High Churchmanship encouraged Kerfoot in that direction. There can be no mistake that, in his biography of Kerfoot, Harrison hoped to distance Kerfoot's churchmanship from that of his mentor, Dr. Muhlenberg.

82. McLachlan, *Boarding Schools*, 132.

power of Kerfoot's own considerable experience, common-sense, and problem-solving skill in regards to running a Christian college.

How *much* did Hobartian religion alter the Muhlenberg-type church school at Fountain Rock? One of Kerfoot's former students who possessed an expert knowledge of education and schools believed that the changes were many and deep. Joseph Coit, writing in the 1880s, insisted that "Dr. Kerfoot's practical temper, knowledge of boys, and power to instill a good spirit among them, were strongly manifested in giving up many of the traditions and rules which had been transplanted from Dr. Muhlenberg's school, which his observation and experience finally pronounced unwise or unnecessary."[83] That Kerfoot found it necessary to make some alterations in the "traditions and rules" would not surprise anyone. Muhlenberg's 1841 "Farewell to Kerfoot" shows that the doctor himself expected changes would have to be made in the program once Kerfoot had a better knowledge of the situation on the ground. On the other hand, the evidence summarized above shows that there is no reason to think that the alterations were either many or particularly significant while Kerfoot was Rector of Saint James. Coit does not say in his "Recollections" what the altered "traditions and rules" were or when they were altered or dropped. Coit was also writing from Concord, New Hampshire, where his brother Henry started a Muhlenberg-type church school from scratch and thus like Kerfoot was able to correct any weaknesses in the tradition. Dr. Muhlenberg visited the Coit brothers at St. Paul's, Concord, at least twice before his death in 1877.[84]

83. Coit, "Recollections," in Harrison, *Kerfoot*, 1:331. Coit contradicts himself in the reminiscences, saying in one place that "the apparatus for help was scant" (332) and in another that every teacher was more than helpful and generous at all times (333). Coit's "apparatus" might mean our *facilities*, which to Kerfoot were of secondary importance. Coit was writing his reminiscence of Fountain Rock from St. Paul's School, Concord, an increasingly well-endowed church school where the facilities used by masters and scholars had become steadily more splendid especially after the older Coit's headship. Joseph Coit's assessment of Saint James creates a problem for the researcher because his testimony is weighty. He worked very closely with Kerfoot for eighteen years as a student, an instructor, and (for over a decade) as the Vice-Rector. Thus, Coit had much opportunity to observe Kerfoot or hear about ways he was intentionally altering Muhlenberg's program. Moreover, Coit would have been somewhat familiar with Muhlenberg's operations at College Point because his brother Henry Coit attended Muhlenberg's school.

84. Henry Augustus Coit (1830–95) was prepared by Muhlenberg at St. Paul's, College Point, between 1842 and 1845. After a year's sojourn in Georgia tutoring Bishop Stephen Elliott's children, Coit earned the Bachelor in Arts degree (classics) from the College of Saint James while serving on the faculty there. Following a brief stint at

By 1860, the ideals, hard work, and daily sacrifices of the faculty, staff, and trustees of the College and Grammar School of Saint James had produced an institution with growing enrollment and an excellent reputation outside the region. Already in 1855, Jared Sparks (1789–1866), just retired as president of Harvard College, remarked to a large gathering of scholars in Boston that he thought Saint James students the best prepared of all the young men coming to Harvard from the South.[85] While high academic status was not the first purpose of the rector and his professors, they were glad for their good repute in the halls of illustrious colleges and universities. The college achieved a solid academic reputation in only eighteen years by stressing the formation of character, then watching how the strengthening inner person enables young men of various gifts to avail themselves of a rich and challenging course of study.

At Fountain Rock they were always short of the resources to enable them to find ease of operation. In certain years, a fear of inadequate funding was felt in the brotherhood. Kerfoot's many letters to Bishop Whittingham constantly mention the need for financial gifts. But the members of this particular scholastic fellowship understood with greater clarity than many members of their profession that there is danger in comfort, luxury, and even national reputation. Kerfoot would have remembered how Muhlenberg favored just this situation for a school: As long as the brotherhood was faithful, hard-working, and achieving its ambitious goals, Kerfoot and the staff knew they were delivering quality according to their ideals. Studiously neutral about developments in the national political scene, at least in his literary remains, Kerfoot remained hopeful about the future. At the time of Lincoln's election to the presidency,

---

Bishop Bowman's school in Lancaster, Pennsylvania (attached to Saint James Parish), Coit headed to upstate New York for service as a mission priest. It was while engaged in missionary endeavor that the nascent Board of Trustees of St. Paul's School, Concord, called Coit to be the first rector. This was the year 1855. The school opened the following year at G. C. Shattuck's farm in Millville near Concord.

85. Sparks quoted in Brand, *Whittingham*, 1:302. The Bishop wrote to Kerfoot on 27 August 1855, "I was greatly pleased, the other day, by hearing from one present on the occasion, that lately, in Boston, in a large company, conversation turning on Southern college students, their negligence, turbulence, etc., Professor Jared Sparks said: 'By the by, there is one institution at the South which has sent some remarkable exceptions. It is, I believe, in Maryland, and called the College of Saint James. Four or five young men have come from it to Cambridge and have been without exception among the best prepared and the best mannered men we have. In all respects they did the very highest honor to their training.'"

the rector enjoyed a sense of accomplishment and contemplated a most promising future for the college.

What developed at Fountain Rock between 1842 and 1864 was as rare and impressive as Dr. Muhlenberg's schools at Flushing and College Point. Under Kerfoot's leadership the College and Grammar School of Saint James became a scholastic brotherhood of uncommon excellence. It was a productive and happy fellowship to which boys and young men were drawn from all over the United States. They left with a lifetime's stock of good memories of a scholastic experience that taught them to aim high, work hard, and live in a community based on Christian faith and high aspirations. Alas, the Southern rebellion finally drove Kerfoot and his companions away from Fountain Rock, but a mission imperative so firmly established must endure.

3

Slavery, War, and Destruction
The College of St. James, 1861–64

Emilie Amt

IN THE FALL OF 1860, the College of Saint James was an uneasy place. With the national political situation intensifying, people at the school were nervous about what the threat of war meant for the college as well as the nation.[1] The election in November of President Lincoln, whose party opposed the expansion of slavery, prompted the Southern states to begin to secede. Rector John B. Kerfoot, worried about pro-secession feeling among the students, felt that he should stay on campus rather than travel for even a few days. The Rev. Joseph Coit, professor of mathematics and physics, described the school community as "excited and disturbed by the progress of the secession movement" but hoping for compromise and peace.[2] This was surely the hope of the schoolmasters, who were mostly clergymen from the North. But other feelings also stirred the Saint James

---

1. For earlier discussions of the college during the Civil War, see Harrison, *Life of Kerfoot*, vol. 1; Duncan, "College of St. James and the Civil War"; Cuthbert, "Naked in the Midst of Armies"; Harvey, "College of St. James During the Civil War"; Pipkin, "(Almost) Battle of St. James College."

2. Maryland Diocesan Archives, Baltimore, John B. Kerfoot letter to Bishop William R. Whittingham, 9 and 19 Nov. 1860 (these letters hereafter cited as Kerfoot to WRW; many are also printed in Harrison); Harrison, *Life of Kerfoot*, 356.

community, which was more diverse than the little knot of Episcopal clergy who ruled it. Like Maryland and like the Hagerstown area, the college sheltered people of many origins and views. Not all of them feared war in 1860; indeed, some welcomed it. And people's views sometimes shifted with almost lightning speed. A closer look at the college community will help us see this.

The largest group at the college was of course the students. The 1860–61 academic year began with 104 of them in residence, nearly two thirds at the college level and the rest in the grammar school. The student population eventually swelled to at least 116. Of these, about half came from Maryland (fifty-one) and Washington, DC (five), and nearly a third (thirty-six) came from other Southern states (Alabama, the Carolinas, Florida, Georgia, Louisiana, Mississippi, Tennessee, and Virginia). The remainder (twenty-four) came from Northern and Midwestern states (Illinois, Massachusetts, Minnesota, Missouri, New Jersey, New York, and Pennsylvania). It is easy to see that Southern opinion might overwhelm Northern views among the students, with much depending on the views of Marylanders. Many young men in 1860–61 were excited about the prospect of war, and their political views often changed quickly.[3]

An example of a Maryland student is W. Wilkins Davis, who came from a well-off slave-holding family easily able to afford the $260 it cost to send a son to Saint James for a year. Their farm in Montgomery County was about sixty miles (by road) from the college.[4] Davis had been at Saint James since 1857; in the fall of 1860 he was an eighteen-year-old junior in the college. His father was a strong Unionist but sympathetic to the South; his mother was at least privately pro-secession in the fall of 1860. Like many Marylanders, young Davis's family members, especially his mother, blamed the looming war on the abolition movement. Davis himself was strongly pro-Union in the late fall, writing to his sister that he thought

---

3. Kerfoot to WRW, 11 October 1860; *Register* (1860, 1862) (the Maryland Historical Society, Baltimore, holds a nearly complete set of *Registers*); Landrum, *History of Spartanburg County*, 346–47; Manning, *What This Cruel War Was Over*, 27–32.

4. Hein, *Religion and Politics*, 36–39. The Davis family letters survive at the Maryland Historical Society. The father, Allen Bowie Davis, held twenty-seven slaves in 1850 and thirty in 1860; in the 1860 census slave schedule his surname is mistakenly recorded as Dorsey, after a string of Dorsey neighbors. Census Data, National Archives and Records Administration, *1860 Census, Montgomery County, MD, First District, Slave Schedule p. 7*, NARA (National Archives and Records Administration) M653. All census citations are from digital images at Ancestry.com and refer to population schedules for Washington County, MD, unless otherwise noted.

"the political demagogues of the South" had "charmed the minds of the ignorant and unthinking" into supporting secession. At school, he was a trusted pupil; in November Kerfoot invited him to teach in a Sunday school being organized for local children. Students like Davis, still holding to the Union or at least not voicing disaffection from it, were in the majority during the fall of 1860, enabling Kerfoot to write, throughout the autumn and winter, that all was quiet on the political front.[5]

While students were the *raison d'être* of the college, other groups were also part of the community at Fountain Rock. Some fifteen instructional staff were engaged for the school year, some residential and others visiting as needed. A few teachers had families living with them at Saint James. Kerfoot's thirty-nine-year-old wife Eliza and daughters Annie (fifteen years old), Catharine (four), and Helen (six months) lived with him at the rectory. His son Abel (seventeen) was a student at the college. The Rev. Julius Dashiell (thirty-four), Vice-Rector and professor of classical languages, had with him his wife Mary (twenty-six). The Prussian-born Rev. Alexander Falk (fifty-seven), professor of history and languages, lived with his wife Martha (forty-nine) and his daughter Bertha (nineteen), who worked as a governess to supplement the family income. The Rev. Joseph Passmore (forty-three), professor of rhetoric, philosophy, and political economy, had his wife Susan (thirty-eight) and two sons (eight and four) living with him. Another resident faculty relative, also an employee, was Eliza Porter (sixty), college matron and grandmother of tutor Lucien P. Waddell (twenty-one); she was also the mother of a career army officer, Fitz-John Porter (1822–1901), who would be a friend to the school in the coming hostilities.[6] We can imagine that these faculty families dreaded the idea of war.

In addition, the college employed many people, both black and white, male and female, who formed overlapping social groups. Some of their names are known to us. Bavarian-born Paul Hartman, the twenty-two-year-old watchman who patrolled the college grounds at night, and gardener George Febri, born forty years earlier in Baden, were among "our

5. *Register* (1857, 1860, 1862); Hein, *Religion and Politics*, 46–49, 51–52, 83–84, 99–103; Kerfoot to WRW, 9 and 19 Nov. 1860; 21 Jan., 26 Feb., and 27 Mar. 1861. The annual charge for a clergyman's son was $175.

6. Census Data, National Archives and Records Administration, *1860 Census, Montgomery County, MD, First District, Slave Schedule p. 7*, NARA (National Archives and Records Administration) M653, Williamsport District, roll 483; Alexander Falk letter to WRW, 8 Oct. 1864 (Diocesan Archives); Harrison, *Life of Kerfoot*, 212n; Hein, *Religion and Politics*, 79.

German servants." Ethnic Germans formed a large part of the local population. Ellen Van Horn, a thirty-two-year-old white woman, worked at the college as a seamstress. A black waiter named Collins, a communicant in the college chapel, had died in 1858; his successor, with the initials "H.U.," was serving the boys in the dining hall in 1863. A black woman named Margaret, married to Collins the waiter, was a longtime servant at the college (at least from about 1846 to 1861) and a communicant in the chapel. Perhaps the nature of Margaret's work is revealed by a Hagerstown newspaper ad in 1853: "Wanted! At the College of St. James—4 Good Trusty *Colored Women*, 2 as Cooks and 2 as Chambermaids. The highest wages will be given." The college cook in 1863 was a black woman who lived with her two children on-site or nearby. Kerfoot employed three black women in 1860, probably in his household, but perhaps in the college: Mary Adley (twenty-one), Ellen Pearce (twenty-five), and Sally Pearce (seventeen). In 1860, the Passmores had two young mixed-race servants in their household, Sophia Jones (eighteen) and Ellen Dorsey (fifteen).[7]

But not all college work was done by paid labor, for there was also a living legacy of slavery at Saint James. Fountain Rock had been a slave-worked plantation before its purchase by the Diocese of Maryland in 1841, with sixty-four souls enslaved there by the Ringgold family in 1820. This made Fountain Rock home to one of the largest groups of slaves in the county. Slave labor had certainly been used in erecting and maintaining the buildings on the estate, including the slave quarters that stood on the school grounds well into the twentieth century. When the college was established, the Maryland Episcopalians who contributed were largely slaveholders, giving money that was made in part from the stolen labor of enslaved people.[8] Slaves were held at the college in its first two decades.

---

7. Census Data, National Archives and Records Administration, *1860 Census, Montgomery County, MD, First District, Slave Schedule p. 7*, NARA (National Archives and Records Administration) M653, Williamsport District, roll 483; Kerfoot to WRW, 27 March and 19 June 1861; Harrison, *Life of Kerfoot*, 310, 330; McLachlan, "Civil War Diary of Joseph H. Coit," 248, 254 (hereafter cited as Coit Diary); Hein, *Religion and Politics in Maryland on the Eve of the Civil War*, 100; *The Herald of Freedom & Torch Light*, Oct. 19, 1853.

8. 1820 Census, Election District 2, NARA M33, roll 46; Nelson, *Reminiscences* (privately printed, 1973), 2; Diocesan Archives, Vertical File "College of St. James," list of local donors in Bishop Whittingham's hand. Listed, for example, were donors Dall, Dorsey, Fitzhugh, and Galloway, who in 1840 held forty-nine, four, twenty, and ten slaves respectively; *1840 Census, Montgomery County, MD*, NARA M704, Williamsford and Hagerstown, roll 169, p. 202; roll 171, pp. 108, 114, 134. For the role of slavery in American higher education generally, see Wilder, *Ebony and Ivory*, esp. 47–111.

Violet, daughter of one of the Ringgolds' slaves, lived on at the College, possibly still as a slave, and others may have been in the same position.[9]

Like many Episcopal clergymen in Maryland, some masters at the College held slaves. Kerfoot owned Kitty Brooks and her children for a few years, though his reasons were expressly to help them to freedom (see below). In 1850, he also owned a thirty-year-old woman.[10] In 1850, the Rev. Russell Trevett, professor of classics, held three slaves: a fifty-year-old woman, a twenty-year-old woman, and a seven-year-old girl. M. C. Clarkson, then-Secretary of the College, held a thirty-year-old male slave in 1850. The ad quoted above, seeking four "colored women," may have meant the college wanted to hire enslaved women from their masters, a common practice in northern and western Maryland. The college's post office was an address for casual slave trading, as in this April 1861 Hagerstown newspaper ad: "Negro Boy for Sale. Will be sold at private sale a healthy Negro Boy, between 13 and 14 years old, slave for life. Terms and prices to suit the times. John Reichard, Executor of John Ringer . . . , College of St. James P.O." A twenty-year-old slave named Matilda Pearce (probably related to Kerfoot's free black servants) was buried in the college cemetery in 1856.[11] Beyond these direct connections, college recruitment benefited from its location in a slave state. Even before its opening, the bishop of North Carolina wrote to Bishop Whittingham, "Your school . . . has the advantage over [St. Paul's] College Point [New York] of being in a slave state." And indeed at least one Southern mother was interested in sending her son to Saint James because she was "unwilling to send him to a free state."[12] These statements remind us that slavery was a key element

9. "She had always lived on the property"; Onderdonk, *Memoirs of Adrian Holmes Onderdonk*, 13. No free black woman named Violet is listed locally in the 1850 or 1860 Census; Violet's story of having seen General Washington, if accurately attributed to her, probably identifies her as a former Ringgold slave.

10. Washington County Circuit Court (Land Records) 1858–1859, IN 13, 298–300, MSA CE 18-18 (online); 1850 U.S. Census, Subdivision 2, slave schedule, NARA M432; Washington County Historical Society, Hagerstown, documents D25 and BS201.

11. *1850 U.S. Census*, Washington County Md. Subdivision 2, slave schedule, NARA M432; Grivno, *Gleanings of Freedom*, 3, 39, 43; *Herald of Freedom & Torch Light*, April 17, 1861, 3B; Boonsboro, MD, St. Mark's Parish Register 1, p. 68. Bishop Whittingham rented a twelve-year-old enslaved boy; Census Data, National Archives and Records Administration, *1860 Census, Montgomery County, MD, First District, Slave Schedule p. 3*, NARA M653, 20th Ward.

12. Diocesan Archives, Levi Silliman Ives letter to WRW, 15 July 1841; William Alexander letter to WRW, 5 July 1845.

in Maryland's southern identity and thus in the college's ability to attract so much of its student body from states to its south. A large proportion of those students and of the Maryland ones—almost certainly a majority—came from slave-owning families.[13] Thus the tuition money that paid the bills at Saint James came in substantial part from slave labor.

A few enslaved persons gained their freedom at the college. In 1843, Kerfoot purchased Kitty Brooks and her daughter Eliza Robison for $476; he freed Brooks (and her three new children) in 1848 after she had worked off $374. In 1851, Kerfoot deeded fifteen-year-old Robison her eventual freedom, while selling her for a term of sixteen more years to clear the rest of her family's purchase price. This whole episode was probably the same one described by a local A.M.E. preacher, who wrote about a white man connected with Saint James helping to rescue a woman (named Catharine Peeker) and her daughter from slavery.[14] These acts of grace, though infrequent, could make all the difference to the individuals concerned. The college benefited blacks through employment and in less tangible ways. Slaves and their free black relatives made up part of the congregation that worshiped in the college chapel. African American children were often baptized, either on campus or elsewhere, by clergy based at the college.[15] In 1859–60, the Rev. John K. Lewis, mathematics tutor and nephew to the rector, ran "a regular Sunday evening service"—evidently more of a Sunday school—"for the colored persons of the College and in its neighborhood," with ten male and seven female

---

13. For examples, see below, *passim*. All evidence indicates, though, that no students brought slaves with them to the college. Students slept in common dormitories, and the austere living arrangements for students made no allowance for personal servants; see, e.g., *Register* (1860); Harrison, *Life of Kerfoot*, 329–30.

14. Washington County Circuit Court (Land Records) 1858–1859, IN 13, 298–300, MSA CE 18-18 (online); Henry, *From Slavery to Salvation*, 43. I believe Catharine Peeker was Catharine "Kitty" Brooks. Although some details of the stories differ, many elements are similar, and it is unlikely two such similar episodes occurred. For fuller treatment of this story, see discussion at www.emilieamt.com. In Maryland at this time, the promise of future freedom was part of 88 percent of local slave sales; Grivno, *Gleanings of Freedom*, 138.

15. College clergy reported baptisms of two black infants in 1847 (p. 146), two in 1848 (p. 102), one in 1849 (p. 95), one in 1854 (p. 90), two in 1860 (p. 88), and one in 1862 (p. 59); *Journals of the Annual Conventions of the Diocese of Maryland* (hereafter cited as *Journals of the Annual Conventions*), *passim*. In 1859 Vice-rector Dashiell baptized free black Rachel Hinton and her three children; *St. Mark's Parish Register*, 1:50–51.

"scholars."[16] In 1861, Kerfoot pleaded vigorously (though in vain) for the bishop to grant a church marriage to the now widowed Margaret Collins, whose earlier marriage to an enslaved man who was probably still living—but had been sold to New Orleans—disqualified her from this rite of the church. For African Americans who lived and worked at or near Saint James, the college may have provided, however inadequately, spiritual comfort, religious education, and even practical improvement of their circumstances. But relations were not always friendly; for example, a free black man named Alfred Howard was arrested in 1853 for allegedly stealing "sundry articles of clothing from the students."[17]

In 1860, there may have been no slaves left at the college itself. But the free African Americans at the college were closely connected with slaves on surrounding farms, such as John W. Breathed's estate. Breathed, the parent of several students at Saint James, was the college's secretary and curator, looking after its finances. Two of his slaves, William (age nineteen) and Ellen (twenty-four) Thompson, were buried at the college in 1858.[18] Slaves like Breathed's, along with their free black neighbors, probably welcomed the prospect of a war they saw as certain to free local enslaved people from bondage. We know that slaves across the South and in Washington County took a keen interest in war news and hoped for a Union victory. Indeed, enslaved Marylanders began to flee to Union lines as soon as the war began; slave escapes from Washington County continued throughout the war.[19]

Although Kerfoot and others connected with the college wrote in this period about sectionalism and unionism, they were almost silent on slavery. Kerfoot blamed abolitionists, among others, for the strife that was

---

16. *Journals of the Annual Conventions* (1860), 86–87. Son of an Ohio abolitionist, Lewis graduated from Saint James in 1857 and served as head of the grammar school for four years. When the war began he moved north; in 1865 he was appointed the founding headmaster of St. Mark's School, Southborough, MA. *Centennial Portrait and Biographical Record of the City of Dayton and of Montgomery County, Ohio, containing Biographical Sketches of Prominent and Representative Citizens*, 362–66.

17. Kerfoot to WRW, 27 Mar. 1861; Brand, *Life of William Rollinson Whittingham*, ii. 102–3; *Herald of Freedom & Torch Light*, Dec. 21, 1853. For local church interaction with blacks before the Civil War, see Amt, "Down From the Balcony: African Americans and Episcopal Congregations in Washington County, Maryland, 1800–1864."

18. *Register* (1857, 1859, 1860, 1862); *St. Mark's Parish Register*, 1:68.

19. Litwack, *Been in the Storm So Long*, 21–27; Mitchell, *Maryland Voices of the Civil War*, 364–65, 368, 372; Miles, *"Grandma," Or, the Life of Mrs. Eliza Miles*; Bingham, "Little Boy in Maryland during the Civil War," 47; "Enrollment of Slaves," *Herald & Torch Light*, March 23, 1864.

rending the country. In a letter written in January 1861 to his friend and pro-Southern trustee William G. Harrison, Kerfoot condemned what he saw as the worst extreme of slavery in the past, commenting that only a revival of the African slave trade would break his loyalty to Maryland, should Maryland secede. (This letter is also interesting in revealing that Kerfoot's staunch unionism emerged only gradually; in it he describes being "more and more" against secession, but says he would be "well content, if God decrees the shattering of our Union, to see Maryland go with the South.") Similarly, the Rev. Cornelius Swope, a former trustee and 1846 graduate of Saint James, wrote to Kerfoot in 1862 lamenting the "the policy of killing slavery" and wishing "there were less abolitionism and more patriotism."[20] Still, these were all abstractions. Reading these letters, one would never know that slavery was a matter of any personal consequence for the writers. Yet the college and the white people who lived there were intimately involved in slave-owning and with enslaved people. It is disconcerting to juxtapose their acceptance of slavery and condemnation of abolition with their strenuous moral teachings in other spheres.

As 1861 began, the college's population faced a quickly changing national political situation. In January, Kerfoot reported to the bishop with typical if misplaced confidence that "3/4 of our Southern boys are—as their families are—*Union*-men." Nevertheless, when some students took the opportunity of an academic debate to speak against secession, the Rector saw the danger of future conflict and forbade any further political speeches. Wilkins Davis, still a unionist, and his fellow students were closely following newspaper reports and rumors about developments in Charleston, South Carolina, and the rector noted, "Any day's news might stir the young blood bitterly." There were also financial strains at the school this winter, apparently due more to the cold weather than to the threat of war. The rector intentionally economized on fuel, light, and other things, and Wilkins Davis complained in a letter home, "They pay such poor prices here for everything that the neighbors wont [sic] bring any but the poorest things."[21] Such conditions would become chronic during the war.

20. Kerfoot to William G. Harrison, 5 Jan. 1861, quoted in Harrison, *Life of Kerfoot*, 193–94; Diocesan Archives, C.E. Swope letter to Kerfoot, 18 July 1862; *Register* (1847, 1859).

21. Kerfoot to WRW, 21 Jan. and undated page, 1861; Hein, *Religion and Politics*, 105–6, 111; Kerfoot to William G. Harrison, 22 January 1861, quoted in Harrison, *Life of Kerfoot*, 200–201.

As the spring of 1861 went on, the school's hold on students grew more tenuous. One South Carolina mother wrote that "outside pressure" would "force her" to remove her son from the college the following year if Maryland did not secede from the Union. In April, students started to leave. Edward Jefferson Dean, a freshman from Spartanburg, answered the South Carolina governor's call for volunteers and left school to join the state's military. Dean may have been among the troops moved to Charleston for the attack on Fort Sumter that began the war in mid-April of 1861. A few days later, federal troops were assaulted by a mob as they traveled through Baltimore. John Boykin Lee, a sophomore from South Carolina, also left for home, where his mother and sister relied on him as the head of the family. By April 27, six students had left the college. Ignorant of Dean's (and perhaps others') military activities, Kerfoot attributed all of the students' departures except Lee's to "parents' panic."[22]

After Sumter, the mood among the students shifted dramatically. "[L]ittle Secession flags" sprouted in their rooms and on their desks, and "secession talk" was everywhere among them. "Most of them are now secessionists," wrote Kerfoot. Wilkins Davis, who in January had been an avowed unionist, declared to his sister that he was now "a straight out 'Southern Rights' man" and "for the 'Southern confederacy' and the right." Moreover, he hoped to "have the pleasure of seeing a battle [at the College] if not of participating in it." With a clear grasp of the college's proximity to militarily significant locations, Davis noted, "We will be able to see the smoke and hear the firing when they get to fighting at Harpers Ferry, and at night we will be able to see the bombshell flying from the Maryland heights batteries."[23] Davis was clearly looking forward to the excitement, and no doubt many of his fellow students shared his outlook.

The students "know that we are Union men," Kerfoot asserted in April, but his assessment of the faculty's loyalty was not entirely accurate. At least one instructor, Greek and Latin tutor Hall Harrison, "was passionately devoted to the South," as his colleague Joseph Coit put it. Kerfoot had every reason to know this. Harrison was the nephew of trustee William G. Harrison, with whom Kerfoot had corresponded frankly in January 1861 about secession and slavery. Kerfoot himself, though, had apparently become more definitely Unionist over the course of the spring. In late

22. Kerfoot to WRW, 27 Mar., 7 and 27 Apr. 1861; Landrum, *Spartanburg County*, 346–47. Dean would serve eventually as a captain in the South Carolina Volunteers, Fifth Regiment, mainly in Virginia.

23. Kerfoot to WRW, 27 Apr. and 19 June 1861; Hein, *Religion and Politics*, 119–21.

April he decided to send his son Abel north, lest he be drafted by a future secessionist Maryland government and forced to fight against the United States. Abel spent some time at seminary in New York.[24]

Once the war had begun, events moved quickly at the college. On May 1, Kerfoot sent a form letter to parents, assuring them "that all is quiet and safe within the College, and in all the district around us," asserting that Saint James would carry on as normal and making practical arrangements in case of difficulties that might arise from the war. Later that month Wilkins Davis reported with pleasure that an "advanced guard of 1500 Virginians has encamped within four miles of us, at Williamsport, and we are daily expecting the advance guard of 10,000 Pennsylvanians at Hagerstown six miles on the other side of us."[25] Unbeknownst to those at the college, the pattern for the rest of the war was being set. Every summer would bring military incursions into Washington County, with increasingly serious consequences for the college. Since school was normally in session from October through July, most of these events—with the notable exception of the Antietam campaign—took place while students were on campus. The rest of each year would be a time of rebuilding, watchfulness, and essentially vain hopes for the future. The gracious thirty-one-acre campus was a magnet to units of both armies because of the unusually abundant spring on its premises, but early in the war the college seems to have suffered fewer depredations by troops than did local farmers, and the adult men at the college, unlike many local Unionists, felt no need to flee or hide at the approach of southern forces.[26]

In May of 1860, the proximity of Confederate troops delighted the southern students, some of whom secretly visited the camp at Williamsport; on May 20, as soon as he learned of the boys sneaking off campus, Kerfoot forbade it under penalty of expulsion. "Lynx eyed John B. got wind of it and made us a stump speech on the subject last night," remarked Wilkins Davis in a letter to his sister. Along with the military situation, students showed a lively interest in Maryland wartime politics. Around June 5, Kerfoot also prohibited the students' private display of

---

24. Coit, *Hall Harrison, 1837–1900*, 5, 10–11; Harrison, *Life of Kerfoot*, 222–25; Kerfoot to WRW, 27 Apr. 1861.

25. Diocesan Archives, printed circular, 1 May 1861, filed with Kerfoot letters to WRW; Hein, 120.

26. Cf. Nesbitt diary, in *Windmills of Time*, 188, 192–93, 196, 201, 203–5, 207; Bingham, "Little Boy in Maryland," 45, 47, 50–51, 54; Davis, "War Remembrances," 18; Smith, Diary in *Hancock, 1776–1976*, 24, 26.

Confederate flags. Meanwhile he was in contact with the Union military leadership in Hagerstown, where Major General Fitz-John Porter, son of the college's matron Eliza Porter, assured him that no federal troops would make camp very close to the school. Students were continuing to melt away; by mid-June, a total of twenty-three had gone. The faculty anticipated further losses before the end of the term.[27]

Troops arrived at Saint James for the first time on the evening of Saturday, June 15, 1861, when Union Brigadier General A. S. Williams and a force of about four thousand Pennsylvanians appeared from Hagerstown and—to the alarm of the faculty and intense interest of the students—camped in a field just south of the college grounds. This first real wartime encounter between the college and the military demonstrated a mix of goodwill and awkwardness. Kerfoot scrambled to introduce himself to Williams and the other officers and assured them of his own loyalty, but he felt compelled to explain that the faculty, as clergy and teachers, had decided to treat both sides in the war evenhandedly. The Rector observed privately that many of the troops were "[r]ude men . . . miners, furnace men, etc." and "of rough make," but that in the "evening the students mixed somewhat with them—and all went on cheerfully." Kerfoot and the general together agreed a demarcation line "across our spring, over the little bridge," to separate soldiers and students, though the officers were given access to the college bathhouse. The rector was still "fearfully anxious," especially that the "sillier" students might "talk South" to the soldiers—as indeed they did. Later the officers arranged a guard at Kerfoot's request to keep soldiers away from the campus; at Sunday morning chapel the headmaster strictly prohibited students from fraternizing with the troops. Still, a crisis arose when some of the soldiers started to grumble that there was no US flag flying at the college and that Saint James was pro-Confederate. The school's German servants heard the rumor in the camp and brought it to Kerfoot, who checked it with a former student in the camp, Lt. John Redmond Conyngham of Lancaster, Pennsylvania (grammar school, 1855–57). Unable to find the college's own flag, the faculty borrowed one from the army and ran it up the flagpole. The soldiers cheered and good feeling was for the most part restored, though "one crazy boy" (as Kerfoot thought him) among the students called out, "Haul down that flag," in front of the soldiers and was nearly beaten up

---

27. Hein, *Religion and Politics*, 120, 125; Kerfoot to WRW, 12 and 19 June 186; Harrison, 211; Coit letter to WRW, undated loose page [June 1861], Maryland Hist. Soc., MS 10, Box 3.

for it. Later on Sunday the troops received fresh orders, and by the end of the day they were gone. Kerfoot followed up this episode with a moratorium on political discussion among the students, giving special attention to those from nearby: "The hottest talkers for months had been young *Marylanders*, all sons of Union men! Each of these I saw privately and gave them the option of abstinence from debates that excite, or a return at once to their fathers." Undoubtedly Wilkins Davis was among those called into Kerfoot's study for one of these chats. The rector hoped that the presence of "6,000 bayonets" had proved "edifying" for the students, but in fact it probably only intensified their existing loyalties.[28]

The rest of the summer passed peacefully enough, but the war with its paradoxes was now a daily reality. Letters from the college were full of troop movements and actions around Williamsport, Hagerstown, and Martinsburg, as young men continued to trickle away from Saint James for the Confederate army. At commencement in July 1861, Kerfoot gave a confident speech, avowing both unionism and toleration as principles of the college. A few days later, the rector would write that Bull Run had thrown "fresh doubts over the immediate future of the College," and in August he described Hagerstown and Washington County as riven by conflict. Yet he was planning for the fall term and hoping for sixty students by January.[29]

The 1861–62 academic year opened quietly in October with only thirty-five students in residence.[30] This number grew unevenly as additional students came and went, reaching forty-five by February, but still the size of the college was at less than half its pre-war level, and only three students were from the South (one from Virginia and two from Louisiana). Throughout the war years the rector watched enrollments anxiously, reporting frequently to the bishop on the prospect of this or that new boy or the likelihood that so-and-so would leave or return.[31] The faculty was shrinking too, mostly through attrition. Fewer teachers were needed or could be supported by the much-reduced student body. Institutional income was reduced by more than half this year, the war

28. *Register* (1856, 1857); Kerfoot to WRW, 19 June 1861.

29. Kerfoot to WRW, 19, 21, and 28 June, 2 and 26 July, and 26 Aug. 1861; Hein, *Religion and Politics*, 16.

30. Harrison is mistaken (p. 216) in saying there were only sixteen; Kerfoot to WRW, 1 Oct. 1861. Wilkins Davis did not return, as he had gone to study medicine at the University of Maryland; Hein, *Religion and Politics*, 129–30.

31. *Register* (1862); Kerfoot to WRW, 18 Nov., 16 and 20 Dec. 1861, 11 Feb. 1862, etc.

meant that debts owed to Saint James went unpaid, and the College itself went more heavily into debt. Faculty salaries were reduced by two-thirds this year.[32]

Like the students, some faculty were anxious to contribute directly to the war effort. Richard Kerfoot, math and history tutor and the Rector's nephew, left to become chaplain at Fort McHenry near Baltimore in early November 1861. The Rev. Julius Dashiell, professor of classics, was hoping for a chaplaincy in the 1st Maryland Infantry Volunteers commanded by William P. Maulsby, Sr., of Frederick, whose son and namesake was a senior at the College.[33] A number of instructors served local churches as clergy. Passmore was rector of nearby St. Mark's, Lappans, while Joseph Coit served St. Luke's, Brownsville, and a Boonsboro mission (and later succeeded Passmore at Lappans). Falk provided pastoral support at St. Andrew's, Clear Spring, and later St. Thomas, Hancock. These positions sometimes brought the individuals extra income but were considerable additional work.[34]

In September 1861 came word of a former pupil, age nineteen, who had met a sad end. Dismissed from the grammar school in 1857 for "hopeless disobedience," Joseph Gabby Duckett had recently attempted to cross the Potomac to join the Confederates, but according to Kerfoot "was *shot* and fell or was thrown into the river. No one knows when or by whom; probably by the Virginia pickets themselves, suspected as a spy." The rector was much affected by the story, visiting the young man's father in Hagerstown to comfort him. December brought renewed federal military activity in the neighborhood and the sound of shelling for several days along the Potomac. In the early months of 1862, sickness and death stalked the school. Disease in the area drove students away. Matron Porter became so ill that her son the general snatched a few hours to visit her bedside. Tragically, the Kerfoots' little daughter Helen died in February.[35]

---

32. Kerfoot to WRW, 2 Dec. 1861; Diocesan Archives vertical file "College of St. James," printed circular from Trustees, 5 July 1862.

33. Kerfoot to WRW, 1, 4–5, and 18 Nov. 1861; Richard Kerfoot letter to WRW, 6 Nov. 1861; *Register* (1862); *1860 Census*, Frederick County, MD, NARA M653, roll 475, p. 770.

34. *St. Mark's Parish Register* 1:1–2; Diocesan Archives, Coit letter to WRW, 31 May 1862; Falk letter to WRW, 22 Jan. 1863.

35. Kerfoot to WRW, 1 Oct., 16, 20 Dec. 1861; 11, 19 Feb., 3 Mar. 1862; *Herald of Freedom and Torch Light*, 2 Oct. 1861.

The rector estimated early in 1862 that two thirds of the students and their families were now secessionists; by now most of these must have been Marylanders. These students were dismayed to learn—their knowledge of current events was always good—that Bishop Whittingham had directed churches across the diocese to give thanks on Palm Sunday, April 13, for Union victories. The boys planned a chapel walkout in protest, and nearly half the students, about twenty altogether, carried it out during the rector's prayers that morning, to Kerfoot's enormous consternation. One of the leaders was senior Arthur George Brown, from Baltimore; the students involved were "among the most orderly and respectable in the College," according to faculty member Hall Harrison. The rector decided to regard the protest as seriously misguided but not insubordinate. Kerfoot addressed the students at dinner, "plainly, unyieldingly but quietly" telling them they had been wrong: "Still, they plead *conscience*." The next day Brown brought Kerfoot a letter from the protestors, which the sympathetic Harrison described as "manly, admirable and respectful . . . explaining their conduct and disclaiming any disrespect to [the Rector] or the College authorities . . . [and doing] great credit to the head and heart of its writers." The rector composed an "affectionate" reply to the students and on Monday evening met with the faculty, who took a formal position of agreement with the rector's response. A new, explicit policy was laid down: Students who, in the future, believed they could not in conscience attend a particular chapel service could ask in advance to be excused, but no one would be allowed to leave a service. This episode at the college became known in Baltimore, where people talked about it and critiqued Kerfoot's handling of it. The students followed it up by observing a Confederate fast day decreed by Jefferson Davis, probably on May 16, 1862. They attended the college's usual voluntary midday chapel service in unusual numbers, and then at dinner, according to Harrison, "the fast was strictly, even ostentatiously, observed. Knives and forks were silent; roast beef and apple-pie for once seemed to have lost their charms, and while the 'Union' boys made the heartiest meal of the session, the Southerners attempted, with more or less success," to be satisfied with no food at all. Kerfoot made light of this incident, but the next fall he would write to his son, "The character of our boys is much better than [in 1861–62]. We had then some ugly stuff."[36]

36. Kerfoot to WRW, 16 Apr. 1862; Harrison, *Life of Kerfoot*, 227–28, 245–47, 250–51.

He may have been referring to these spring 1862 demonstrations or to other, unrecorded, confrontations.

When the Diocesan Convention met in Baltimore in May 1862, it was clear that the overwhelming majority of Maryland churchmen were pro-Confederate. Kerfoot would come to describe many of these men as his and the College's firm supporters, even though they were aware of his Unionist position. Yet Whittingham later judged that the College's wartime difficulties were due in part to lack of support from pro-Confederate Maryland Episcopalians, and the want of funds was certainly a problem already by 1862. Seeking to operate more effectively under wartime conditions, in June the College's trustees formed a Special Committee of three laymen to conduct business "during the present crisis." In July 1862 the College held what would prove to be its "last regular public commencement," with three graduates. In July, too, the Rev. Joseph Passmore, longtime professor of rhetoric, philosophy, and politics, left to take a position at Racine College in Wisconsin.[37]

II.

As early May 1862, the war's summer activities were beginning to be felt in the College's neighborhood: troop movements, rumors of invasion, even riots in Hagerstown. The continuing consequences of war were on everyone's mind. In June, more than a thousand refugee slaves from the Shenandoah Valley crossed north into Washington County in a ten-day period, many of them camping in local fields on their way to Pennsylvania. After Congress passed the Militia Act in July 1862, the draft became imminent in Maryland.[38] Late in July, a Saint James alumnus from Raleigh, North Carolina, Lieut. Duncan C. Haywood (B.A. 1858) of the 7th North Carolina Infantry, was killed in action at Cold Harbor, Virginia. Haywood, a law student from a slave-owning family, was killed "carrying forward the Regimental Colors." News of his death reached the college sometime this summer.[39] In August, Kerfoot heard from a Maryland alumnus of the

37. Diocesan Archives, loose document, 19 June 1862, filed with Kerfoot letters; Kerfoot to WRW, 9 Sept. 1863; WRW draft letter to Israel Condit, 15 Aug. 1863; Harrison, *Life of Kerfoot*, 228–32, 250n.

38. Kerfoot to WRW, 26 May 1862; *Herald of Freedom & Torch Light*, 4 June and 9 July 1862; Hait, *Civil War Draft in Maryland: Lists of Drafted Men, 1862–1865*, i.11.

39. Haywood had enlisted in June 1861; his younger brother William had been a freshman in 1860–61. Harrison, *Life of Kerfoot*, 233; *Register* (1862); *1860 Census*,

college, Edward Belt of Upper Marlboro, who mistakenly hoped that his two nephews would be exempted from the draft if they were enrolled in the college, or that Bishop Whittingham could obtain some special draft exemption for all the college's students; instead Kerfoot sent him a newspaper clipping about purchasing substitutes. Prospects for fall enrollment were up, perhaps because other parents had similarly mistaken ideas.[40] But almost everyone's hopes for the fall were about to be smashed.

In early September, Lee's army crossed into Maryland, just to the east of Washington County. The seriousness of the situation was immediately clear at the college. Teenagers Abel and Annie Kerfoot were dispatched to New York with the Kerfoot family valuables, on the last train leaving Hagerstown before rail service stopped. The Falks and the rest of the Kerfoots had planned to follow, but were unable to do so. College officials postponed the opening of the academic year from September 24 to the end of October. It was obvious that student numbers would be disastrously affected by this new situation. Those left at Saint James fretted anxiously, prey to every rumor. On September 11, several former students now serving in the Confederate forces stopped by the campus to greet their old teachers. In his diary Kerfoot described the day as "full of excitement." Among the visitors were Col. Edward Graham Haywood from Raleigh (BA, 1851), of the 7th North Carolina Infantry, and cavalry Sgt. John Boykin Lee of South Carolina's Holcombe Legion, who had left school in April 1861 purportedly to care for his family.[41]

Raleigh, NC, NARA M653, roll 916, p. 285, and Slave Schedule, Raleigh, pp. 3, 17; NARA, *Carded Records Showing Military Service of Soldiers Who Fought in Confederate Organizations*, Catalog ID 586957, Record Group 109, online at fold3.com (hereafter cited as NARA, Carded Records), Roll 173.

40. Kerfoot to WRW, 21 Aug. 1862.

41. Harrison, *Life of Kerfoot*, 232–33n; Kerfoot to WRW, 10 Sept. 1862; *Register* (1851, 1860). Haywood was probably the older brother of Duncan Haywood '58, mentioned above. A slaveowning lawyer, Edward Haywood enlisted as a lieut. col. in fall 1861; was promoted in June 1862; had been in some nineteen battles and wounded three times by Oct. 1862; was court marshalled for being AWOL and drunk on duty, cashiered, and had his sentence set aside because of his "long and gallant service"; claimed disability by Aug. 1863; was "retired" from field duty in Aug. 1864; and survived the war. Lee, of Camden, South Carolina, enlisted as a private in Sept. 1861, joined the cavalry battalion of the Holcombe Legion when it was organized in Nov., and was promoted in June 1862. NARA, Carded Records, Rolls 173, 376; Census Data, National Archives and Records Administration, *1860 Census, Raleigh, NC, Slave Schedule, p. 3* M653; Historical Data Systems, comp. *U.S., Civil War Soldier Records and Profiles, 1861–1865* (database online).

The Battle of South Mountain, on September 14, was fought just northeast of Boonsboro, about nine miles from Saint James. The sounds of artillery and muskets could be heard on the college campus. Someone at the college penned a new circular on the same day, again postponing the opening of the school year, this time until early or mid-November. Parents were assured that a "proportionate reduction of the year's charges will be made," and also that "no part of the College buildings or property has been used for hospital purposes."[42]

The next day, thousands of Confederates retreating from Boonsboro to Sharpsburg passed through college grounds. Eliza Kerfoot and Eliza Porter (the College Matron), assisted by others, handed out water, bandages, and the Kerfoots' food—"to the last scrap," wrote faculty member Harrison—from the porch of the rectory. Valuables were packed in trunks and hidden in the cellars. Evacuation of the family members remaining on campus proved impossible because the local roads were jammed with armies on the move from South Mountain. Throughout these days, the intermittent sounds of artillery were heard.[43] On the 16th, Kerfoot and Falk visited the South Mountain field hospitals and battlefield. It was a searing experience for both of them. Though they would also visit the battlefield at Antietam within the next few days, Kerfoot found South Mountain more horrifying, perhaps in part because it was his first experience of wounded, suffering, and dying soldiers. He wrote, "My most fearful ideas of battlefields [are] more than fulfilled."[44]

Worse, of course, was to come. The following day, September 17, was the bloodiest in American history, the Battle of Antietam. The little community at Saint James, five miles north of the battlefield at Sharpsburg, "watched it anxiously from [the] top of the College" and listened to the "fearful cannonading." In the afternoon Falk and Kerfoot, in the latter's words,

> took bread and biscuits and bandages and drove to the hospitals three miles this side of Sharpsburg (just in the rear of the battle-line). Our biscuits, etc., most grateful to the wounded men. We needed much more. The battle-lines were in sight. We went up nearer, three-fourths of a mile short of our batteries; all the first lines in full view. Strange sight for us! ... The shells whistled

---

42. Diocesan Archives, "College of St. James" vertical file, manuscript draft of circular, 14 Sept. 1862; Harrison, *Life of Kerfoot*, 233.

43. Harrison, *Life of Kerfoot*, 233–34.

44. Harrison, *Life of Kerfoot*, 233–34.

fearfully. The terror, strangeness and sadness were vast and soul-stirring... Terrible work to-morrow!⁴⁵

On that morrow, Kerfoot and Falk repeated their mission to the battlefields and hospitals, and, like so many of their neighbors, walked the battlefield of Antietam. Back at Saint James they met three former students from Pittsburgh who were now serving temporarily in Pennsylvania militia units mustered for the emergency, defending their state's nearby border: George Aston Gormly (sophomore in 1857–58), Charles Avery Howe (BA, 1861), and Oliver Franklin Wharton (sophomore in 1859–60).⁴⁶ "Kept them to evening family prayer. Read 91st Psalm," wrote Kerfoot in his diary, the brief words hinting at the emotion of the occasion. On the 20th, nearly three thousand Confederate troops retreated through the college grounds. Eliza Kerfoot took charge of first-aid efforts for about forty wounded soldiers as they passed through.⁴⁷

On Sunday, September 21, US and Confederate troops positioned themselves on opposite sides of the campus. With a clash seeming possible any moment, Kerfoot evacuated his wife and six-year-old daughter to Hagerstown for the day (though Eliza herself wanted to stay), leaving Falk in charge of the college. Federal troops swept across the grounds, damaging the spring-house, digging up the potato field, and looting various buildings. After this the college more or less gave over the spring to the federal troops but acquired guards for the rest of the school property. Bai-Yuka spring continued to do impressive service. Dr. Elias Marsh, a surgeon with the 5th Regiment, US (Regular) Cavalry, which was encamped at the college throughout October with a horse depot and tent hospitals for humans and horses, called it "the finest spring that I have ever seen. One spring furnishes water in abundance for the horses and men of 4 regiments of cavalry and a battery of artillery." College buildings provided some housing for officers and their wives during this period. These troops moved on to Virginia in early November.⁴⁸

---

45. Harrison, *Life of Kerfoot*, 235.

46. It seems these men had not fought at Antietam. Harrison, *Life of Kerfoot*, 236; *Register* (1858, 1860, 1862); Bates, *History of Pennsylvania Volunteers, 1861–1865*, 1182–83, 1205–6.

47. Kerfoot to WRW, 23 Sept. and 18 Nov. 1862; Harrison, *Life of Kerfoot*, 235–38.

48. Kerfoot to WRW, 23 Sept. and 18 Nov. 1862; Harrison, *Life of Kerfoot*, 238–39; Elias J. Marsh, "The St. James Campaign of 1862" [letters], St. James School Archives, p. 5.

Antietam changed life in Washington County beyond the changes the war had wrought before now. Makeshift hospitals full of terribly wounded men were everywhere; indeed Kerfoot had to expend some energy to assure the bishop that Saint James had *not* become a hospital, contrary to rumors that reached Baltimore immediately after the battle. Both Kerfoot and Falk were seized by a new mission, and would spend many days in the fall and winter months ministering to the wounded and other troops, in addition to their academic duties. Eventually seventeen-year-old Annie Kerfoot also began nursing, at Smoketown hospital near Sharpsburg. When the much-delayed academic year finally began on November 12, one of the first activities, on Saturday the 15th, was to take the thirty newly-arrived students walking over Antietam battlefield, and to visit with Lt. Carlyle Norris, a former grammar school student (1849–50) who had been seriously wounded in the fighting. Over the course of the academic year, the college chapel collected $20 in offerings for "the sick and wounded soldiers of both armies in the hospitals in our vicinity."[49]

In some ways, life took up again its by now familiar wartime pattern: Kerfoot resumed hoping for more students and fretting about tuition income; tutors came and went; supplies were hard to get. But the situation and the mood were definitely grimmer after Antietam. In early October, Kerfoot suggested that Bishop Whittingham consider moving the college. In November he asked the bishop to advertise the college by writing an editorial. Logistical challenges were piling up. The armies had stripped the neighborhood of firewood, including fences; the college had to send away for winter fuel to replace the stores that had been looted. Other supplies were difficult to obtain. Tutor Lucian Waddell, the matron's grandson, was ill with an apparently fatal lung disease. With the full-time faculty reduced to just five (including Robert Coster, who had arrived in September as "instructor in book-keeping, etc."), teaching duties were heavier, and by January the faculty was largely working without salaries. The college's unpaid bills swelled. Kerfoot began to express more openly to the bishop his doubts about the college's ultimate survival. Confidence was further shaken in mid-January when a student from Hagerstown,

---

49. Norris, from Carlisle, PA, enlisted in the 71st Pennsylvania Infantry and was later promoted captain. His Antietam wounds were at first thought fatal, but he recovered. Harrison, *Life of Kerfoot*, 239, 253; Kerfoot to WRW, 18 Nov. and 30 Dec. 1862; NARA, *Index to Compiled Service Records of Volunteer Union Soldiers Who Served in Organizations from the State of Pennsylvania* (1965), M554; *Journals of the Annual Conventions* (1863), 52.

Frederick Schley, came down with a mild form of smallpox. Five or six students left campus, the student population was revaccinated and Kerfoot sent a reassuring circular to parents. Those who had left began to return by early February.[50]

The new year of 1863, which opened with the Emancipation Proclamation on January 1, brought political turmoil of several kinds to Saint James. The most severe concerned three vacancies on the college's small Board of Trustees. Kerfoot nominated three laymen who were Confederate sympathizers, including tutor Hall Harrison. Bishop Whittingham flatly refused to appoint representatives of Maryland's "disloyal" element, who already dominated the board and with whom he felt less and less able to work. He proposed, in effect, a loyalty test for further appointments, and threatened to resign from the board if it were not implemented. Kerfoot, though a Unionist himself, begged the bishop not to pursue this course, arguing that it would wreck the school's future in the state: "The four laymen now on the board will leave, and 2/3 of our boys." Kerfoot proposed a different plan: to set aside the political question and to fill the vacancies with faculty members—specifically Falk, Coit, and Harrison. Whittingham agreed to this compromise, dropping his objection to Harrison since he was being proposed *as a faculty member*. Peace was restored.[51] Kerfoot had won an awkward point, though—that the college need carry its loyalty to the United States only so far.

At the same time that the rector and the bishop were having this "first . . . grave difference," over the makeup of the board, they also disagreed about the court martial (November 1862 to January 1863) of Major General Porter, the Matron's son, for his conduct at the second battle of Bull Run. Kerfoot, who counted Porter a friend to the college and himself, rebuked Whittingham sharply when the latter assumed the officer was guilty as charged and convicted. He felt confident that he knew enough about the case to declare that Porter had been framed for political reasons. This contributed to bitterness on Kerfoot's part toward the government.[52] But it was not the only factor.

Emancipation was also causing concern at Saint James. While local slaves were not freed by the Proclamation (because it applied only to the states in rebellion), they were intensely interested in the spread of

50. *Register* (1862); Kerfoot to WRW, 10 Oct., 18 Nov., 30 Dec. 1862; 20 and 26 Jan., 2 Feb. 1863; Diocesan Archives, Falk letter to WRW, 22 Jan. 1863.

51. Harrison, *Life of Kerfoot*, 254–59; Kerfoot to WRW, 26 and 27 Jan., 2 Feb. 1863.

52. Kerfoot to WRW, 26 Jan., 2 Feb. 1863.

freedom and its implications. So were local whites. The idea of recruiting African Americans into the Union army attracted much interest in Maryland and would become a reality later in the year. Black men around the college were no doubt wondering about the possibility of joining up to fight for freedom; by the end of the summer a black unit would be recruited in Hagerstown and another seventy-some African Americans would enlist in Clear Spring. But Kerfoot was appalled. In February he read in a Baltimore paper a vitriolic screed against recruiting black soldiers and (unusually) drew the bishop's attention to it with what seems to be approval: "See how the *American* (Editorial of Saturday) speaks of the idiotic folly of negro enlistment. If the party in power go on, we will even have a counterrevolution in the north."[53] Kerfoot's disaffection found a focus in President Lincoln, whom he called "a stubborn imbecile—manipulated by reckless, fanatical partisans."[54] These winter months seem to have been a low point for Kerfoot, when he was writing about politics more frankly and pessimistically than usual in his letters. A national fast day on April 30 demonstrated the changed *modus vivendi* on campus. Kerfoot announced ahead of time that students would be allowed to skip chapel that day in order to avoid participating in the special prayers. The students this year, who numbered at least forty-two, came largely from Maryland and Pennsylvania, a mix of returners and newcomers. As usual, many or most of them supported the Confederacy.[55]

In May 1863, the terrible Union defeat at Chancellorsville, though more than a hundred miles to the south, sent refugees flooding north through the Shenandoah Valley and into the College's neighborhood. Joseph Coit described the impact of the evacuees, especially the African Americans:

> The poor, terrified darkies, who were themselves the *avant-couriers* of this rout, filled the country with exaggerated and frightful stories of the fierce and ruthless temper of the Confederate cavalry, and of the slaughter from which they had escaped. And although, when we heard the wild, incoherent talk of a trembling negro, or the noisy, boastful accounts of a cowardly

---

53. Kerfoot to WRW, 2 Feb. 1863; "The Negro Regiment Bill before Congress," *The American and Commercial Advertiser* (Baltimore), Jan. 31, 1863, p. 2; "Recruiting Colored Men," *Herald of Freedom and Torch Light*, Sept. 2, 1863; "Volunteering of Colored Men," *Herald of Freedom . . .* , Aug. 26, 1863.

54. Kerfoot to WRW, 26 Jan., 2 Feb. 1863.

55. Harrison, *Life of Kerfoot*, 259; Kerfoot to WRW, 26 Feb. 1863.

and demoralized soldier, calm reflection pointed out that their narratives were in the main preposterous and incredible, yet the ferment was so general, and the voices humming and buzzing danger around us were so numerous and incessant, that it was impossible not to be disturbed a great deal.[56]

War rumors were nothing new by this point. But June 1863 brought Lee's army north into Maryland again. The massive invasion rolled into Washington County in the middle of the month, sweeping up horses and supplies and local black people, and convincing everyone that something momentous was happening.[57]

At the college, it was now impossible to carry on as usual. As the Confederates drew near, students from states north of Pennsylvania (that is, from the most distant places) were sent home.[58] The dining room's black waiter spent Sunday, June 14, in Hagerstown and stayed there into the wee hours; at breakfast on Monday the 15th he was able to share the latest news of federal troops and black refugees fleeing north across the Pennsylvania border. A few hours later another black man brought the college news that the Confederates had crossed the Potomac at Williamsport. In the late afternoon, Confederates appeared on campus, a troop of cavalry riding across the grounds. While Kerfoot and Coit watched quietly, a group of students and faculty member Hall Harrison ran out "cheering and waving their hats," according to Coit. This was a fateful mistake for Harrison, who lost Kerfoot's confidence (though not his friendship) by this action and resigned his position at the college the following day. In chapel the next morning, Kerfoot "strongly reproved" such demonstrations, and indeed there were no more of them.[59]

Still, the near presence of so many Confederate troops was simply too exciting for many of the students. On Monday the 15th, seventeen-year-old freshman William G. Harrison and sixteen-year-old Thomas G. Edmundson had slipped away with a Confederate soldier who was

56. Harrison, *Life of Kerfoot*, 363. Although Coit's language and perspective are often demeaning, he is the only Saint James faculty member from this period whose writings notice African Americans and their concerns with any frequency.

57. Keller, *Events of the Civil War in Washington County, Maryland*, 123–32; Alexander, "'A Regular Slave Hunt': The Army of Northern Virginia and Black Civilians in the Gettysburg Campaign," 85–88.

58. Firsthand accounts of the college evacuation stages differ, but there were still Pennsylvania students on campus on June 18. Harrison, *Life of Kerfoot*, 364; Coit Diary, 250–51; Kerfoot to WRW, 24 June 1863.

59. Coit Diary, 248–50; Kerfoot to WRW, 20 July, 9 Sept. 1863.

in the neighborhood taking horses from a nearby farmer. When more cavalry passed through campus the following morning (June 16), two fifteen-year-old students, Jacob J. Bankard and Silas Boteler, left with them. Four more students left secretly during the course of the morning, going to Hagerstown with the intent of enlisting in the Confederate army there: Richard S. Latrobe (eighteen) of Baltimore, H.P. Hayward (eighteen) of Baltimore, J. C. Heighe (sixeen) of Baltimore, and Joseph Motter (nineeen) of Williamsport. It seems that none of these young men successfully enlisted. Latrobe, Hayward, and Motter came back to the college the same day they had left; Edmundson and Heighe returned the following evening. Ex-tutor Harrison, who was a relative of young William Harrison, wrote to the colonel of the unit in Hagerstown that William was trying to join, asking him not to accept William, and then went into Hagerstown to retrieve him; William was packed off to his relatives in Baltimore. Most of the other returnees were also sent to their nearest parents or guardians, either because it was too risky to try to keep them on campus now, or because of the grave disciplinary breach they had committed. "The neighborhood is full of absurd stories with regard to the conduct of the students," remarked Coit on June 18, without being specific. Meanwhile, sophomore Francis Lewis of Baltimore was still wrestling with his loyalties. Late on the night of June 21, according to Coit, this student went quietly to the Rector "to tell him that he felt it his duty to join the S[outhern] army. Dr. K. said what he could to dissuade him." The next morning Lewis "informed him that he had not changed his mind and would go while we were at chapel. And so he is gone." But the conditions in camp thwarted Lewis's plans, too; he fell sick and was back in the college by July 5.[60]

In the charged atmosphere, other students left campus just to visit the Confederate camps. Thomas D. and Charles H. Pitts, Confederate-minded cousins from Baltimore who enjoyed the rector's confidence, visited Williamsport on June 16. They brought back the sad news that two former students, Ives Smedes (BA, 1861) and John Archibald Weddell (a freshman in 1853–54), had been killed at Chancellorsville. Smedes was one of five brothers who had attended the college from Raleigh, where their father was the rector of St. Mary's College and Grammar School.

---

60. Coit Diary, 249–51, 253; Kerfoot to WRW, 17 June, 20 July 1963; *Register* (1862). The fate of the two fifteen-year-olds, Bankard and Boteler, is less clear; it was believed at the college that they were going to enlist or had enlisted, but I have found no military records for them.

Ives was especially loved and admired by the faculty at Saint James, who were devastated by this report.[61]

While current students were excited by the presence of Confederate troops in the neighborhood, former students in the invading Confederate army were delighted to find themselves near Saint James and visited the campus in unprecedented numbers. Current students also received visits from soldier friends and kin. For the old Jacobites, the college was a serene and nostalgic oasis, and their few old teachers who remained there were cherished friends. On June 16, Pvt. Isaac B. Snodgrass (a freshman in 1860–61) of the 2nd Virginia Infantry, who had been wounded in the fighting at Winchester a few days earlier, stopped by for tea.[62] On June 19, Sgt. Francis Atherton Boyle (a freshman in 1853–54) of the 12th North Carolina Infantry visited "for several hours."[63] Pvt. John Mackall Heighe, who had been a freshman in 1860–61 and was now with the 1st Maryland (Confederate) Cavalry, spent the night at the College on June 20–21.[64]

---

61. Weddell came from a slaveholding family in Petersburg, Va.; he enlisted April 1861 in the 12th Va. Infantry; was promoted to 2nd lieut. in May 1862; transferred to 41st Virginia Infantry; and was promoted to capt. same year. Smedes was the son of the Rev. Aldert and Sarah Smedes of Raleigh, NC; he enlisted Feb. 1862 in the 3rd NC Cavalry; was promoted to corp. in Aug. and sgt. in Sept. of the same year; was captured in Sept.; was released in Oct. 1862; re-enlisted as pvt. in 63rd NC Infantry. In early 1863, through efforts of family and connections reaching as high as Jefferson Davis, he was promoted to 2nd lieut. and adj. in the 7th NC Regiment; was wounded at Chancellorsville; died a week later on May 10, 1863. His older brother Lieut. Edward Smedes (B.A. 1860) was killed in action at Spotsylvania Courthouse in May 1864. Three other Smedes brothers also attended Saint James: Lyell (BA, 1856), Bennett (BA, 1857; served as a Confederate chaplain and held as a prisoner), and Abraham (freshman 1860–61). Coit Diary, 249 (where Weddell is misidentified in the footnote); Kerfoot to WRW, 29 June, 10 Oct. 1863, 11 Jan. 1864; *Register* (1854, 1857, 1858, 1862); Census Data, National Archives and Records Administration, *1860 Census, Raleigh, NC*, NARA M653, roll 916, p. 145, and Petersburg, VA, South Ward Slave Schedule, p. 10; National Archives and Records Administration, *Carded Records*, Rolls 24, 178, 227, and 533; Munson, *North Carolina Civil War Obituaries*, 31; Sharpe, *Growing Up with Raleigh*, 399–411.

62. Isaac B. Snodgrass of Martinsburg, WV, is the most likely identity of this visitor, out of several Snodgrasses who had attended Saint James. Coit Diary, 250; National Archives and Records Administration, *Carded Records*, Roll 380; *Register* (1862).

63. Coit Diary, 251; National Park Service, *U.S. Civil War Soldiers, 1861–1865*; *Register* (1854).

64. Heighe, from Baltimore, was not the current student who had tried to enlist a few days earlier, but almost certainly a relative. He was captured late in the war and survived. Coit Diary, 252; *Register* (1860); National Archives and Records Administration, *Carded Records*, Roll 3.

On Sunday, June 21, the Pitts cousins had a visit from three officers who were acquaintances of theirs. The same day, Capt. J. J. Nicholson (BA, 1859) of the 12th Alabama Infantry came to chapel and spent most of the day on campus. He "seemed cordial" and shared welcome news of other old students in the Confederate army, but Coit noted that Nicholson "was rather rude in his remarks."[65] The next day a student named Turner had a visit from his brother, who had been a student of Coit's brother in New Hampshire.[66] On June 23, Pvt. Henry Hollyday of the 2nd Battalion Maryland (Confederate) Infantry (freshman in 1851–52) visited campus.[67] Two old students from St. Mary's County, Maryland, Pvt. Edwin Thomas of the 1st Maryland (Confederate) Cavalry (a junior in 1860–61), and Henry Aisquith (grammar school, 1853–56), visited for a few hours on June 24.[68] The next day, Major Osman Latrobe (grammar school, 1845–49), serving on Gen. Longstreet's staff, stopped in for "a few moments."[69] Walton Hughes, who had been a freshman in 1855–56, spent the night of June 29–30 at Saint James; a civilian living in Hagerstown, he had been talking with Confederate officers and passed on gossip from them. The college heard news of other old students who "passed near us, though unable to come and see us."[70]

65. John Joseph Nicholson, of Mobile, Alabama, enlisted as a lieut. in June, 1861; was promoted to capt. in 1862; was wounded at New Market, VA, in May 1864; was captured and paroled in 1865; and retired from service because of wounds in 1865. Coit Diary, 253; National Archives and Records Administration, *Carded Records*, Roll 214.

66. Coit Diary, 253. Coit's brother, the Rev. Henry Augustus Coit, was Rector of St. Paul's School, Concord, NH. Both Coits were alumni of Saint James.

67. Hollyday, from Queen Anne's County, Md., enlisted at Richmond in 1862; was hospitalized in summer 1864; and survived the war. Coit Diary, 255; *Register* (1852); National Archives and Records Administration, *Carded Records*, Roll 19.

68. Thomas had enlisted in the 1st Maryland Infantry at Fairfax Station, VA, in 1861; joined the 1st Maryland Cavalry in Charlottesville, VA, in Sept. 1862; was wounded near Winchester in Nov. 1862; was hospitalized in Sept. 1863; and survived the war. I have found no military records for Henry Aisquith. Coit Diary, 257; *Register*, 1856, 1862; National Archives and Records Administration, *Carded Records*, Roll 17.

69. After the college, Latrobe (of Baltimore) attended the Maryland Military Academy in Oxford, MD, and then began a legal career. He enlisted as a captain; was promoted major by July 1863; was a staff officer to Gen. D. R. Jones and then Gen. James Longstreet; was promoted to lieut. col. in Dec. 1864; and survived the war. Coit Diary, 257; *Register* (1846–49); Bunting, "Did You Know? Oxford Cadet Accepted Truce at Appomattox," 1–2; National Archives and Records Administration, *Carded Records*, Roll 153.

70. Coit Diary, 255, 258; *Register* (1856).

Though these visitors were benign, the overall situation was perilous in the extreme, especially for those without the privileges enjoyed by white men of wealth and rank. North of the Pennsylvania border in mid-to-late June, Confederate troops were rounding up and abducting hundreds of African Americans in Mercersburg, Chambersburg, and Greencastle.[71] Marylanders were not immune from such dangers. On the afternoon of June 22, the college's black cook was preparing tea as usual. Given the frightening conditions, she probably had her two children near her. Suddenly a white man from Winchester, Virginia, appeared, saying that his name was Sever (or Seevers) and that he was looking for his father's escaped slaves. Since this was 1863, anyone who had been enslaved in Virginia was now free under US law, which certainly applied in Maryland. But Sever seized and "carried off" the cook and her children. Not long after this, the teachers at the college would show considerable courage in protecting their families, students, and white neighbors. But they did nothing to prevent this woman and her children, whom they knew, from being abducted by a stranger. Coit wrote in his diary, "It was a sad sight."[72]

Even before this violent incident on campus, the faculty were working on a plan to evacuate about twenty of the remaining thirty students, specifically those whose homes were in Baltimore, Pennsylvania, or other places more than an hour away. Several routes away from campus were blocked by the military, and transportation was difficult to obtain, but by June 24 the plan was in place. Early that morning two local men named Lynch and Knode arrived with "omnibuses"—large, enclosed horse-drawn passenger vehicles—and the twenty-some students set off for the railroad junction at Frederick accompanied by Kerfoot and Coit. Both Confederate and Union pickets stopped the party at different points, but the clergy talked their way through and got the students onto the Baltimore train in Frederick, at which point the youngsters were on their own. Two brothers from Baltimore, Henry C. (seventeen) and George G. Hooper (sixteen), were charged with visiting Bishop Whittingham the

---

71. Alexander, "Regular Slave Hunt," 85–88; Creighton, "Living on the Fault Line," 213–30.

72. Coit Diary, 254. No more is known of the cook and children, not even their names. George W. Seevers, age sixty-three, held twenty-four people as slaves in Winchester in 1860 and had a twenty-seven-year-old son Robert; *1860 Census, Winchester, Frederick County, VA*, NARA M653, roll 1347, p. 450, and *Winchester Slave Schedule*, p. 11.

next day to deliver a full report on the evacuation, which they apparently failed to do. Kerfoot and Coit headed back to Saint James, not without further challenges on the road, and arrived home late that night.[73]

The invasion proceeded for the next few days, with the Confederates passing in large numbers northward on roads just a few miles from the campus. According to Coit, "late at night, the rumble of the long trains of ammunition and baggage wagons over the stony turnpikes became audible."[74] Twelve students, four faculty, a handful of family members, and an assortment of employees were still left on campus. Food was hard to obtain, but fortunately the college had laid in good supplies of sugar, tea, coffee, and flour in mid-June, had sufficient bacon on hand, and could bake its own bread. The faculty tried to carry on with lessons, but in an abbreviated form, as the college waited nervously for news from the armies in Pennsylvania. Tensions rose between the faculty and their pro-Confederate neighbors, even with such a good friend as John Breathed. A few more boys left for home, including Charles Pitts of Baltimore, whom Coit and Kerfoot were sad to see go. Both men also recorded their deepening sense that the college would not be able to carry on after the summer. After more days of anxious waiting, in early July word of the Union victory at Gettysburg reached Saint James, not long before the retreating Confederate army swept back into Washington County, pursued by federal troops.[75]

What followed was perhaps the most perilous time of the whole war for the college.[76] From July 6 until July 15, the Union and Confederate armies faced each other in Washington County, as Lee tried to get across the rain-swollen Potomac into Virginia and Meade's forces trapped him on the Maryland side of the river. The two armies were entrenched on opposite sides of the college. The Confederate lines began west of Hagerstown and ran roughly south-southeast until they reached a point about half a mile north of the college grounds, where they swung southwest and ran along a wooded ridge to join the road to Downsville and stretch

---

73. Coit Diary, 250–51, 253–58; Harrison, *Life of Kerfoot*, 260–61n, 267, 364–66; Kerfoot letters to WRW, 24 and 27 June 1863; *1860 Census, Baltimore, MD*, NARA M653, roll 468, p. 581.

74. Harrison, *Life of Kerfoot*, 366.

75. Coit Diary, 251–52, 257–59; Harrison, *Life of Kerfoot*, 261, 366–67; Kerfoot to WRW, 27–29 June, 2 July 1863.

76. The events of July 1863 are expertly detailed in Pipkin, "(Almost) Battle of St. James College."

almost to the Potomac. Williamsport lay two and a half miles behind the line. The federal lines began just west of Funkstown and ran roughly south, coming within a mile of the college buildings.[77] Had there been a full-scale battle, as many anticipated or even called for, the grounds of the college of Saint James would have been smack in the middle of it.

Instead, there was a kind of organized chaos. Those at the college saw or heard skirmishing most days from July 6 onward. Things started relatively quietly on July 7. Kerfoot and others talked with the 9th New York Cavalry "in the woods opposite our gate," before Confederates arrived from Williamsport to attack. The college folk watched "from the top of the College" as the two sides clashed and the federal troops retreated "right under our eyes." Later that day, at the behest of a Confederate surgeon, Kerfoot and Falk went out with a wagon to pick up a badly wounded Union soldier and brought him back into the college, where the students were assigned to nurse him. (The pro-Confederate students were as gentle as the Unionists in caring for him, according to Kerfoot, and by July 20 he would be on his feet.) College folk also buried a dead soldier in the school cemetery.[78]

That night Confederate troops flooded across the campus, broke into the spring-house, and stole 100 pounds of butter. On July 8 Confederate guerilla cavalry ("bad fellows" in Kerfoot's view) camped immediately south of the college; the next day these soldiers were all over the campus searching for food. On the 10th the two armies moved nearer, with Confederate batteries placed on campus. At this astonishingly late date, the faculty sent home the students who lived in Hagerstown, while making other preparations for what seemed an imminent battle. The next morning, July 11, two Confederate generals came to urge Eliza Porter to leave campus immediately. Friends of her son (the Union general) from West Point, they were concerned for her safety. They also pressed Kerfoot to move the other women and children away from the college, and their counsel carried the day, though Eliza and Annie Kerfoot left only reluctantly. The Kerfoots, Mrs. Porter, young Bertha Falk, and two invalids—Lucian Waddell and a student, Charlie Harrison (yet another relative of Hall Harrison, and apparently the last student remaining on campus)—took a harrowing ride in a wagon and a carriage to Hagerstown early that afternoon. As Kerfoot described the scene:

77. See the "Map of the Vicinity of Hagerstown . . . 1863," in Phillips, *Maps of the Civil War*, 116–17.

78. Harrison, *Life of Kerfoot*, 261–62; Kerfoot to WRW, 20 July 1863.

> The cannon of *our* United States army were already throwing shells, visible and audible, against the batteries at our outer gate; and the brigade of cavalry (Confederate) wheeling into position on our lawn as we drove off. Our ride for two miles was right along the Confederate sharpshooters, who were crouching under the fence, ten feet on our left. Our United States sharpshooters three-quarters of a mile on our right. God's mercy took us safely through.

At the college Falk, Coit, Coster, and the remaining staff took the best cover they could. On the night of July 12 the three professors fled from the college to John Breathed's house, which was also under fire. As the skirmishing and foraging continued, every campus building was broken into, every room looted, every storage space plundered, and a great deal stolen and vandalized. But Union troops did not engage the Confederates in battle at this time, and on July 13 and 14 Lee's army was able to cross the Potomac into Virginia.[79] The college was safe, for the time being.

Finances now became a priority. Apparently the four remaining faculty put the terrors of July behind them fairly quickly and were willing to carry on at Fountain Rock, even though job offers from elsewhere were beginning to appear. But Kerfoot put it plainly to the bishop that a substantial infusion of money ($2500) was needed if the college was to carry on. Whittingham himself pledged $1000 if necessary; he also approached the wealthy Israel Condit, who gave at least $500 in October. Dr. George Shattuck pledged $500 and promptly sent half of it.[80]

The summer's violence had left the local military hospitals full again. Among the hundreds of cases was Confederate Sgt. William Thomas Blakiston, who had been a freshman in 1857–58. His parents arrived from St. Mary's County, MD, to be with him at the Seminary Hospital in Hagerstown, and Kerfoot visited frequently, until Blakiston died on August 1. Kerfoot, Falk, and Coit suffered variously from overwork, the weather, and illness during this summer, as they ministered to the local wounded.[81] And there were further deaths among old Jacobites in the early fall. On September 23 George Hayden (sophomore, 1860–61), another native of St. Mary's

79. Harrison, *Life of Kerfoot*, 261–66; Kerfoot to WRW, 19 and 20 July 1863.

80. Kerfoot to WRW, 23 July; 13, 15, and 19 Aug.; and 10 Oct. 1863; Diocesan Archives, Whittingham draft letter to Israel Condit, 18 Aug. 1863; Condit to WRW, 1 Oct. 1863, 5 Jan. 1864; Harrison, *Life of Kerfoot*, 268–72, 360.

81. Blakiston seems to have been a member of Weston's regiment. Kerfoot to WRW, 13 Aug. 1863; *Register*, 1858; National Archives and Records Administration, *Carded Records*, Roll 22; Harrison, *Life of Kerfoot*, 266.

County, died of wounds. Lt. William Creighton Meade (BA, 1857) died of typhoid fever in Washington on October 3; he was mourned as, "perhaps, our brightest alumnus." Another graduate, Dr. Daniel Weisel of Williamsport (BA, 1858), was with Meade when he died. Alumni and friends of Saint James reported such deaths when they could, and they often wrote to Kerfoot that the values and character instilled by the college had remained strong in the young man to the end.[82]

The college opened again in early October, full of more optimism than a year earlier. By December there were thirty-four students: four seniors, five juniors, five sophomores, nine freshmen, and eleven boys in the grammar school.[83] All four seniors had been freshmen in the fall of 1860. As they reached the milestone of their senior year, one of them, James Belt Chesley of Upper Marlboro, MD, inked his and the others' names into his two-year-old copy of the 1861–62 College *Register*: Edward W. Mealey (from Hagerstown), Samuel Earp (Danville, PA), and Thomas D. Pitts (Baltimore). Since 1862 the annual charge for students had risen to $275, which was penciled into Chesley's *Register*. Perhaps because of more energetic advertising, a third of the students this year were non-Episcopalians from Maryland.[84] Although the student population still included a large pro-Confederate element, there was—according to the teachers at least—less conflict on campus this year. Kerfoot wrote in December, "secessionism is among us very polite and quiescent. Really our Sec. students comport themselves quietly and cheerfully. There seems to be an almost, if not an entirely, habitual avoidance of political wrangling. Both sides mingle together in common things better than for the two years preceding." Joseph Coit, looking back, remembered this as a year when there were "no disastrous collisions with the students, but, on the contrary, good feeling and kind and affectionate relations prevailed." This was the case even though political bitterness was, if anything, worsening in the neighborhood around the college. Southern partisans in Hagerstown "slandered" the college faculty, Kerfoot complained, even though they sent their sons to the school. Occasionally the rector's patience wore

---

82. Meade had been commissioned a 2nd lieut. in the 42nd NY Infantry in Sept. 1863. Kerfoot to WRW, 10 and 22 Oct. 1863; *Register* (1858, 1859, 1862); *New York, Civil War Muster Roll Abstracts, 1861–1900*. I have not located Hayden's military records.

83. Four more students would be added by spring; Kerfoot to WRW, 10 Oct. and 14 Dec. 1863; 22 April 1864.

84. *Register* (1862), copy at Maryland Historical Society, Baltimore; Kerfoot to WRW, 22 April 1864.

thin, as when he vented in confidence to the bishop about a particular pro-Confederate student, whom he called "very self-complacent and prone to harsh and unreflecting words."[85]

By January 1864, the college had heard of a dozen former students dead in the war, about half of them lost to disease and the rest killed outright. The most recent blow was the loss of Maj. John Redmon Giles (BA, 1859), who had died of typhoid outside Savannah. Johnny Giles had been close to the rector's family and was considered one of the college's best and brightest graduates. His younger brother William Giles (a sophomore in 1858–59) was reported disabled around the same time.[86] Otherwise the spring went on quietly. In June, the remaining faculty members again began to receive employment offers from other institutions. Dr. George Shattuck, who had been a generous donor to Saint James within the past year, invited Kerfoot to become president of Trinity College in Hartford, and Falk and Coit were also offered teaching positions there. Because Eliza Kerfoot's health was very poor, Kerfoot felt some duty to move her to a less stressful environment; his son Abel was suffering from long-term illness as well. Every overworked faculty member had similar concerns: their small salaries were not guaranteed; their families lived in uncertain conditions; and the war made their work discouraging and at times dangerous. And yet they were usually willing to work on at the college, if financial support could be assured.[87]

Meanwhile, the college community had somehow, after the unsuccessful invasion of the previous summer, convinced itself that the Confederates (in Kerfoot's words) "never could come again." So it was a doubly discouraging blow when, in early July 1864, the Confederates once more began to cross the Potomac in Washington County, raiding, possibly invading. A Federal force occupied Hagerstown, and skirmishing ensued throughout the neighborhood. Locals reported that this summer's

85. Harrison, *Life of Kerfoot*, 368; Kerfoot to WRW, 14 Dec. 1863.

86. The Gileses were sons of Savannah lumber merchant William B. Giles, who owned more than a dozen slaves and acted as agent for slaveowners. After graduation John Giles went into his father's business as a clerk; enlisted Feb. 1862 as a lieut. in the 63rd Ga. Volunteer Infantry; was elected capt. in the 13th Battalion (Phoenix Riflemen) in April 1862; was promoted maj. in Dec. 1862; and died on July 5, 1863. I have not located William's military records. Their brother Clayton attended the grammar school in 1860–61. *Register* (1859, 1860, 1862); Kerfoot to WRW, 11 Jan. 1864; *1860 Census, Savannah, Ga., District 3*, NARA M653, Roll 115, p. 245, and *Savannah Slave Schedule* p. 62; National Archives and Records Administration, *Carded Records*, Roll 564.

87. Kerfoot to WRW, 25 and 29 June 1864.

activity was more damaging than ever, perhaps in retaliation for recent severe Union raids in the Shenandoah Valley. The college certainly felt the effects of the new military activities. The older students, regardless of political sympathies, were sent by the faculty as "scouts" around the area, posted on "watch" at night, and also required to do much of the manual labor of "absent" servants. Frightening incidents abounded. On July 6, 1864, Dr. Falk was out driving a carriage when he saw hostile-looking soldiers approaching him on the road and, thinking quickly, stuffed into his boot the large sum of money he was carrying. He saved the money but lost his watch and cigar case. Later in the day, the same men arrived at the college and made off with its three horses. Another rough group of soldiers, claiming that the Saint James students were enemy "cadets," wanted them to come out and fight; Kerfoot had to pacify this officer and his men with calm words. On July 11 Federal troops threatened the life of John Breathed, the college curator, but the faculty intervened to protect Breathed and his property. These and similar events throughout July complicated exams, shortened the commencement on July 12, caused the hasty dispersal of the students at mid-month, and altogether shook people's faith in the college's survival. Kerfoot wrote repeatedly in his diary and letters that this was the end of his time at Saint James, and on July 14 a letter arrived from trustee William Harrison "reluctantly advising" that the college suspend operations for the duration of the war. Yet indecision reigned—the college must close; the college might go on.[88]

If a sign was needed, it came in August. On Friday the 5th, the day the college faculty had planned to make a final decision about carrying on or not, a large body of Confederate troops arrived on campus. Despite a strong undercurrent of antagonism, civility predominated for most of the day. An old Jacobite, Maj. Richard C. Badger (grammar school, 1852–54) of the 45th North Carolina Infantry, advised Kerfoot to hide the College horses. Kerfoot pressed Gen. Dodson Ramseur to dine in College with his family, despite an initial rebuff from staff officer Henry Kyd Douglas (whose home was in Washington County). Also at dinner were two former students, a Capt. Phillips and a Capt. Moore.[89] But suddenly, in

88. Harrison, *Life of Kerfoot*, 282–88; Kerfoot to WRW, 5, 15, and 27 July 1864; Diocesan Archives, Kerfoot letter to William G. Harrison, 16 July 1864. Kerfoot consulted with trustees and friends during a trip to New York and Boston in late July; Kerfoot to WRW, 27 and 28 July 1864.

89. Badger, from Raleigh, NC, enlisted May 1861; was promoted captain April 1862; was promoted major July 1862; and resigned from army 1865 to serve as clerk of

the evening, Ramseur informed Kerfoot and Coit that they were being arrested by order of Gen. Jubal Early in retaliation for the recent arrest by Union troops of the Rev. Dr. Hunter Boyd of Winchester, Virginia.[90]

Now prisoners, the two clergymen were moved into Kerfoot's parlor in the rectory for the night. Coit was allowed to spend a few hours in his own study. The Kerfoot family and Coit passed the time in extreme anxiety, writing letters, packing a few necessities, and otherwise preparing for the two men's removal to Richmond the next day. But Eliza Kerfoot calmly sent for John Breathed, and, first thing in the morning, the pro-Confederate curator went to see General Early personally to negotiate for his clerical friends. Early then came to see the prisoners, and, after delivering a forty-five-minute lecture about Dr. Boyd's treatment and the egregious behavior of Federal troops, he granted Kerfoot and Coit three weeks' parole, on condition that they secure Boyd's release or else turn themselves in again to be sent to Libby Prison in Richmond. Early also gave the college a written order of protection, but soon after his departure, his soldiers made off with Kerfoot's and Coit's horses.[91] Within a few days Kerfoot and Coit left for Washington, all their energies now focused on obtaining Boyd's release from President Lincoln and the War Department. Kerfoot and Coit had to make extensive investigations into Boyd's case. On August 19, with the help of influential friends, they finally managed to obtain a federal order for Boyd's release.[92]

In the course of these tense weeks the decision to close the college was made. Before leaving Saint James for Washington, Kerfoot and Coit had packed up their own libraries and other personal belongings and called on employees and local friends to help close up the buildings.[93] Now it was time to dismantle what remained. The campus and buildings would remain in the hands of the diocese, but the contents were to be dispersed. Robert Coster, the last faculty member remaining on-site, helped oversee the sale of the college effects on September 15–17, 1864.

NC Senate. I have been unable to identify Phillips and Moore with any certainty. Harrison, *Life of Kerfoot*, 292; *Register* (1854); NARA, *Carded Records*, Roll 12; Douglas, *I Rode with Stonewall*, 303–4.

90. Harrison, *Life of Kerfoot*, 292, 302–3.

91. Harrison, *Life of Kerfoot*, 292–95, 303–9; Douglas, *I Rode with Stonewall*, 304–6. Falk and Coster may have been absent from campus on this day, thus escaping arrest; *Journals of the Annual Conventions* (1865), 72.

92. A detailed account is in Harrison, *Life of Kerfoot*, 292–318,

93. Harrison, *Life of Kerfoot*, 309–10.

"It has been a painful duty to me to assist in the disposal of the College property and to see the dear old place stripped of all the appliances of school life," wrote Coster. Nearly $6500 was realized from the sale, more than expected; this sum was applied to the existing college debt. The science equipment and the library of some eleven thousand volumes were shipped to Baltimore to be stored for future use.[94]

Left behind at Saint James, on and around the campus, were the people who had worked for the college and some who had been enslaved there. On November 1, 1864, slavery was abolished in Maryland, and more than a thousand African Americans in Washington County became legally free for the first time, including those with ties to the college. Some of these individuals still lived there when the school was refounded after the war. Violet, the daughter of a Ringgold slave, was still living and working at Saint James School in the 1880s. Letitia Diggs, born into slavery somewhere nearby in the 1850s, would work as the Onderdonks' maid and housekeeper. She may have been one of the children who was baptized at the college or attended its Sunday school.[95]

What the employees and students thought of the closing of the college has not survived in written form, though the students and old Jacobites had made their strong attachment to Saint James clear by their actions throughout the war years. Robert Coster, studying for ordination, wrote a pious epitaph: "It looks like the death of our work, but God sees not as man and I trust He will resuscitate in His own good time and way." Alexander Falk, taking up a professorship of German languages and literature at Franklin & Marshall College in Lancaster, Pennsylvania, mused that "it was very hard to leave the dear old place! Nine years of work had made it a home for me. It was hard to see the place . . . entirely desolated. But we must consider of course all the circumstances, which led to the breaking up of St. James, as providential, and as one of the sacrifices, which the war against the rebellion involved." Joseph Coit went to St. Paul's School in Concord, New Hampshire. He eventually succeeded his brother Henry as rector, the two Jacobites solidifying the legacy of Saint James at the increasingly successful New England school.[96] Joseph

---

94. Diocesan Archives, Robert J. Coster letter to Bishop Whittingham, 26 Sept. 1864; *Journals of the Annual Convention* (1865), 73.

95. *Memoirs of Adrian Holmes Onderdonk*, 13, 31; for Letitia (née Warfield) Diggs's background, see "Family-Papers-Warfield-Allen-Doleman."

96. Heckscher, *St. Paul's*, chapters 1–6.

Coit kept his memories of the college green and would later contribute them to Hall Harrison's 1886 biography of Kerfoot.[97]

Kerfoot went on to a brief presidency of Trinity College and then was elected the first Episcopal bishop of Pittsburgh. But the twenty-two years he had spent at Saint James were perhaps what he considered his most important work. Eight months before the end of them in 1864, he wrote sadly of the war deaths among the college's old students and what they meant to him personally: "I find that I have thought much of my College sons as treasures and honors and friends here, this side [of] the great river—I feel poorer—I shall not have so many of them as I thought I should—as *my* old School Father has—to come around me if I live to be old, as Dr. Muhlenberg is old—and rich now." Each death was a sadness to him, though in truth just over a dozen young men were then known to have died, out of well over 700 who had been educated at the College.[98]

A better measure of the college's work is those hundreds of youths who passed through its doors and were the better for it. As Kerfoot said at the 1862 commencement, even if the college were to close, "none of us would deem the past a vain expenditure of time and work." But they would work on, he said, until they heard God's word bidding them to cease. "And should that word come to us"—as now in 1864 it had—"none the less has the work thus far done been worth the while. It will stand. It will repeat itself through other agencies, in better times. Other Christian Colleges, preceptors and pupils will grow out of this work here. The foundations laid are deep and sure."[99] Imperfect, divided, lacking in funds, the college foundered when civil war tore the nation apart. That it nevertheless endured through most of that war, teaching and ministering, is a testament to its strength and commitment.

---

97. Diocesan Archives, Coster letter to WRW, 26 Sept. 1864; Falk (two) letters to WRW, 14 Sept. 1864; Harrison, *Life of Kerfoot*, 302–70.

98. Kerfoot to WRW, 11 Jan. 1864; *Register* (1862).

99. Harrison, *Life of Kerfoot*, 231.

4

Reconstruction of a Vision
The Onderdonk Era Begins
Saint James School, 1869–95

John McCardell

It is a great story, the stuff of legend, related most colorfully by the subject's son:

> He was not enthusiastic about making a change . . . But . . . he felt that it was due to his Bishop to at least make a visit to the School . . . He found the buildings and grounds in a deplorable condition . . . and so made a hasty exit in order to catch the stage back . . . A short distance from the School he found the road blocked by a number of wagons, buggies, and people who had assembled to watch the dancing bears which some gypsies were showing . . . [H]e realized he would not be able to catch the stage [and] therefore returned to the School [and] devoted the afternoon to going through the buildings, studying the possibilities. As a result, his statement to the Bishop on his return was quite the opposite from what he had intended had it not been for the dancing bear.[1]

---

1. Onderdonk, *Memoirs*, 3.

Historians wrestle repeatedly with differing accounts of an event. This is a case in point, for the record appears to indicate that the very same unenthusiastic "he" had in fact written his bishop the following:

> Dear Sir:
> You may remember that a few weeks since, my brother-in-law, the Rev. B. B. Griswold, called on you in reference to the College of St. James. He mentioned at the time his intention to associate a layman with him. The layman referred to was myself. Mr. Griswold, upon reflection, has determined to abandon all further consideration of the subject, thinking his strength does not lie in keeping boarding school. Immediately . . . I called upon you to ascertain whether a proposition from myself would be considered.[2]

The year was 1869, and the prospect of reopening the College of Saint James was surely daunting. Poised at the crossroads of North and South, the institution had fared poorly during the Civil War. Enrollment in 1860–61 included fifty-five students in the college and fifty-eight in the grammar school. Its students, mostly Southerners, had gone off to serve the Confederacy. By June 1861 enrollment had dropped to eighty-one. Its rector since 1842, the Reverend John Barrett Kerfoot (ordained by Bishop Benjamin Onderdonk in 1837), was a Union sympathizer. He had struggled to keep the school afloat as battles raged at nearby Sharpsburg in 1862 and Gettysburg in 1863. In 1864, Confederate General Jubal Early, passing through on a raid north that would culminate in the battle of Monocacy, arrested Rector Kerfoot and held him as a hostage. Enrollment by then had dropped below fifty, and the College of Saint James closed down.[3] Distraught but unbowed, the Reverend Dr. Kerfoot accepted the presidency of Trinity College in Hartford, Connecticut, in 1864. The following year he was elected the first bishop of Pittsburgh.[4]

---

2. Henry Onderdonk to Right Rev. W. R. Whittingham, July 15, 1869, Maryland Diocesan Archives, Episcopal Diocese of Maryland, Baltimore (hereafter MDA). The editor and authors owe a great debt to Mary Klein, Director of the Maryland Diocesan Archives, Baltimore, who led us to innumerable files and drawers containing original sources and useful secondary literature. Many excellent sources are available electronically from the Project Canterbury website, anglicanhistory.org, created and managed by Richard Mammana. Ted Camp, Senior Master and History Chairman of Saint James School, and Archivist of the Owens Library, has pointed the authors in the right direction for some years.

3. Duncan, "Impact of the Civil War," 37–52; Saint James School Archives, Document produced for "The 125th Anniversary of Saint James School," 1.

4. Duncan, "Impact of the Civil War," 8.

The "he" was Henry Onderdonk, born in 1822 in New York, of old Knickerbocker lineage. A graduate of Columbia College, Onderdonk studied for a year at the General Theological Seminary before determining that he was not called to the priesthood. He moved in 1846 to Baltimore, to teach at St. Timothy's Hall, an Episcopal school in Catonsville. After seven years at St. Timothy's, he went on to several other teaching assignments nearby and, in 1861, was elected president of the Maryland Agricultural College, later the University of Maryland.[5]

The Onderdonk family was no stranger to the church, to Maryland, or to controversy. Henry's uncles, Henry Ustick (1789–1858) and Benjamin Tredwell (1791–1861) both served as bishops, of Pennsylvania and New York, respectively. Henry Ustick, a Columbia graduate, was consecrated assistant bishop in 1827 and diocesan in 1836. Benjamin, also a Columbia graduate, was consecrated in 1830.

Although thought by a colleague to be "not a man of exceptional ability, but immensely hard-working," Benjamin served as the first Professor of Nature, Ministry, and Polity of the Church at the new General Theological Seminary in New York, founded in 1817. Caught up in the controversy spawned by the Oxford Movement in England in the 1840s, Benjamin became an increasingly vocal advocate of the "High Churchmanship." The Oxford Movement was given forceful articulation in a series of pamphlets bearing the general title of *Tracts for the Times*. One historian succinctly summarized the essential purpose of the Oxford, or Tractarian, Movement as a "revolutionary recall of the Church of England to the knowledge and recovery of her essentially Catholic heritage of doctrine and spirituality," this in contrast to those "thoroughly wedded to the Protestant heritage of the Reformation."[6]

To this ecclesiastical strife were added, in the mid-1840s, serious charges of alcohol abuse. The House of Bishops, meeting at the General Convention of 1844, accepted the resignation of Bishop Henry Ustick Onderdonk, who admitted his "habitual use of spirituous liquor as a remedy

---

5. Prehn, "Saint James School at 175," 8.

6. Dawley, *The Story of the General Theological Seminary*, 147–48. For some taxonomical helps for mapping the development and views of religious parties in the Episcopal Church and in Anglican Christianity generally in the nineteenth century, see the early notes to chapters 1 and 2 of this book. The difference between the traditional High Churchman, the follower of the leaders of the Oxford Movement (1833–1845), the Anglo-Catholic, the Ritualist, the Low Churchman, the Broad Churchman, and the Evangelical are a subtle but important consideration in the study of the church school movement in nineteenth-century America and England.

for disease." In response, the House formally suspended the bishop indefinitely as "the administration of discipline." Historians differ over the degree to which this punishment was as much theological, given Onderdonk's embrace of the Oxford Movement, as behavioral. In any case, the suspension was not lifted until 1856, two years before his death.[7]

William Whittingham of Maryland appeared frequently in the lives of the Onderdonks. Born in 1805, Whittingham was an 1825 graduate of General Seminary and "universally admired for both his scholarship and character." A generous gift to the seminary by Peter G. Stuyvesant in 1835 established a professorship of ecclesiastical history, under the terms of which the donor himself would choose the appointee. Stuyvesant selected Whittingham, who served four years until his election, in 1840, as the fourth bishop of Maryland.[8] Benjamin Onderdonk served as one of Whittingham's four consecrating bishops in a diocese where Henry Ustick Onderdonk had served as an interim bishop, replacing James Kemp, second bishop of Maryland, who had died in an accident returning from Henry's consecration in 1827.

Thus, the connections between the Onderdonk family and Bishop Whittingham were multiple. They were also, at times, trying, even stressful. Soon after the resignation and suspension of Henry Ustick Onderdonk, the House of Bishops brought charges against Benjamin Onderdonk for "immorality with deliberately impure intent." Three of his fellow bishops alleged that, "improperly excited by vinous or spirituous liquors," Benjamin Onderdonk had, "at sundry other times . . . impurely and unchastely laid his hands upon the bodies of other virtuous and respectable ladies." In January 1845, by a vote of eleven to six, he was found guilty and suspended. Whittingham, along with five other "high church" bishops, voted consistently in the minority. "Never," wrote the bishop, "have I so desponded with regard to the Church as I do now . . . What is to become of us who are set as marks for everybody to shoot at, God only knows."[9] Ensnarement in the tangled web of sexual behavior and theological dispute is not a modern phenomenon.

Suspended but not deposed, Benjamin Onderdonk continued to hold the title bishop of New York, though he could no longer perform the duties of office. He died in 1861. He is buried in Trinity Church, New

---

7. Dawley, *Story of the General Theological Seminary*, 164.
8. Dawley, *Story of the General Theological Seminary*, 140.
9. Dawley, *Story of the General Theological Seminary*, 172–74 (see esp. n52).

York, where in a cenotaph he is depicted in eucharistic vestments, lying in repose, but crushing a serpent labeled "Scandal" at his feet.[10]

Perhaps it is understandable, then, why, after a year of study at General Seminary, young Henry Onderdonk chose the path of teaching over the path of ministry. A protégé of William Augustus Muhlenberg, Libertus van Bokkelen had founded St. Timothy's Hall in 1845 and brought with him his mentor's belief in a holistic education. Onderdonk made his way to the Catonsville, Maryland, school to take up a new vocation.[11]

By the time of Onderdonk's arrival in 1846, according to a local historian, "St. Timothy's Hall was prospering." By 1850 "there were one hundred and thirty-two students enrolled at the school, with a staff of fourteen professors." Students wore military uniforms and participated regularly in military drill. The course of study, as might be expected at a "Muhlenberg school," was at once rigorous and traditional and included art, history, philosophy, and the natural sciences. Most students came from well-to-do families. Headmaster van Bokkelen had a strict set of regulations. Not only were boys required to wear uniforms while they attended classes; they were also not allowed to receive food from home or to engage in singing, dancing, or studying in groups.[12]

Among the students at St. Timothy's was young John Wilkes Booth, who spent but a single year there, 1852–53. According to a Booth biographer, Booth "easily made friends with his classmates, some of whom included Fitzhugh Lee, nephew of Robert E. Lee, the commanding general of Confederate forces, and a future Confederate general himself, and Samuel Arnold and Michael O'Loughlin, both future co-conspirators in Booth's initial plot to kidnap the president."[13] On January 23, 1853, the fourteen-year-old Booth was baptized at St. Timothy's Church in Catonsville.

Little, however, is known of Onderdonk's tenure at St. Timothy's Hall, and, in fact, even its duration is not certain. One account states that he left the school in 1853 to teach "at several other Baltimore schools." Another places him at St. Timothy's until 1861. It is reasonable to assume that however many there may have been, his years there were successful,

---

10. Lawrence, "Episcopate of Benjamin Tredwell Onderdonk."

11. Prehn, "Saint James School at 175," 9.

12. Norris, "Catonsville's Connection to Lincoln Assassin John Wilkes Booth," para. 13.

13. Norris, "Catonsville's Connection to Lincoln Assassin John Wilkes Booth," para. 22. See also Alford, *Fortune's Fool*.

especially since, in 1861, he was elected president of the Maryland Agricultural college, which later become the University of Maryland.[14]

A slave-holding state that remained in the Union, Maryland during the Civil War was deeply divided. To manage an institution so close to Washington, DC, in a state where Confederate sympathizers were both numerous and vocal posed severe challenges. In April 1864 Union troops camped at the college en route from Annapolis to Washington. Later that year Confederate troops under the command of General Bradley Johnson, a Marylander, arrived on the grounds as part of General Jubal Early's move on Washington.

What happened next remains a matter of controversy. Yet the evidence makes clear that Johnson and his four hundred soldiers were warmly received. The historian of the university has noted that "partying lasted into the night," as Johnson established his headquarters at a nearby inn and singing and dancing around the campfires commenced. "The neighborhood's ladies also found their way to the campus for the party."[15]

From these general facts emerged the story of an extravagant "Old South Ball," supposedly hosted by Onderdonk, who ordered his kitchen staff to lay on a feast, including "the delicacies of the season."[16] Though Johnson's force moved on the next morning, the tale of the lavish event spread quickly and prompted a federal investigation. A member of the college's board urged that the inquiry proceed quickly, lest the start of a new academic year be put at risk.[17]

Newspapers carried many versions of this event. The investigation queried local residents and faculty members. Onderdonk himself denied even being present. "The only truth in the whole thing," he wrote, "is that General Johnson's 'band of raiders' passed through the College grounds. I am mentioned by name as having invited them. I did not invite them."[18]

In the end the investigation produced no clear-cut findings. Yet Onderdonk's reputation never recovered, and he resigned his presidency soon thereafter. He went back to Baltimore to teach. He also published, in 1868, *A History of Maryland... For the Use of Schools*. In his preface to this volume, which was an abridgment of a larger work by James McSherry

14. See "Henry Onderdonk"; Prehn, "Saint James School at 175," 10.
15. Steven, "College Divide"; "Henry Onderdonk."
16. Minaya, "Divided by War."
17. See "Henry Onderdonk."
18. See "Henry Onderdonk." See also Callcott, *History of the University of Maryland*, 163–64.

first published in 1849, Onderdonk expressed his hope that "our youth ... will be animated to deeds worthy of their sires and ... will hand down the State to posterity with untarnished lustre." Readers would search in vain for authorial vindication. Of the 1864 event Onderdonk simply wrote: "The troops posted there, four hundred in number, precipitately retreated, without waiting to fire a shot."[19] This history would go through at least six editions.

Thus, after a career of what must have seemed a series of dead ends, Onderdonk made his approach to his old friend Bishop Whittingham. It is difficult to credit the "dancing bear" story in light of all that had taken place up to 1869. At age forty-seven, Onderdonk had not yet found a place to put down roots or to avoid controversy. For him, the opportunity to revive and lead a school must have been welcome.

The conditions existing at Saint James in 1869 were daunting. War had taken a severe toll, and its effects lingered well beyond the end of hostilities. Years of neglect had rendered the physical plant virtually inoperable. The school's main building, Claggett Hall, now served as a stable for horses, a barn for cows, and a coop for chickens. Much of the campus had been given over to the production of wheat and corn. In his 1885 commencement address, Onderdonk recalled that "the buildings were so ruined and dilapidated as to be uninhabitable."[20]

Then of course there were questions of even more fundamental importance. Where were the students to come from? Who would teach them? How could the campus be brought back into serviceable condition? And where were the funds to make these things possible to come from?

A man of lesser energy or vision would want no part of such a futile enterprise. That undoubtedly explains the decision of the Reverend Mr. Griswold, as Onderdonk, his brother-in-law, put it, to "abandon all further consideration of the subject."[21]

Yet Onderdonk saw in this challenge an opportunity, which he laid out in detail in a letter to Bishop Whittingham:

> To take the property ... for 7 years—rent free.
> To put the buildings required for the use of the school in habitable order, and keep them so.

19. Onderdonk, *History of Maryland*, 3, 247.
20. Onderdonk, "St. James Commencement," 3.
21. Henry Onderdonk to Right Rev. W. R. Whittingham, July 15, 1869, Letter in the MDA.

> That the school shall be a diocesan school, and known as the Grammar School of the College of St. James, and as such enjoy the influence of the Bishop and the Bishop of the Diocese shall be visitor.
>
> That as soon as the patronage of the school will admit of it, say 20 full pay pupils—to employ a chaplain to hold religious services and take charge of the religious instruction. This chaplain to be the one whom the Bishop approves of.
>
> That for every 15 full pay pupils from every source excepting the Diocese of Easton, to receive free of expense for board and tuition one son of a clergyman of the Diocese of Maryland, and for every ? of like character from the Diocese of Easton, one son of a clergyman of that diocese upon the same terms.

He concluded by writing that, with the bishop's assent, the school could be in operation that fall.[22]

The bishop quickly agreed, with one perhaps notable exception: Saint James would not be a diocesan school. The bishop would give his unflagging moral support, but the school would not become a diocesan dependency.[23]

With that, Onderdonk went to work. He and his wife would eventually spend more than $5,000 of their own money to help revive the school. Students initially came from nearby and not farther away than Baltimore. In 1869 the price of tuition for "The College of St. James School" was set at $375. The academic year ran from September 15 to June 24, with "no protracted vacations at Christmas or Easter."[24] In an advertising circular, Onderdonk described the course of study as "a thorough English education," and went on to explain what that meant:

> The minds of those attending this school being regard[ed] not so much as vessels to be filled at a stipulated price, as organisms to be developed and trained, the aim is to cultivate the habits of thought ... A well-disciplined mind is regarded as the most practical preparation for any walk of life. ...
>
> The one-sided education, therefore—the exclusive training of the faculties that are already strong, the neglecting of those

---

22. Henry Onderdonk to Right Rev. W. R. Whittingham, July 15, 1869, Letter in the MDA.

23. Henry Onderdonk to Right Rev. W. R. Whittingham, July 15, 1869, Letter in the MDA. At the top of the letter the bishop wrote, "Assented, except as to its being 'Diocesan.'"

24. Saint James Senior Master Theodore Camp to John McCardell, January 5, 2018.

that are weak, or, as it is called, consulting the taste and genius of the pupil as to what he shall study; the making of education a sort of passive pleasure, instead of a dutiful, studious, and strenuous energy—in this school will meet with no sympathy. The aim is to make *cultivated men*.[25]

Of the governing-board membership at the time the school closed in 1864, two—the Reverend Joseph Passmore, ordained by Bishop Whittingham in 1848 and from 1844 to 1862 a member of the Saint James faculty, and J. Mason Campbell, a prominent attorney—had died. The remaining six included Bishop Whittingham, as president; the Right Reverend Cleveland Coxe, bishop of Western New York; the Right Reverend John B. Kerfoot, bishop of Pittsburgh; and Baltimoreans William G. Harrison, Frederick W. Brune II, and Samuel G. Wyman.

Bishop Coxe had been ordained to the priesthood by Bishop Benjamin Onderdonk in 1842, had received a Doctor of Divinity degree from the College of Saint James in 1856, and, from 1854 to 1863 was rector of Grace Church in Baltimore. Bishop Kerfoot, of course, had served as rector of Saint James. Harrison had served as president of the Baltimore and Ohio Railroad for two years in the mid-1850s and had represented Baltimore City in the Maryland legislature while the southern states were leaving the Union. A pro-secession member, Harrison had been arrested in September 1861, refused to take an oath of allegiance to the Union, and was held until February 1862.

Brune, a Harvard graduate, also harbored southern sentiments but, as partner with Baltimore Mayor George Brown in the firm Brown and Brune, favored the gradual emancipation of slaves. Wyman, a successful Baltimore merchant, was a director of the Bank of Baltimore and lived from 1839 to 1861 at "Homewood," built by the son of Charles Carroll of Carrollton on what would become the campus of The Johns Hopkins University. These were men of mark and substance, and their identification with the revived Saint James undoubtedly attracted both attention and students.[26]

A letter from Onderdonk to Bishop Whittingham in February 1871 provides some insight into conditions at Saint James after eighteen months. Onderdonk expresses gratitude for a gift of altar cloths, the

---

25. Onderdonk, *Sources by and about Henry Onderdonk*, 9.
26. Onderdonk, *Sources by and about Henry Onderdonk*, 9.

receipt of which addressed an "unsightly" furnishing, one "so far from being suggestive of anything sacred."[27]

But he goes on to acknowledge the "limited patronage the school has yet received." Still, there is hope that "increase seems likely to be realized. In fact, it has already been so by the addition of two pupils last week." Moreover, "I hear of rumors of several more to come."[28]

Despite limited means, Saint James was able to contribute five dollars to the Diocesan Missions Fund in December 1870, with the hope of additional gifts the following April and July. Then as now, participation mattered almost as much as gift amount in any sort of fund-raising activity. And, "though small," this gift represented "at least evidence that, though small and quiet, we are neither dead nor asleep."[29]

By 1874, five years in, Onderdonk with merited satisfaction could report great progress. A major renovation to Claggett Hall added, by the design of a French roof, an entire floor of 300 square feet, "admirably ventilated and for the purpose of a dormitory."[30]

Onderdonk's vision continued to be ambitious, as he wrote to Bishop Whittingham:

> It is my effort to make St. James equal in all its appointments to the celebrated school at Concord [St. Paul's], and yes, at the same time, one where Churchmen of the moderate means that characterize those of this latitude may enjoy all the advantages that cost so much at St. Paul's . . . And if the character of the instruction is not equal to that at Concord, it will be either my fault or the fact that our own people will not foster [their] own institutions and thus build up among us what everybody acknowledges is wanted.[31]

---

27. Onderdonk, *Sources by and about Henry Onderdonk*, 10. For information on Coxe, see Perry, *Bishops*, 159; on Harrison see "War of the Rebellion" and "Presidents of the Baltimore and Ohio"; on Brune see McCoy, "Frederick W. Brune"; on Wyman see "Samuel Gerish Wyman."

28. Henry Onderdonk to Right Rev. W. R Whittingham, February 11, 1871, Diocesan Archives.

29. Henry Onderdonk to Right Rev. W. R Whittingham, February 11, 1871, Diocesan Archives.

30. Henry Onderdonk to Right Rev. W. R. Whittingham, December 6, 1870, Diocesan Archives.

31. Henry Onderdonk to Right Rev. W. R. Whittingham, September 28, 1874, Diocesan Archives.

By 1874, Onderdonk had abandoned any plan to eventually make Saint James a college again. Such an initiative, he concluded, would be "dissipating our efforts and accomplish nothing," owing to the "enormous endowments that are necessary to compete with those already established and so richly endowed."[32]

Onderdonk's work had, however, reached beyond the simple daily operation of the school. Every Sunday, "children of the neighborhood" along with "a large number of colored adults" attended a weekly Sunday school. Attendance numbered as many as fifty, but the effort had not been without "many discouragements, especially as far as the whites were concerned, owing to the well-known prejudice to the Church in this quarter."[33]

That so much had been "accomplished in a barren field by taking *Nil Desperandum* as our Motto" was in no small way attributable to the energy and persistence of Onderdonk's wife, Mary. Henry's first wife, Harriette S. Henry of Somerset County, Maryland, whom he had married in 1849, had borne three sons—Henry Ustick, Robert, and Andrew—but died in 1861. Mary Elizabeth Latrobe, born in New Jersey in 1836, became the second Mrs. Onderdonk in 1869. The two had met while Henry was teaching in Baltimore. A seven-year courtship led, at last, to marriage.[34]

Mary had been reared in a household of wealth and comfort. Her father, Benjamin Henry Latrobe, was Chief Engineer of the Baltimore and Ohio Railroad, and her grandfather, also named Benjamin, was a distinguished architect, best known for designing the US Capitol building but also was the architect for the park at the Bai Yuka on the Saint James campus. To her, Saint James might have presented a true challenge. But she plunged right into a life of "everything from cooking, cleaning,

---

32. Henry Onderdonk to Right Rev. W. R. Whittingham, September 28, 1874, Diocesan Archives. Onderdonk admired the good work being done at St. Paul's School, Concord, New Hampshire. While St. Paul's had been founded in 1856 by men affiliated with the College and Grammar School of Saint James, the founders saw themselves as specialists in secondary education and never intended to offer the BA degree.

33. Henry Onderdonk to Right Rev. W. R. Whittingham, September 28, 1874, Diocesan Archives.

34. Henry Onderdonk to Right Rev. W. R. Whittingham, September 28, 1874, Diocesan Archives. One son from the first marriage, Robert Jenkins Onderdonk (1852–1917), moved to Texas after Saint James and was a promoter of and instrumental to the rise of fine-art painting in that state. Robert's son Julian (1882–1922) graduated from the Episcopal School of Texas (West Texas Military Academy at that time and later Texas Military Institute), then studied art with William Merritt Chase (1849–1916) in New York. An impressionist who appreciated the Texas Hill Country, Julian is considered "the father of Texas painting." See Rudolph and Sheerin, *Julian Onderdonk*.

laundry and sewing to nursing sick students."[35] But, as is the case for "first ladies" in positions of prominence, Mary Onderdonk also had public responsibilities. She became a leader of the Dorcas Society, a circle of women who did sewing for the poor. She also served on the board of the County Orphans' Home.[36]

But it was her "never flagging persistency" in establishing the Saint James Sunday School that most endeared her to her husband. "White and Black," he wrote, "are learning, whether they can read or not, the responsive parts of the service as well as the Lord's Prayer, the Creed, and Ten Commandments."[37]

Mary also gave birth to two sons, one of whom, Latrobe, died of a ruptured appendix in 1883 at age eleven. The other, Adrian, born in 1877, would serve as headmaster of Saint James from 1903 until 1939 and as a member of the faculty until 1947. As mother and as spouse, Mary had a substantial influence in the growth of the school.[38]

Student life in the Onderdonk years produced insightful and even colorful memories. Adrian Onderdonk recalled that "in those days cows grazed on the campus and so one had to watch one's step. Much amusement was caused us boys on one occasion when we overheard a certain swain say to the girl he was with, 'It's a crime the way cows are permitted to graze on the grounds.' *We* knew what had happened."[39] There were rules and also consequences. "The use of tobacco, of profane and coarse language, and the hunting or destroying of birds' nests will be regarded as a withdrawal, on the part of the pupil, of any claim to the honors of the school."[40]

Principal Onderdonk endeared himself to his students, who referred to him, affectionately, as "the Old Man." On Friday nights, himself a Shakespeare scholar, he would read selections from the Bard's works aloud. When a former student was jailed in Ecuador as a political prisoner, Onderdonk interceded with President Chester Arthur to secure

---

35. Henry Onderdonk to Right Rev. W. R. Whittingham, September 28, 1874, Diocesan Archives.

36. See "Mary Onderdonk"; "At St. James Dies Mrs. Onderdonk."

37. Henry Onderdonk to Right Rev. W. R. Whittingham, September 28, 1874, Diocesan Archives.

38. Saint James School Archives, Document produced for "The 125th Anniversary," 8.

39. Onderdonk, *Memoirs*, 3–4, 7–9.

40. Onderdonk, *Memoirs*, 9.

his release—and would henceforth always try to have at least one student from Ecuador at the school.[41]

One cold January evening, the entire school community gathered for the wedding of two African Americans. A dance followed and lasted late into the evening. The noise made sleep impossible. Eventually, Mary demanded: "Henry, are you going to allow them to keep this up?" He replied: "It will be old man winter and not the Old Man who will bring their dance to a close." His nickname, it turned out, was no secret.[42]

Adrian Onderdonk noted that "there were fine boys and bad boys in the School, but they were for the most part an honorable bunch. A liar had no place among the larger group . . . Boys were required by the 'Old Man' to be gentlemen." The only sport played was baseball, but football was introduced in 1894. "Football was some game in those days," Adrian remembered. "There was no head gear. Our only head protection was our hair, which we were allowed to grow very long."[43]

Principal Onderdonk persevered, and slowly but surely the school began to grow, this in spite of a protracted depression that struck the country in 1873 and lasted much of the decade. Annual reports to the Diocesan Convention afford glimpses of progress. In 1877, $155 was raised "to paint and refurbish the Chapel."[44] In 1878 there were forty-two students in attendance, from Maryland, Pennsylvania, New York, New Jersey, West Virginia, Illinois, and Iowa. Of these, eighteen were communicants and four had been confirmed. Of the Class of 1878, two students each matriculated at Hobart College and the College of New Jersey (later Princeton), and three more would soon enroll at Trinity College, Hartford. In his report to the diocese of Maryland, Onderdonk commended the general "healthfulness" of the school, noting that there had "not been a professional visit by a physician for any case of sickness, originating on the place, for two years."[45] In 1880, the gymnasium had "been, at considerable expense, renewed," and the school in general "gives earnest of returning prosperity."[46] By 1883, the library held eleven thousand volumes. Enrollment stood at forty students. Annual tuition

---

41. Onderdonk, *Memoirs*, 12.
42. Onderdonk, *Memoirs*, 14.
43. Onderdonk, *Memoirs*, 14.
44. Diocese of Maryland, "Journal of the Ninety-Fourth Annual Convention," 165.
45. Diocese of Maryland, "Journal of the Ninety-Fifth Annual Convention," 55, 56.
46. Diocese of Maryland, "Journal of the Ninety-Seventh Annual Convention," 72–73.

was $300. In that year the chapel walls were "colored and stenciled," the chancel "enlarged . . . and newly furnished," and a "complete set of stained-glass windows, eight in number, replaced the old windows."[47]

By 1887 the school had thirty-two students and five instructors. Three students had gone on to Trinity, Lehigh, and Johns Hopkins. Steam heat and gas had been installed. The cost of these improvements had come "at the expense of the Principal."[48] Indeed, the convention journal noted that the work of the school was "carried on at the risk of the Principal, at whose expense the school is maintained."[49]

"The College of St. James Grammar School" observed the fiftieth anniversary of the founding of the institution in 1892. As part of the commencement exercises on June 21, 1892, the celebration was becomingly modest. The Reverend Hall Harrison, the rector of St. John's Church, Ellicott City, Maryland, was the speaker. Harrison was an alumnus of and later taught at the college before departing in 1864 to join the faculty of St. Paul's, Concord. He was also the biographer of the Right Reverend John B. Kerfoot. His principal address included a "justly merited eulogium" on the service of Principal Onderdonk.[50]

Having now reached the age of seventy, Henry Onderdonk could look back with satisfaction at the good work he had accomplished since his arrival in 1869. Though his health had begun to fail, he and his family made a trip to the Columbian Exposition in Chicago in the summer of 1893. There they beheld the "white city" illuminated by electricity and witnessed the power of the dynamo, which the historian Henry Adams would identify as the symbol of a new and potentially terrifying future.[51]

In 1895, on August 14, Henry Onderdonk died of kidney and heart failure.[52] He was seventy-three years old. The funeral took place in nearby Hagerstown, Maryland, with interment in Greenmount Cemetery in Baltimore. Six of his former students, as pallbearers, carried his body to its final resting place: Shirley and Julian Carter, Joseph Wilkins, Ernest Rich, Harry Slingluff, and Robert Bowie.

47. Diocese of Maryland, "Journal of the One Hundredth Annual Convention," 27. When Endicott Peabody opened Groton School in 1884, the price of tuition was $300.

48. Diary of John Moore McCalla, July 25, 1893.

49. Diocese of Maryland, "Journal of the One Hundred Fourth Annual Convention," 219.

50. *Baltimore Sun*, June 24, 1892.

51. Adams, *Education of Henry Adams*, chapter 25.

52. *Baltimore Sun*, August 14, 1895.

Of his legacy, one historian has written: "Unceasing labor was rewarded by the love his pupils bore him and the rank they obtained in college and subsequent life."[53] But perhaps an editorial in the *Baltimore Sun* said it best: "He was a man who did good in his generation and adorned the profession which had engaged his best efforts for fifty years."[54]

---

53. *Baltimore Sun*, August 14, 1895.
54. *Baltimore Sun*, August 19, 1895, 2.

Rt. Rev. William R. Whittingham, D.D. (1805–79), bishop of Maryland

Reverend Dr. William Augustus Muhlenberg (1796–1877), Founder of the Church Institute, Flushing, and St. Paul's College and Grammar School, College Point, on Long Island, New York.

Rt. Rev. John Barrett Kerfoot (1816–81), founding rector

Claggett Hall before 1910 fire

Kemp Hall fire in 1857

Saint James School Chapel today

Chapel Tower

Claggett Hall today, with original Fountain Rock Manor steps

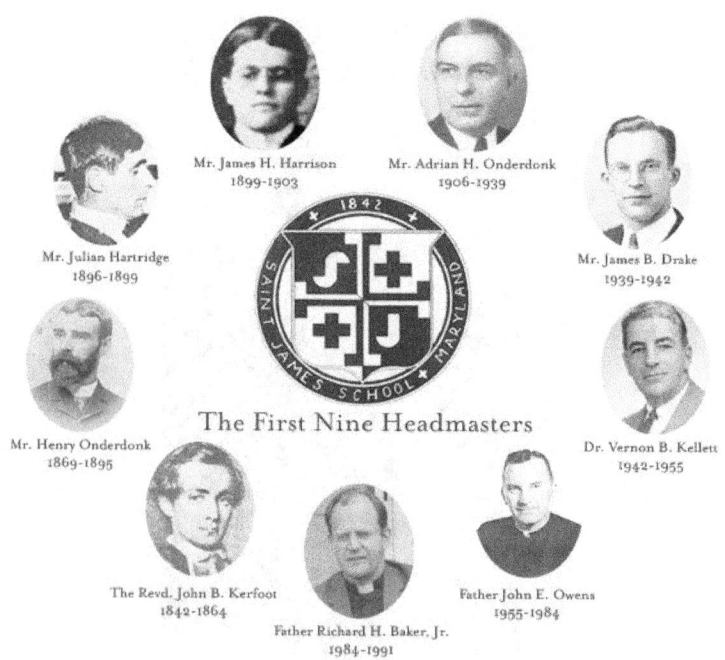

The First Nine Headmasters

Mr. Julian Hartridge
1896-1899

Mr. James H. Harrison
1899-1903

Mr. Adrian H. Onderdonk
1906-1939

Mr. James B. Drake
1939-1942

Mr. Henry Onderdonk
1869-1895

Dr. Vernon B. Kellett
1942-1955

The Revd. John B. Kerfoot
1842-1864

Father Richard H. Baker, Jr.
1984-1991

Father John E. Owens
1955-1984

Headmasters, 1842–1991

Rev. Dr. D. Stuart Dunnan, tenth headmaster

5

Adrian Onderdonk's Memoir
Saint James School, 1903–39

ANNOTATED BY W. L. PREHN

From the age of six up to and including my tenth year, I had learned not only my prayers and ethics but also the 3 R's at my mother's knee. During that period I must have tried her patience to the Nth degree. I was eleven when my father said to me, "Son, sit down; I wish to have a talk with you."[1]

> 1. Thus begins Adrian Onderdonk's memoir: "I was the second and youngest son born to Henry and Mary Latrobe Onderdonk. My father was the son of William, a New York merchant, brother of the Rt. Rev. Benj. Treadwell Onderdonk, D.D., Bishop of New York, and the Rt. Rev. Henry Ustick Onderdonk, D.D., Bishop of Pennsylvania. My father, on graduating from Columbia, entered the [The General Theological Seminary] in preparation for the priesthood. At the end of his first year at the seminary he accepted an invitation from a Mr. [Van Bokkelen] to become a teacher in his school at Catonsville, Maryland. The school was known as St. Timothy's School for Boys. Although his intention was to return to the seminary to complete his course and enter the ministry, he never did so. While at St. Timothy's, he met a Miss Henry of the Eastern Shore of Maryland and married her. He had three sons by that marriage, Henry Ustick, Robert Jenkins, and Andrew. His first wife died several years after the birth of Andrew. Later he was appointed President of the Maryland Agricultural College (now the University of Maryland). While there, he met my mother, Mary Latrobe, daughter of the Chief Engineer of the Baltimore & Ohio Railroad, and granddaughter of the Architect, Benj. H. Latrobe, best known as the architect of the National Capitol. At the

As in the case of a drowning man, there flashed through my mind all the things I had done which I ought not to have done. Was I in for a "necker." In those days a "necker" meant a severe scolding. Imagine my surprise and joy when he told me I was to enter School as a regular student in September. I would not have been so joyful at the prospect had I

outbreak of the war between the States, because of his sympathy for the Confederacy, he found it necessary to resign from the College. After his resignation he established a school on the Falls Road near Baltimore, which became very successful. For seven years he courted my mother, whose home was on Mt. Vernon Place. Shortly after his marriage to my mother, he was asked by Bishop Whittingham in 1869 to reopen as a secondary school the College of St. James near Hagerstown, Maryland. He was not enthusiastic about making a change as his school near Baltimore was very successful and he also felt that Hagerstown was too remote from patronage. But as he felt that it was due to his Bishop to at least make a visit to the School and give a report on the advisability of reopening St. James as a preparatory school, he made the trip, which involved a train to Frederick and stage coach to Hagerstown. He found the buildings and grounds in a deplorable condition. The caretaker had converted the west wing of the main building into a stable. Horses, cattle, and chickens occupied the rooms on the first floor. The campus had been plowed up for corn, wheat, and potatoes. He realized that there was little money available to restore the buildings and grounds, and so made a hasty exit in order to catch the stage back to Frederick. A short distance from the School he found the road blocked by a number of wagons, buggies, and people who had assembled to watch the dancing bears which some gypsies were showing. When he was able to get through the crowd, he realized that he would not be able to catch the stage. He, therefore, returned to the School (college). After finding a place to spend the night, he devoted the afternoon to going through the buildings, studying the possibilities. As a result, his statement to the Bishop on his return to Baltimore was quite the opposite from what he had intended had it not been for the dancing bear. Because of the bear, I was born at St. James and lived there all my life until my retirement in June, 1947." We have allowed Mr. O. to speak in his own words in what follows.

Stevenson W. Webster wrote a foreword to this memoir in May 1974, when it was printed or reprinted. The foreword reads as follows: "Adrian Holmes Onderdonk was the Headmaster of Saint James School from 1903 until 1939. He then continued until 1947 as Head of the Latin Department. Born at Saint James in 1877, and reared there during his father's Headmastership, he probably had a closer relationship to the School and knew more of it than anybody before or since. And certainly Saint James School has owed him, and still owes him, as much as it has owed anyone. He gave to it both his worldly goods and himself. A man of firm character and splendid personality, he fostered in the school a background of integrity and accomplishment and an atmosphere of loyalty and devotion. Few who came into contact with him as students or faculty were uninfluenced by the association. He was a fine man and an outstanding headmaster. In preparing his Memoirs for publication, the editors have omitted those parts which had no connection with Saint James, such as the accounts of his college life and a few brief remarks of a very personal nature which seemed to merit the privacy of his family."

Libertus Van Bokkelen was another of Muhlenberg's school sons specially trained at Flushing and College Point, New York.

foreseen the agonies I was to suffer at the hands of my teacher, Mr. Wallis. I shall have plenty to say about that gentleman later on.

As my father sat beside me with his hand on my knee, he impressed upon me that I should never be a talebearer either to my mother or to him, that I was to pay no attention to the nasty things boys might say about him, that I was not to mingle with the older boys more than I could help, and that, in my contact with the other boys, I was to forget that I was the son of the headmaster. He felt so strongly on this last bit of advice that I was never allowed to forget it. He rode me harder than any other boy so that the other boys felt sorry for me.

I had no trouble in keeping from mingling with the older boys, for whenever I approached a group, they would chase me away by saying, "Get out of here, you kid of misery." I used to wonder if they had been so directed by my father.

My greatest antipathy was my teacher, Mr. Wallis. Wallis was a student in the School. In his senior year my father arranged for him to teach us younger boys and continue his courses. At first I thought it was wonderful to have one of the older boys teach us, but I soon changed my mind. He had certain pet names for me such as numbskull, block-head, stupid, and empty wagon. He was careful to explain that an empty wagon made a lot of noise but delivered no goods. He had a very loud voice so that everyone in School knew that I was a block-head.

My father I feared, but I adored him. My feeling toward my father was the same as any Christian should have toward God. As to Mr. Wallis, I not only feared him but I hated him. There was scarcely an afternoon which I did not spend in his class-room, for he had formed the habit of keeping me in after School. As I recall it, I was kept in every afternoon. School was over at 3 P.M. for boys who were not kept in.

My father took charge of the older boys who were kept in and stayed with them. Wallis would come into his classroom with the usual greeting, "Well, block-heads, do you know your lesson?" Those who could answer his questions were dismissed. I never was. I was too scared to open my mouth. He would then say to me, "You stay here until I come back," and, like the boy on the burning deck, I stayed. I would watch him from the classroom window out for a walk headed away from the School, and yet I stayed.

I must admit that Wallis was a good teacher, but I still think that much of my stupidity was due to my terror of him. He made me hate

Latin to such an extent that it took my father two years to change my attitude toward that subject.

A number of years later in Baltimore I happened to see Wallis approach me. I crossed the street, hoping he would not see me. No such luck. He had seen me and followed me. His gushing was most cordial. When he invited me to come to his room with him, I tried to make some excuse, which he would not accept. He never would accept any of my excuses. I meekly followed him. I had a wonderful visit with him and left him, wondering why I had always felt about him as I did.

"Doc" Harry or "the little Doc," my half-brother, taught mathematics. We boys were under the impression that he knew more mathematics than anybody in the world. He could take the cube root of a number in his head—whatever that means. Someone once remarked the only small thing about Doc was his size. Boys were crazy about him, but they were scared of him. The flash of his eyes, which he inherited from our father, would make a boy or a group of boys feel like the proverbial Two Cents.

Because my father was instrumental in persuading President Arthur to send a gun boat into Ecuadorian waters to get one of his old students out of prison, where he was held as a political prisoner, we could always be sure of one or more students from Ecuador. On one occasion one of these Ecuadorian students rolled a huge snow ball which stranded on the boardwalk leading to the School room. It was about four feet in diameter. That night was the "Doc" study hall. The boys saw to it that none of the kerosene lamps in the school room were lit, for these lamps illuminated the walk as well as the room.

The windows were crowded with boys waiting to see the fun when "Doc" would hit the snow ball. Did he hit it? I wish you could have seen the fire flying from his pipe! We knew where he landed. The lamps were soon lighted, and Doc came into the room amid shouts of laughter. He made no effort to quiet the boys down for several minutes. After he had touched the bell with the suggestion that they had had their fun, the room became quiet. One boy, however, could not contain himself and his burst of laughter aroused the Doc's ire. He hit the bell so hard that he almost broke it. "You may not know, and it is time you did, but it is considered a very cowardly act to trip a person in the dark." There was no more laughter.

It was the "Old Man's" custom to read to the boys on Friday nights . . . [One Friday night,] a boy in his anger hurled a pyramid ink well at another boy who was sitting three desks in front of him. Fortunately the flat side of the ink well hit the boy's head; otherwise, there would have been a funeral. The "Old Man" fairly leaped over the desk, yanked the culprit to his feet and catapulted him through the door, with an order to go pack his trunk and get out. The boy who was hit made such an earnest appeal for the boy that the "Old Man" allowed him to stay on probation. Later on he was expelled, and no one was sorry to see him go.

The Reverend Mr. M. was appointed by the Bishop to be the Rector of Smithsburg and Clear Spring. Arrangements were made with my father to have the Reverend gentleman live at the School, and for his room and board he was to give us one Communion Service a month and teach one sacred studies class. We boys were delighted, because the Rector of St. Mark's Church, Lappans [a nearby village], who heretofore held this monthly service, preached anywhere from fifty minutes to one hour and twenty minutes, and this after the full normal service including the Litany followed by the Communion service.

This service under the Reverend Mr. E. lasted at least two hours. We used to envy his wife, who always slept through his sermons. Naturally to us boys anyone was preferable to Mr. E. The first Sunday Mr. M. was here everything went off on schedule. The following Friday he met the class in Sacred Studies. Although this Sacred Studies class was scheduled to meet every Friday, it seldom did. It was an occasion for a good time, for the Reverend Mr. M. did not honor us. We, of course, were careful to keep the fact a secret. We liked that class 'sans' teacher.

The second month came around, when Mr. M. was to celebrate Communion. Everything had been prepared for him. The Reverend Gentleman failed to put in his appearance. I don't know what excuse he made for his absence, but it seemed to have satisfied my father.

The next Sunday he was to be here, I happened to be on a tour of inspection with my father. When we were at the stables, Nathan, the coachman, said to my father, "I wonder what kind of an animal that am crawling along the inside of dat fence." The three of us ran to see what it was. It was his Reverence making his get-away. I had seen my father sore, I had seen him provoked, I had seen him angry, but that morning he was the maddest man in seven states. I thought he would pull his beard out. He couldn't tear his hair, because he was bald, as Nathan remarked afterwards. "Boy, he skeered me he was so mad. I sho' would hate to be in dat man's shoes when he come back heah."

When Mr. M. returned that night, he was met by my father. Outwardly my father was calm, but inwardly a fiery furnace. I happened to be present when they met. Father did not mince words. Without preamble he said, "Your trunk has been placed in your room. You will pack tonight and be off this place the first thing in the morning. That is all, sir. Good night!" Mr. M. went to the Bishop with some cock & bull story which, unfortunately for my father, the Bishop believed, and for a while the Bishop was unfriendly to my father. Later the Bishop discovered what manner of man the Reverend M. was, and I think he was unfrocked.

There were fine boys and bad boys in the School, but they were for the most part an honorable bunch. A liar had no place among the larger group. There was no honor system. Boys were required by the "Old Man" to be gentlemen, and with some exceptions they acted as gentlemen. Although I never got into a fight myself, fights were common. Some of them were fought in my behalf, for each of us smaller boys had his champion among the older boys. Unfortunately, my champion was usually licked. A champion saw to it that his kid was not bullied.

Athletic teams were not directed by a master. Baseball was the only major sport until the year before I graduated, when a boy from Elizabeth, New Jersey, introduced football. This boy coached us, and we had a real team, defeating an all-star team from Hagerstown by a score of 69 to 0. Ernest Rich was the outstanding player. Football was some game in those days. It was a fight to the finish. To stop the flying wedge took nerve and a total disregard for broken bones. There was no head gear. Our only head protection was our hair, which we were allowed to grow very long.

The latter part of my last year was made very sad for the boys and especially for me. My father was taken ill and was no longer able to meet his classes or take any active part in the School. Commencement came and my half-brother handed me my medal. That was a sad commencement, for we realized that the "Old Man's" days were numbered. He passed to his great reward in August.[2]

---

2. Henry died in 1895 at the age of seventy-three. "Harry" Onderdonk was a child of Henry's first marriage to Henriette Stevenson Henry (1822–61), whom he met in Maryland soon after he arrived in the state. Henry and Henriette had three children: Henry Ustick was born in 1850; Robert Jenkins in 1852; and Andrew in 1853. Robert (1852–1917) moved to Texas and became a celebrated artist. Robert's son Julian Onderdonk (1882–1922) is called "the father of Texas painting." In 2013, three of Julian Onderdonk's paintings sold for a total of $1.1 million at a Heritage Auction event. Julian was an alumnus of the Episcopal School of Texas in San Antonio (formerly West Texas Military Academy, then from 1926 to 2004, Texas Military Institute). Henry's second marriage to Mary Elizabeth Latrobe (1836–1916) gave rise to two sons, Latrobe (1872–1883) and Adrian, the headmaster.

It was during my last year at Saint James that my father asked me where I would like to go to college. Without a moment's hesitation I said, "The University of Virginia." "Why the University of Virginia?" he asked. "Because," said I, "there are no gentlemen north of the Mason-Dixon Line." Then he, without a moment's hesitation said, "Because of that remark, even if there were not other reasons, you will go to a New England college where you will learn better."

Many of the Saint James boys entered Trinity College [Hartford, Connecticut]; so it was decided that I was to go to Trinity. I was reconciled because one of my closest school friends, Julian Carter, had entered Trinity the year before, and two of the boys in my class were headed for Trinity. After my father's death I felt that I should go to a college near home in order to be a comfort to my mother in her great sorrow and loneliness. She would not have it so, for she felt that she should carry out my father's wishes. So to Trinity I went.

During my college course I gave little or no thought to my future work. When asked what I planned to do after leaving college, I answered, "I don't know, but I am not going to be a civil engineer." Many members of my mother's family were civil engineers. They all advised me against taking civil engineering up as a profession. It was not so much their advice as the fact that mathematics was a closed book to me. I managed to get through my freshman course in mathematics, which was required of all freshmen, but I did not make the mistake of selecting any math courses in my sophomore year.

My roommate was the son of the president of the New York Shipbuilding Company located at Camden, New Jersey. I had been a frequent visitor at my roommate's home. His father, a most jovial man, seemed to take a fancy to me. I asked for a position in this new concern and was told to report on a certain day.

When I blew into the president's office, I told his secretary to inform Mr. M. that I was there. "Have you an appointment?" asked the secretary. "No," said I, "but he will be mighty glad to see me." "Please take a seat," said the secretary. After two hours the secretary said, "Mr. M. will see you."

I knew that he would appease my anger at being kept waiting by his usually affectionate greeting to which I had grown accustomed. In this I was greatly mistaken. His greeting was short and to the point. "Well, Onderdonk, what do you want?" I felt like telling him I wanted him to go to a warmer climate. Here was I—a BA—come to add prestige and success to his old shipbuilding company, feeling sure that the entire works were held up awaiting my arrival, and he wanted to know what I wanted. I was trembling with rage, or was it stage fright, as I told him the object of my visit. "Report to Mr. Phillips at the yard at seven o'clock tomorrow morning. Good afternoon."

I was so darned mad that I left Mr. M's office determined to ruin his old company by refusing to work for it. Needless to add, I reported to Mr. Phillips promptly at 7:00 A.M. Mr. Phillips was seemingly a grouch, but he wasn't. He asked me if I knew a transit when I saw one. "Yes," said I. "Well, look around this God-forsaken lot and when you see a man with his eye glued to a telescope, tell him you are a member of his corps." I sat down in the nearest chair and laughed. Mr. Phillips turned on me and said, "What the H——are you laughing at?" The very thing I was not going to do was the very thing I did do. I never advanced beyond a stake driver, although I carried the title of rodman.

That yard was a Godforsaken place. There was a story told about that sandy strip of land. A goat could find nothing to eat and what was worse, nothing to butt except a bee hive. The bees objected and chased the goat out of the yard having registered numerous stings. As the goat jumped over the fence, he was heard to say, "Damn it." One day I was sent out in a row boat to bury level stakes.

That job in Camden ended my career as an engineer. The old football injury opened up, so I was transferred to the office. I had been living in a very cheap boarding house in Woodbury, New Jersey in order to be nearer the shipyards. The offices at the time of my transfer happened to be in Philadelphia, so I moved to Philadelphia where I shared a room with an old college friend in a most delightful home. I hated office work and I disliked the Chief Clerk. What I greatly enjoyed that year was the social life of Philadelphia. Thanks to my cousins and friends of my cousins, I attended most social functions except the famous Philadelphia Assembly.

In May of the year 1900 I decided that I could not stand office work and the chief clerk any longer, so I gave notice and left the last of May. I had decided that I wanted to be a teacher and returned to Baltimore to look for a position in one of the Baltimore schools.

The first headmaster I called upon was Mr. Dunham of the Boys Latin School. His secretary called him to the door of the study hall, which he happened to be holding at the time. I introduced myself and told him the object of my visit. While I was talking to him, he had his back to me, watching the large group of boys in the room. When I finished speaking, he turned to me, gave me the once-over and said, "Do you think you could control that crowd?" "I am quite sure I could," said I. "I don't agree with you," said he; so out I went.

Several other calls on schools netted the same result. A saddened man, I dropped in at the Hopkins chapter of Alpha Delta Phi. While I was there, one of the members happened to mention that L. Baxter was leaving the Country School and that I might possibly secure his place as teacher of French and Greek. I had never heard of the Country School. The School's full name and address was The Country Day School for Boys of Baltimore City Charles Street Avenue Extended. It took a long envelope to handle that address.

This school, later to be known as the Gilman School, was the first country day school. It occupied the Carroll Mansion, now a part of Johns Hopkins University. Mr. Frederick Winsor was the first Headmaster.[3] He left the spring I was engaged as a member of the faculty, in order to found the Middlesex School at Concord, Massachusetts. The only Headmaster I had ever known was my father, who had a long beard. I thought that a gray beard was the badge of a Headmaster. I was quite overcome to find that the new Headmaster of the Country School was a young man and had no beard.

The only fall sport the boys indulged in was soccer. The boys were quite young, and the boys of the other Baltimore schools were quite sarcastic about the "Baby School on Charles Street." I asked permission to coach a football team. We played one game that year and won it. The next year I was influential in getting my closest friend, Ernest Rich, to come to the School as Athletic Director. From that year the Country School was no longer spoken of by the boys of the other schools as the Baby School on Charles Street.

For the next two years I was the head of the Latin Department, which was made possible by the resignation of Mr. Chase, a great teacher.

---

3. Frederick Winsor (1872–1940) was an alumnus of Roxbury Latin School and founded the Middlesex School in Concord, Massachusetts (1901). The Country School for Boys was founded in Baltimore in 1897. In 1910 its name was changed to the Gilman Country School for Boys to honor one of its founders, Daniel Coit Gilman, the first president of Johns Hopkins University. In 1951 the Gilman Country School became simply the Gilman School. Winsor was one of the great headmasters of the twentieth century. Onderdonk would have come into contact with Winsor at least once a year at gatherings of the Headmasters Association, founded in 1893. That the headmaster of small and struggling Saint James was invited to be a member of the Headmasters Association suggests both that Saint James held a place of honor among American preparatory schools and that Adrian Onderdonk was esteemed by his peers.

I did better in Latin than I had done in French, and I no longer gave written tests when a committee of Trustees came to my class. Soon they discontinued their visits, for I always asked their opinion on certain questions which I knew they could not answer.

It is not my intention in these Recollections to speak of my many mistakes and failures at the Country School, and so I shall pass over any reference to my experience as a teacher of French, except to say that I had for a time made a point of giving the class a written test whenever a committee of the Trustees came out to visit classes. Those were three happy years at the Country School. It was a hard decision I had to make when the opportunity was given me of returning to my old home at Saint James.

It was in the winter of 1903 that I awoke one morning to find a letter from the Headmaster of Saint James School informing me that he intended to leave Saint James at the end of that school year and suggesting that I consider taking it over. Although I was only twenty-four years old, I felt that I was fully qualified to become the head of any school. Such is the conceit of youth. But I did not want to leave Baltimore and the Country School. I was completely happy in my work and was thoroughly enjoying the social life of Baltimore. The summer before, I had been invited to go abroad with a family whose boys were at the Country School. This family later became most helpful financially and otherwise in my first years at Saint James.

Plans had been made for another European tour the coming summer, when my own mother would be in the party. My mother had been looking forward to this trip and to give it up would prove a most grievous disappointment to her. Balancing her disappointment about the European trip with the happiness she would feel at the thought of returning to her old home, and, recalling my promise that some day I would bring her back to Saint James, I gave her the letter from the retiring headmaster, Mr. Harrison, to read. She expressed no joy at the thought of returning. She, too, was happy in her life and church work in Baltimore. She never even mentioned her disappointment at not going abroad that summer. She wanted to do what was best for me, but she urged me not to act hastily.

On my way up to have an interview with Mr. Harrison, I visualized the Saint James as I had known it, one of the most beautiful places I had ever seen. It was a cold bleak night when I arrived. The drive from Hagerstown, which is now made in ten minutes, took one hour and ten minutes and I was stiff with cold. I was greeted by the Headmaster in the main hall.

What a different hall from the one I had known! Instead of the pure white of the columns and wood work, I saw a pinkish color. The paper was falling in festoons from the wall. At the end of the hall there were school desks and in front of these desks a partly drawn green curtain.

The only thing which seemed familiar was the temperature. It was still cold in the hall. I was ushered into the Headmaster's room, where there was a fire burning in the fireplace. It took me at least one-half hour to thaw out. In spite of Mr. Harrison's effort to inspire me with a desire to take over the School, I left him with a feeling that the last thing I would consider was to do so.

That night I slept in my mother's and father's old bedroom, which was occupied by Mr. Harrison's Senior Master, an old Saint James boy, Henry W. Keating. Before retiring we had a long talk, and it was agreed that, if I should decide to come back, we could form a partnership. It was a long time before sleep overcame me.

I was not encouraged by what I saw the next day as I made a tour of inspection. I had another long talk with Mr. Keating and left in the afternoon after telling Mr. Harrison and Mr. Keating that I would give them my answer within a week or ten days. The next day I called upon Mr. Bernard Carter, President of the Board of Trustees. I had a talk with Bishop Paret, who had been most antagonistic to the School and had resigned from the Board when Mr. Harrison had been appointed Headmaster because Mr. Harrison was a Presbyterian.

I called on other gentlemen whose opinion I valued. All of them advised me not to give up a position which was certain and where I was so content to undertake a work which was most uncertain and where a failure might end my career as a schoolmaster. In spite of the unanimous advice against making the change, my love for my old home, my youth, and a spirit of adventure fairly whipped me into making my decision.

I handed in my resignation to the Trustees of the Gilman Country School and accepted the call to go to Saint James. From February to June, I was a teacher in the morning, a soliciting agent in the afternoon, and a correspondent late into the night. By June I had signed up twenty-three boys plus the three who expected to return.

One day early in my headship, an old gentleman appeared at the School. He said he had come to enter his son. We entertained that "Bird" for three days. I was bound to get him to enter not only his own son, but also the son of his friend, who was to attend the same school elsewhere, as the two boys were inseparable. I shall never forget my joy when the father told me to expect both boys in September. It looked as if the School would open with a capacity enrollment. He was a bit short of cash, so I consented to cash his check for $25.00. It was foolish, as I afterwards learned, but I was not going to lose those two boys. The check came back. Two months later I saw his picture in the *Baltimore Sun* paper. He had been arrested for doing the same thing at other schools. The only consolation I found in my unfortunate transaction was that I was not the only sucker.

Several days before the opening of School, the two masters whom we had engaged arrived at the School. One, John G. Campbell, I knew. He was a brother Alpha Delta Phi of the Johns Hopkins Chapter. The other, William G. McDowell, had graduated the year before from Washington & Lee University. As I write this in August 1941, Mr. Campbell has completed his 37th year at Saint James. Mr. McDowell entered the ministry and later was elected Bishop of Alabama. He was one of the men considered for Presiding Bishop.[4] He died shortly after the Convention which had elected Bishop Tucker.[5]

It is not my intention to bore my readers with a detailed account of the blood-sweating years from 1903 to 1912. I should like to say at this point that those years made me love the School as nothing else could. As I said above, the School opened with 31 boys, and with but few exceptions they were a fine group and most cooperative under trying circumstances. The making out of a recitation schedule was in the beginning our most serious problem. Every night Mr. Campbell and I would work on it from 9 P.M. to 4 A.M., only to tear it up because we could not eliminate the numerous conflicts in classes.

In my many, many discouragements, my partner, Mr. Henry B. Keating, was a tower of strength. Because of his wisdom and experience, we surmounted many difficulties of administration. Mr. Keating was small

---

4. A gifted and popular priest who had a way with young people, William George McDowell (1882–1938) served as the fifth bishop of Alabama from 1928 to 1938, when he died of pneumonia at the age of fifty-five. From a family of staunch Presbyterians living in the Valley of Virginia, McDowell was a native of Lexington. A brilliant student, he graduated from Washington and Lee in 1902 (age nineteen) with both bachelor's and master's degrees in languages. In the autumn of the same year, McDowell began teaching at Saint James School. McDowell taught at Saint James from 1902 to 1906. At Fountain Rock he converted to the Episcopal Church and began to feel the vocation to the priesthood, to which he was ordained in 1909 after a distinguished record at the Virginia Seminary in Alexandria.

5. In 1937 Henry St. George Tucker (1874–1959) was elected presiding bishop of the Protestant Episcopal Church in the United States of America, beginning his tenure in January 1938. See Hein, "Henry St. George Tucker," 21:895–96.

of stature, but in other respects he was a giant. The boys both loved and feared him. I have known boys to be deliberately dismissed from class in order to return to the school room to hear Mr. Keating "riding" a boy. His caustic wit was stinging. Strange to say, the boys he "rode" the hardest were his greatest friends.

Jerningham Diggs, known as "Jern," had been in my father's service as headwaiter for twenty-seven years. After my father's death he was the butler for a wealthy family in Hagerstown. When he learned that I had returned, he asked if he might serve me as he had served my father. I was very happy to have Jern back, but unfortunately he was with me for less than a month. He died in the buckboard which he was driving to Hagerstown. Several of us from the school attended his funeral. We were ushered into the front seat. We were the only white people present.

I felt Jern's death very deeply, for not only had the school lost a valuable servant, but I had lost a life-long friend. He was a wonderful man. As boys we used to say to him, "Did you know that Negroes were not allowed in heaven?" To which he replied, "The Good Book says 'De sheep shall be on the right hand of God and the goats on the left'; and we ails got the wool." On the south wall of the main building there was a large sun dial. Jern would use the sun dial to set the dining room clock.

The servant problem was pretty serious. My father had a wonderful gardener who had been with him for many years. When I learned that John Futterer was in the neighborhood, I got in touch with him, and he seemed only too willing to return. Unfortunately I had to fire him after a short interval. He just couldn't keep sober. The problem was a real problem in spite of the high wages we paid, *viz.* $20.00 a month for a cook; $12.00 for head waiter; $8.00 for second waiter and janitor $15.00; $12.00 for stableman; and the chambermaid got $8.00. The tuition was higher than other schools in this section of the country, $400.00 a year including laundry.[6]

6. In the 1920 edition of his *Handbook of the Best Private Schools in the United States and Canada*, 197, Porter E. Sargent wrote that the price of tuition at Saint James had risen to $750, which was competitive to expensive for 1920. Compare this to the following schools in the region and beyond in the same year: Mercersburg was $800, the Hill School $1400, Woodberry Forest $750, Episcopal High School $650, and St. Albans $900. (St. Andrew's, Middletown, Delaware, was not yet in existence; it was founded in 1929.) In the same year 1920, St. Paul's, St. Mark's, and Groton charged $1200, $1100, and $1250, respectively. Perhaps the school most like Saint James was the Kent School in Connecticut (founded by Father Sill in 1906). Kent was only $550 in 1920. Salisbury charged $1000 and Taft, Lawrenceville, Middlesex, and Pomfret were $1300, $1250, $1200, and $1150. One US dollar in 1920 would be worth almost eleven today; hence the price of Saint James was about $8,250 in today's dollars, but we

The janitor was our greatest difficulty. The furnace, which I was told was in good condition, proved quite the reverse. Until Isaac Barnum arrived on the scene, I was the furnace man. That was one job I hated. Up at 6 A.M. to fire the furnace, shoveling coal between classes and banking the furnace at 11 P.M. During this period one of the boys wrote to his parents, "The trouble with this School is too much religion and too little heat."

One man I engaged was proving to be quite satisfactory. After he had been here several weeks, a deputy sheriff appeared and told me he wanted to interview this man. We went everywhere looking for him. At last we went into the chapel. No luck. We were about to leave the chapel when the sheriff noticed that the altar was standing out from the reredos. He looked behind the altar and found the janitor curled up inside it. Again, I was the furnace man.

My job of fireman was over after the Christmas holidays when we were fortunate enough to secure Isaac Barnum, step-son of Jern. Isaac was a real genius. He should have been a mechanical engineer. I recall one night being awakened by the steam hissing in my radiator—an unheard of occurrence. I was worried for fear that the furnace would burn itself out, and as a result, there would be no heat in the morning. I jumped out of bed, dressed, and hurried to the furnace room. Imagine my surprise to find Isaac there watching the fast revolving wheel of a steam engine.

"Where in the world did you get that engine, Isaac?" I asked. Isaac's grin reached from ear to ear. "I made it, Sir," he said. "Where did you get the parts?" I next asked. "Found them around the place. I hope you don't mind my trying it out. I figure it is making 2000 revolutions a minute." I could well imagine it was, for the wheel was a blur. All I could think to say was, "Well, I'll be damned."

Some years later an engineer came down from the Mills Boiler Co. of Philadelphia to see about the installation of the new boiler we had purchased. When I told the engineer that I thought our Isaac was qualified to set it up, the engineer said that the company would not permit anyone

---

must compare this to the buying power of the dollar: In 1920, one could buy a decent four-bedroom house for $2,500. Sargent wrote in his *Handbook* that "Mr. Onderdonk is a man's man, a strong and lovable personality, and a great teacher. A hero to his boys, he instills them with the spirit of courtesy and of service. He intimates rather than requires what a boy is to do. Were he stronger in business administration he would undoubtedly occupy a larger position in the educational world." (In an editor's box in the front of his guides, Sargent did promise "intimate information and unprejudiced advice in regard to any school"! But it is obvious he liked Saint James and the Headmaster.)

but an expert mechanic to do the work. I called Isaac and told him to help the engineer to get the information he needed. At the end of two hours the engineer came to my office and said, "That man, Isaac, is remarkable. He very politely pointed out several mistakes I had made. He certainly is qualified to install the furnace, and when he completes the job here, send him up to us, for we sure can use him."

There is one other servant of whom I wish to speak, and then I'll pass to other subjects. Letitia Diggs, Jern's widow and Isaac's mother, was my mother's housekeeper. We all loved Letitia and Letitia loved us. I shall never forget the day in 1914 when she came to my mother and told her that she would have to leave to take care of her own old mother, who needed her. My mother just couldn't believe that she could get along without Letitia. As her mother was over 80 years, we had the consolation that her mother would soon die and Letitia would then return to us. The old woman outlived my mother 15 years, dying at the age of 98. Then Letitia was too old to carry the work of the School. When Letitia died, I felt that I had lost a dear and faithful friend.

The only illumination we had my first year at Saint James came from kerosene lamps. It was a one-man job to keep the lamps in good condition and filled. Thanks to the great generosity of one of our patrons an acetylene gas system was installed. This was indeed a great improvement over lamps, but every once in a while something would happen and the gas machine would fail to deliver the carbide to the water and suddenly every light would go out.

This happened one night in chapel during the evening service. My great friend, the Reverend Ernest Rich, was holding the service. He was reading that portion of the Old Testament which had to do with the death of Samuel. He arrived at that verse where it said, "The light in his eyes went out," when *flick* and we were in total darkness. Mr. Rich immediately started up the creed and followed it with the Lord's Prayer and a few collects which he knew by heart. When he started the prayer, "Lighten our darkness," Mr. Keating appeared through the chancel door with a lamp and stood behind Mr. Rich while he finished the regular prayers for Evensong. As far as the boys were concerned, one would have never known that anything had happened.

Mr. William McDowell was a very brilliant young man, an excellent teacher, and an outstanding musician. Although at first his discipline was poor, he later developed into a splendid disciplinarian. His spiritual influence was felt by all of us. He also had a great sense of humor.

During these first years we developed excellent teams. At that time schools played masters on teams. We at Saint James decided that it was a great mistake to do so, as such teams did not represent a student body. Most games were won by masters on whom the boys relied too much. For example, when Mr. John Campbell was the catcher and Mr. Tom Campbell the pitcher, if a player on the opposing team by any lucky chance arrived at first base, he was thrown out at second.

When Saint James had the Campbell battery, all our team needed was the infield. The outfield just didn't operate. Even the infield had very little to do. We therefore took the stand that we would play no teams on which there were masters. One school after another came to see our point of view and eliminated masters as players.

My greatest worry in these early years was not the fact that, in addition to my duties of administrator, fireman, plumber, etc., I carried a full teaching schedule of from 25 to 30 periods a week. Every cent of profit had to go toward the improvement of the property. Additional dormitory space to meet the demands of increasing numbers, new boilers to be installed, and a thousand and one other improvements were required. I was constantly reminded that I was investing a good deal of money in property in which I had no equity.

My one hope was to make Saint James a school of which my father, who had given his all to make it successful, would be proud. I also wanted to have Saint James recognized as a school of sound scholarship and spiritual training. To teach boys perseverance, punctuality, politeness, and truthfulness was our aim. The very first thing I did was to establish the honor system. At first it may not have been a success, but as years went by it was working almost 100%. Many, many boys in after years have told me that it did work, even if not perfectly. The student council saw to it that it did.[7]

God must have had me by the hand when he sent us Charles Hartwell to fill Mr. McDowell's place. For sound scholarship and wonderful tact I have never known his equal. He was beloved by everyone. The boys almost worshipped him. Hartwell was the son of a famous Baptist missionary

---

7. Until relatively recently in boarding schools on both sides of the Atlantic, older students were relied upon to ensure the discipline of the younger. Most boarding schools had small staffs. Depending on the prefects to assist in keeping order was a necessity and had a positive effect on the development of leadership skills in the students. One of the innovations of Dr. Arnold of Rugby School (Headmaster 1828–42) was that he relied on his Sixth Form leaders even more than customary. This practice was taken up by many reforming headmasters in the British Isles and the United States.

in China. He spoke Chinese (Mandarin) as fluently as he did English. I cannot overemphasize what he meant to the School and especially what he meant to me. Because of our great friendship, he would spend most of the summer at Saint James.[8]

While he was here, I was always saddened by the thought that his plans were to go back to China. The school mentally went into mourning when he did leave. In China, he was made the head of a Chinese mission school. When he took charge, the enrollment numbered 80 boys. In the first month, he fired thirty boys and was on the point of being fired by the Missionary Board. When he returned to Fountain Rock for his first Sabbatical after several years, I asked him about the enrollment. "Slightly over 1400," he said.

When Mr. Hartwell was on his way back to the States on his third Sabbatical and was waiting at Chefoo for his boat, word came to him that there was a serious epidemic at Hwang Hien, where his school was located. The school was a three days' trip by litter. Far from well himself, and the doctor at Chefoo telling him he must not return, he went back to Hwang Hien. He fought the epidemic as long as he had the strength to do so. It was too much for him in his weakened condition, and God called him to some greater work across the Great Divide. Truly can it be said of him, a Christian gentleman and martyr. How I loved that man.

[Saint James] School continued to increase in numbers, and I am happy to say that the School became well known for both clean sportsmanship and sound scholarship.

About this time, my college friend Mr. A. M. Langford came to visit me. Later I persuaded him to become one of our masters. The first year he was here was the year that Halley's Comet was to appear [April 1910]. Langford was in charge of the upper school dormitory. Halley's Comet was to appear at its best at 4 A.M. in the eastern sky. I was awakened that morning by hearing someone call me by name. As no one replied to my answer, I jumped out of bed, calling down the stairs and running up into the main building in an effort to find out why I was wanted.

---

8 The older Charles Hartwell (1825–1905) worked for fifty years in China and was a native of Massachusetts. He was prepared at Westford Academy and earned both the bachelor's and master's degrees from Amherst (1849 and 1852). He was ordained in the Congregational Church in 1852. The American Board of Commissioners for Foreign Missions (ABCFM) was very active in China. Hartwell took over the ailing Foochow College and it thrived under his leadership. He was a respected Sinologist and a master of the Foochow dialect. See "Charles Hartwell" in biographical resources.

Returning to my room, having had no success, I looked at my watch. It was two minutes of four. I therefore decided that it must have been Halley. I went out on the front porch and beheld that magnificent sight. As Mr. Langford could see the comet merely by looking out the window from his bed, I ran over to his room, and shouted, "Langford! Halley's Comet!" The only response I got from him was this statement made in loud voice, "To Hell with Halley's Comet." The next morning several boys said to him, "You weren't interested in the comet, were you, Sir?"

One of the serious problems was stealing by some boy. This usually involved a small amount and not always money. There was one occasion when the amount involved was serious. Over a period of months the thief had stolen about $80. Marked money was used in order to trap the thief, but he was too smart. One boy was strongly suspected, but there was no proof.

Toward the end of the year a boy who had received quite a large amount from his parents to visit Cornell University for his final examination reported that ten dollars had been taken from his pocketbook, which he had carelessly left in his room when going out for baseball. Fortunately he had taken the numbers of all the bills so that he was able to give me the number of the bill which had been taken. As we had tried so many methods of locating the thief with no success, I decided to make a direct appeal to the boy who was guilty in a school assembly, assuring the guilty one that no effort would be made to trap him.

After my appeal, I stood at the door and as the boys filed out, I told each boy where he was to go, having selected four locations. I felt that this would make it impossible for the boys to check up on the boy who was absent and thus make it possible for the guilty boy to replace the money without being discovered. When the bell was rung, all boys were to return to the assembly room. After an interval of twenty minutes, the bell was rung, and all boys returned. I then asked the boy from whom the money had been stolen to go to his room and see if my appeal had had any effect.

In a few minutes he returned. I had not caught the thief, but I felt very happy that my appeal had been effective. Later, as I sat in my office, the boy whom others suspected burst into my room and without preamble said, "Sir, I may be a ratter but I am not a thief." "Who said you were?" I asked. "The boys say I am, and I demand that I be cleared of the charge they have brought against me." I confess that I thought he was the guilty one. Although it was late, I called all boys, pajama clad, back to the assembly room. I explained that I must rescind my statement that no effort would be made to find out who stole the money as a certain boy who had been charged with the theft demanded to be cleared.

The next day the $10 bill was located at the country store near the school. The description of the boy who had passed it was hard to believe as he was the last boy anyone would suspect. The boy later confessed that he had not only taken the $10 in question but was also guilty of all the thefts over a period of months amounting to $80. Later I had to witness the sad scene of a broken-hearted father who came into my private den after a talk with his son, who had made a full confession.

The father, after he had recovered from weeping, took out his check book, and as he started to write out a check for the amount involved, I stopped him and suggested that the boy himself pay back the money in order that he might learn the hard way the value of money. The father finally consented. I secured a job for the boy, not an easy job, which would pay him $5 a week. The School made good the losses, and the boy made good to the School. It took him four months to do so, but it taught him a much needed lesson.

Fifteen years later the boy now become a man dropped in to see me. Before he left, he told me in a very embarrassed way that for the past ten years he had been in charge of a department in a very large department store which involved the handling of large sums of money, and then he grasped my hand and said, "Sir, I want you to know that my accounts always balance." Does anyone wonder why I think school mastering is a profession where discouragements are forgotten because of the encouragements?

While Mr. Langford was a master at Saint James, he was continually giving penalties to one of the boys who was something of a mischief maker. The boy was a fascinating kid and used to say to Mr. Langford, "I'll get even with you some day." After graduation the boy received a commission in the army. When we entered the First World War, this officer was stationed at Fort Myer, Arlington, Virginia, where there was an officers' training school. Mr. Langford was sent there for officers' training.

To his amazement and fear, he found that 1st Lieutenant White was in command of his platoon. What a chance for the Lieutenant "to get even." It turned out quite the opposite. Lt. White did everything he could to be of assistance to "Zig," Langford's nickname. (Few people ever heard Langford's given name for he tried to conceal the fact that it was Archibald. He was Zig Langford to all his host of friends.)

No husband ever had a more wonderful partner and co-worker than my wife. Her greatest pleasure has always been in doing for others. In all the years of our married life, I have never known her to nag. The boys found in her a counselor and friend. As our life together has been so very close, from now on this ceases to be an autobiography but the biography of a man and his better half.[9]

I prefer to pass over the next two years for they were made up of School worries and sadness due to the death of my mother-in-law in the early winter and of my own mother in June. It was a problem to secure good masters, because we were then in the war. I shall never forget our joy when news came that the war was over. But that joy was short-lived because of the flu epidemic. Fortunately, I read in the paper that schools were required to close. I knew that this referred to public schools only, but I took advantage of the ignorance of someone in the health department and was glad to have him say that we were included in that order.

Before I might hear differently, I had all the boys who were not yet affected on the train for their homes. The order later came "not to close," but it was too late. As it was, we had thirty cases. A number of boys volunteered to remain and help. No nurses were available. Most of the cases were light but required constant attention. Two of the cases were very serious, and for these cases I was able to secure Mrs. "Zig" Langford, who was a R.N., to take over. All cases came through in good shape.

One of the boys who had been so seriously ill could not travel to his home alone, so I arranged to drive him there in my car. My senior master, Mr. Harry Keating, and my sister-in-law, who lived across the campus, decided that they would like to go with me. All went well until our return home. A car, driving without lights, following a car with very brilliant lights, decided to pass and in doing so hit my car. Mr. Keating, who saw what was going to happen, stepped out of our car, lost his balance, fell on hard macadam, and fractured his skull. His death the next day was a terrible blow to me and to the School.

After the war the School was most fortunate in securing excellent masters. One of our old boys, Steve Webster, came back, and the previous

---

9. Adrian Onderdonk married Evelynne Richardson (1887–1947) in 1912. Stricken suddenly, she died at the age of 59. Evelynne was the daughter of the Reverend Dr. William C. Richardson (1854–1914), rector of St. James Episcopal Church, Philadelphia, from 1901 to 1914, when he died at the age of 60. (This St. James was located on 22nd and Walnut Streets and thus should not be confused with the Church of St. James the Less.)

year a Mr. Ernest Black, who proved to be a source of constant amusement, had become a master. Both he and Mr. Webster were Trinity men. The School was also most fortunate in securing three other great teachers and a very outstanding athletic coach. Mr. and Mrs. Russell Nelson were very serious-minded teachers. Mr. Robert Dinsmore was all that a School could desire as a dormitory master and teacher.[10]

Mr. Stark's one great ambition was to develop outstanding teams, and he did. His talks at halftime of football games were classics. He was equally good as a basketball and track coach. His football team won most of their games even against schools of several hundred students. We won all our track meets, and the basketball team was equally successful. Blinded by the success of his teams, I did not see that his methods of coaching lacked the real sportsmanship for which the School had always been famous. When my eyes were opened, I suggested a change.

The Fire—March 3, 1926. Things were flourishing at Saint James. The School was full to overflowing. The only worry I had outside of the usual school problems, to which I had long become accustomed, was the fact that the home which I had purchased to protect the School from undesirable neighbors was without a tenant. It was a lovely home, and I had known that a certain person had had his eye on it for some time. The School could not tolerate such a person almost on the School grounds.

Over a period of years, the tank room situated on the third floor and directly over the beautiful "Dolly Madison" room was given to leaking. When it leaked, it poured. I can recall in my boyhood days when I occupied this room with my mother and father hearing my mother say to my father, "Henry, wake up! The tank is leaking." Out of bed we would all jump. Basins, foot tubs, and any kind of receptacle were placed under the downpour. It seemed to be a tradition of the School that the tank should leak at stated intervals in spite of much money and effort spent to rectify the situation.

The finances of the School at last permitted the installation of a pressure system. On the afternoon of March 2nd the man who installed this system came to me and said, "Well, sir, the work is completed, and I shall be out tomorrow to drain your tanks and 'cut in' the new system." The next day was cold and dreary. No one appeared to "cut in" the new

---

10 Henry Webster Keating earned a BA degree from Johns Hopkins in 1891. Robert Mitchell Dinsmore graduated from Harvard College in 1916. John G. Campbell (1879–1946) served the school for almost forty-three years and was a beloved, respected master.

system. I phoned to ask the reason. "We'll be out in the morning. I guess you can stand the old system another day." I was disappointed, but after all, it was only for another day, and the weather was pretty bad for me to work outdoors, with possible leaks in the pipes to repair. Besides, the tank hadn't leaked for a long time.

At about eight o'clock that night it began to leak with a vengeance. On investigation it was discovered that a pipe had frozen. In order to stop the leak this pipe had to be thawed out. It was thawed out, and the leak stopped. It was about 12:30 A.M. when I heard the sound of glass breaking. I went to the window to investigate. When I saw flames pouring out of the tank room, I rushed to the main part of the building and was told that every boy was out of the dormitory, which was next to the tank room. Not satisfied, I, with the master-in-charge of that dormitory, rushed up the stairs and examined every bed. All beds were empty. Thanks to fire drills, they had beaten their former record by emptying the dormitory in less than a minute.

I shall not go into details about that dreadful night except to mention a feat of remarkable strength and the fact that the fire engine from Hagerstown was unable to reduce the basin of the spring, although it was pumping 800 gallons a minute. Feats of strength were many, but one especially I recall.

A neighbor picked up a mahogany and glass case five feet tall and three feet wide, filled with glass ware, and carried it out, without much damage to the glass ware. Most of our furniture in the West Wing, or Rectory, was saved as well as the dining room furniture and things which could be removed from the chapel in the East Wing.

At 4:30 A.M., all boys had been transported to the Hotel or private homes of friends in Hagerstown with such scanty clothes as they were able to grab when they left their rooms. When Mrs. o. and I stood and looked at the ruins of our efforts, we had but one thought—ON THESE RUINS WE SHALL BUILD AGAIN.

The next day, arrangements were made with a building contractor to put up temporary buildings and to convert the gymnasium into a dormitory to take care of those boys who had had quarters in the main building. During the day, many friends from Hagerstown arrived and with the aid of farmers, placed all our furniture in the empty house for which, only the night before, I had regretted not having secured a tenant.

That night, worn out with fatigue and half asleep, I stumbled into our new home. I paid slight attention to the fact that the house was furnished. I went immediately to the telephone and called Central to ask her not to put any calls through as I had to get some sleep. I made one exception, any ultra-important message, to call me.

I was in that first deep sleep when I heard the phone ringing and ringing. Out of bed I jumped, thinking that the call must be a serious one, to have Central call me. By the time I had arrived at the telephone, the house was still in darkness, for I did not know where to find the lights. I had located with my shins most of the furniture in the house. Anxious in mind and sore in the shins, I lifted the receiver.

"Yes," said I, "What is it?" Mr. Dinsmore was on the phone. "Is that you, Mr. O? I thought I'd call you up to say that everything over here seems to be all right and to ask if there is anything I can do for you." "Thank you, R.D.," said I. "There is something you can do for me." "Splendid!" said R.D., "What is it?" "R.D.", says I, "You can go to Hell." I managed to get back to bed without further injury.[11]

Three days later as I stood above the ruins of the building, in which I had been born and in which my father had spent all profits from the School and for the beautifying of which his son had done likewise, a letter was handed to me from Mr. Charles W. Strout, the Headmaster of St. Luke's School, Wayne, Pennsylvania. In this letter he asked me to take over St. Luke's School as he wished to retire from active service.[12]

St. Luke's was a beautifully equipped School and at that time most successful. The temptation was tremendous, for St. Luke's contained everything I had always wanted for Saint James. It seemed foolish to pass up such an opportunity, especially as I had no means of knowing whether I could raise a sufficient sum to rebuild. The School had been my personal venture.

Before I left the place on which I was standing above the ruins, I had decided that Saint James must not die. It had weathered too many storms in the past, and it was going to weather this one. I was not going to

---

11. Nathaniel Burt (1913–2003) was a Saint James alumnus (Princeton, AB, 1936) who published a novel in 1953 about a boys' boarding school where a fire destroys the main building. *Scotland's Burning* was based on the 1926 fire at Saint James.

12. St. Luke's School was founded in 1863 by Mrs. Jane Crawford at her house in Fox Chase, northeast of Philadelphia. It was called Ury House School until 1902, when Strout relocated it to Wayne on the Main Line and named it after the Episcopal parish in which it was situated. Strout was unable to hand St. Luke's over to another proprietor and it closed in 1927. That its campus and some buildings were beautiful and commodious can be known by the facts that the directors of the St. David's Golf Club purchased them, Valley Forge Military Academy later acquired them, and several of the old buildings still adorn the VFMA campus.

allow a devastating fire to destroy entirely my blood-sweating of twenty-five years. I wrote Mr. Strout a letter expressing my appreciation of his wonderful and tempting offer and my regret that I could not accept. I got this letter off on the next mail, fearing that if I delayed I might change my mind.

The School had two outstanding friends whose influence would help in rebuilding. One was Bishop John Gardner Murray, the Bishop of Maryland, who a few months before had been elected Presiding Bishop of the Episcopal Church. The other was Mr. Charles O. Scull, Vice-President of the United States Fidelity and Guaranty Co. of Baltimore, and a great power in the Diocese.

Bishop Murray was at the time confined to his bed. I was granted a short interview and he inspired me with this statement, "Go to it, Adrian. I'm back of you. Full steam ahead and don't let fogs or storms cause you to reduce speed or turn back." Mr. Scull also gave me his full support as well as a very generous pledge for the rebuilding fund.

The greatest inspiration I had came from the faculty. I was quick to call them together to tell them that the future of the School was uncertain and that they were free to make other arrangements for the coming School year. Every member of my staff in no uncertain terms assured me that he was standing by and along with me and would stick with the ship.

The work on the temporary buildings was progressing rapidly, and we had every reason to hope that we could recall the boys at the end of the normal Spring Recess, which we did. Disaster certainly brings out the best in people. We found this to be the case with the boys. On their return to School—not one boy failed to come back—there was no task too menial which they would not cheerfully perform.

There was one job which had to be taken care of every other day. It was a nasty job. It was the emptying of the temporary chemical toilets. It took about twenty minutes. First I approached an employee who had been a faithful servant for many years. I offered him $2.00 for this twenty minute job. He needed the money but told me most regretfully that he would quit before he would do it. I then made the same proposition to an "extra" who also needed money. He refused to speak to me for over a month. I then tried to persuade two men who were at work on the foundation at $2.00 a day. Nothing doing. I was desperate.

A group of older boys approached me to say that the boys themselves would take care of that job. I insisted, however, in paying the $2.00, this to be divided equally among the four boys on each detail. Finally they agreed to accept it just to satisfy me. Each day a record was kept of the amount due each boy who had served on that detail known as the "Wagon Brigade." The boys preferred to have their pay accumulated until the end of the School year. The day before commencement I was presented with a letter from the "Wagon Brigade" in which the following statement was made:

> We, the Wagon Brigade, request that the sum due us be applied to the building fund. It is not our wish or intention to accept personally one cent for doing what we did for our School.

We ended the year without the loss of a single recitation period. The loyal attitude of the faculty and boys during these trying days made me feel more keenly than ever that I would not change places with anyone on God's green earth.

I love teaching. I love school administration. I love the daily contact with boys. I love solving the many problems which come up. I love everything about Schoolmastering, and I feel sorry for people who are not School masters. But I hate to raise money. I hate being away from the School during term time.

Thanks to the influence of Bishop Murray and Mr. Scull, the School was included in the yearly budget of the Diocese. Generous friends in New York, Pennsylvania, and Delaware as well as the splendid support of the Alumni made it possible for the contract for the main building, Claggett Hall, to be awarded. The cornerstone was laid on Commencement Day.

One of my jobs was to make my plea to the congregations of the Baltimore churches. The Rector of St. Michael and All Angels, one of Baltimore's largest churches, introduced me at such length that when my time came to appear in the pulpit, I had great difficulty in controlling my knees, to say nothing of my voice.

At another church I made a most impassioned appeal, as I thought. That appeal netted the fund $1,000 from a gentleman who was so deaf that he didn't hear a word I said, and who was the only contributor from that congregation. I only hope that my speech was not responsible for the death of the rector three days later. It seems he was taken ill during my address.

Building operations went on day and night during the summer in an effort to complete Claggett Hall before cold weather. In spite of the fact that boys on their return to the School in September would be required to occupy temporary quarters until Thanksgiving Day at least, not a single old boy failed to report. To our surprise a goodly number of new boys were enrolled. Again, that same spirit of cooperation prevailed. The boys, however, changed the name of the gymnasium from Coit Hall to Cold Storage, and the Barracks was dubbed the Ice House.

Many of the old boys, on their return, handed over to the Building Fund goodly sums which they collected over the summer vacation. I shall never forget the case of one boy who handed me $24.30. He was the last boy who I thought would be able to raise money, so I asked him how he managed to do so well. He seemed so embarrassed by my question that I regretted having asked him. Finally it came out that it represented his pay for work he had done during the summer, less five dollars which he had kept for spending money. Fifteen years later that boy was killed by a subway train in New York.

Thanks to the great generosity of my cousins, the Laidlaw family of New York, a beautiful modern and fully equipped infirmary was built in memory of the father and mother of that family. Following almost immediately upon the building of the infirmary, work was begun on the west wing of the main building. "Whittingham Hall" featured a beautiful sixteenth-century Dining Room, a memorial to Mr. Strout.

Two years before, Mr. Strout had closed St. Luke's and became a much beloved member of the faculty of Saint James. It was a strange course of events that, instead of my going to St. Luke's at the time of the fire, Mr. Strout should come to Saint James. I was fortunate in securing pledges which would almost cover the cost of Whittingham Hall, but before these pledges could be redeemed, the crash of 1929 and the subsequent depression made it impossible for me to collect on these pledges.

It was in 1933 when another serious blow to the School occurred. The Hagerstown Bank, which had on deposit all funds from the second-term tuitions, closed its doors. This bank held the mortgage on Whittingham Hall, so we had every reason to suppose that there would be an offset, as the amount of the mortgage was approximately the same as the amount of money the school had on deposit. As the offset was not forthcoming, the School entered suit, which it won in the circuit court. The Bank Commissioner of the State of Maryland was ordered to make the offset. At the time this decision was handed down, I was attending a reunion meeting of the New York Alumni.

The announcement to that group of the court's decision changed that gathering from a quiet well-behaving group to a riotous one. The bar of the Amherst Club did a land office business. No longer did the old boys look upon me as their dignified headmaster but as a fellow alumnus. Had I yielded to their efforts to get me to celebrate, I would have found it necessary to request help to get back to my hotel. Suffice it to say, I was able to navigate under my own steam.

My joy was short-lived, for the Bank Commissioner appealed the case and won. The failure of the Hagerstown Bank had a two-fold effect upon the School. Not only did the School lose all the money on deposit, but an impression was abroad that the School would be forced to close. The fact that the Donaldson School at Ilchester was to "fold up" at the end of that school year started the rumor that it was Saint James. Thanks to the great generosity of my cousin, Mr. Elliott Laidlaw, President of the Banking House of Laidlaw Company, the School was permitted to draw on that firm to the amount of $10,000 for which amount the Trustees gave a note.

I have failed to mention that after the fire I ceased to operate the School as a private venture. A Hagerstown man, who was regarded as a financial expert, was appointed by Bishop Murray to be the Treasurer of the School and was to be responsible to the Board. At the time of the appointment, this gentleman was the First Officer of the Hagerstown Bank & Trust Company. Several years prior to the closing of the bank, he resigned in order to give his entire attention to his private business. The summer prior to the closing of the bank I tried to persuade him to withdraw our account from the Hagerstown Bank as sidewalk gossip had it that the bank was in bad shape.

He gave me three reasons why this need not be done. First, the bank was in no danger of closing; second, the bank might in retaliation call the mortgage; and third, if by any chance the bank closed, the School would have an offset. This last was also the opinion of the School's attorney. It was this last reason which decided me to let the matter drop. The Hagerstown Bank had been the depository of the School from its founding in 1842, and many times during my administration and that of my father the bank had been most helpful to the School. The fact that the School did not secure the offset shows that there was something wrong.

To return to the situation after the bank's failure, something had to be done to make up for the loss. It has always been my policy to consider the gentlemen of the faculty, not as employees, but as members of the firm. No headmaster up to this time ever had a more loyal faculty. To a man they were 100% back of the administration. As was the case after the fire, they were willing to stand by even though it meant a personal sacrifice.

At the end of the third year, the treasurer reported to me that the School was almost out of the red. I felt very keenly the School's obligation to Laidlaw & Company, for Mr. Laidlaw, I was certain, had come to its rescue on my account. Because of this good news from the Treasurer, I left for my summer vacation feeling pretty happy over the fact that all salaries could be restored to the original figure.

On my return from my vacation, I found a letter from Mr. Laidlaw telling me that the School had overdrawn several thousand dollars. I was dumbfounded, as I had been given to understand that the School's obligation to Laidlaw & Company had been paid. I lost no time in calling on the Treasurer. It developed that his head clerk, in whom the Treasurer had complete confidence, instead of sending the money to Laidlaw, had falsified his books and had gotten away with $16,000. The fact that this absconder was sent to the penitentiary did not help the School. That blow almost got me down.

What hurt me terribly was the attitude taken by the President of the Board and several of the Trustees. In a measure, I suppose I was to blame. But when Bishop Murray appointed the Treasurer, he said to me, "Now, Adrian, your job is to send all the money to the Treasurer and he will be responsible to the Board. It is up to you to see to the enrollment and to run the School. The finances will in the future be our responsibility." Had Bishop Murray been alive at this time, I am sure he would have taken a different stand.

The thing which gratified me in these dark days was the splendid cooperation of the School's creditors. Mr. John Ridgely, Jr., and I visited every firm to whom we owed money and whom I had been informed by the "absconder" had been paid in full, and, with but one exception, all cut our indebtedness in half. Of course, the School had to suffer from a whispering campaign that the School was in serious difficulties, and as a result I had to combat such rumors with very little help from the Board. But I am getting ahead of my story.

I shall now return to my story where I left off after the fire. Before the fire, the School numbered 99 boys. I tried to get in one more to make it 100 but it was impossible to do so. The new building could accommodate no more than seventy-two boys and so the number had to be reduced. Later, when Whittingham Hall was built, the number was increased to 85. The School ran at its maximum capacity until after the bank failure, when rumor had it that the School would be forced to close. There was absolutely no foundation for that rumor. There were a few changes in the faculty.

In spite of fire, bank failure, and the absconding with the School funds; in spite of the fact that the President of the Board and several of the Trustees failed to give me the support I greatly needed at that time, I still could say that I would not change places with anyone on God's green earth. I had to combat the unfortunate attitude that the success of a school was measured not by the type of boys in the School and the quality of instruction but by the balance sheet.

In 1938, under pressure I took certain boys whose only recommendation was that their parents could pay the tuition. Yes, we had a full school, but not one in which I took any pride. Several of these boys were dismissed during the year, and a number of others were requested not to return.

Because of my attitude I was constantly dodging bricks hurled at me by some members of the Board. I was no longer asked to attend trustee meetings. The fact that I had rescued the School when its numbers had been reduced to eight boys, that over a period of years I had spent out of my own funds many thousands of dollars to improve a property in which I had no equity, that with the help of my faculty I had built up the School to its full capacity—all this was forgotten. So the only course left to me was to retire as headmaster but to remain as head of the Latin Department.

My wife suffered more from my act than I did. After 38 years, it was a relief to me to be free from responsibility. I loved the house across the road that we had bought and were living in, but unfortunately it caught on fire from a defective furnace pipe. Most of the furniture was saved, but the house was a complete loss.

Fortunately the house was covered by insurance, which enabled me to rebuild. Our new home was later featured in the magazine *House & Garden*. We did not move into the new house immediately on its completion but rented it for three years. Because of the sudden death of our tenant, the house was vacated, and, instead of re-renting it, we decided to move in. Our two oldest sons were in the army at the time. It was good to get back into a home where we could be surrounded by our "lares and penates."[13]

Two months later came Pearl Harbor. Fortunately, the end of the war did come and our boys returned to us safe and sound.[14] That year,

---

13. Proving here that he was an experienced Latin teacher, Onderdonk refers to the gods protecting the family and the Roman state.

14. All three Onderdonk sons graduated from Saint James School: "Henry II" went to Princeton and earned two master's degrees from the University of Michigan. He

however, was made very unhappy for us because of the sudden death of that noble man John Campbell, my dearest friend and for so many years my coworker.

Henry II was a student at Princeton, Richardson (Dick) started in to complete his college course, and Adrian took Mr. Campbell's courses at Saint James. The next year we were all together for Christmas for the first time in five years, and it was a most happy occasion. Little did we realize in the midst of our rejoicing that in less than three weeks I would no longer have my darling wife constantly at my side. She had always been so well and strong that I never thought that I would outlive her. The only reason I felt reconciled to going on without her was my three boys.

No longer could I remain at Saint James without her, so I am now spending my last days in the home of life-long friends in the suburbs of Baltimore. As I write these lines, one and a half years later, I am at Essex on Lake Champlain, where I first met Evelynne and where we spent many happy days during the summer holidays. And so on her birthday I bring these memoirs to a close.

---

became a composer. Richardson Latrobe (1917–99) earned the AB degree from Trinity College and a master's from the University of Delaware; he served in the Signal Corps during World War II and made a career teaching history, political science, and social studies in both public and private schools. He was a long-time master at West Nottingham Academy in Maryland (founded 1744). He died in Tucson, Arizona, but was buried in the family plot in the churchyard of St. Mark's Church, Lappans, Maryland, just a few miles from Saint James School.

6

Father Owens, Eighth Headmaster of Saint James[1]

1955–84

Stuart Dunnan

On 26 March 1945, during the assault crossing of the Rhine River near Willmich, Germany, Captain Owens, Commanding Officer of Company "C", 354th Infantry, saw one of the boats containing leading elements of his company capsize in midstream, leaving heavily laden men drifting helplessly downstream under heavy

---

1. This chapter is an expansion of the talk I offered in 2014 at the annual memorial service of the Headmaster's Association, and that was based on the homily I preached at Father Owens's Requiem at the Church of the Ascension and St. Agnes in Washington, DC, in May of 2013. In remembering Father Owens and considering his legacy at Saint James, I am drawing on my own conversations with him, his friends and colleagues, alumni, and past parents. I am also drawing on some additional school resources such as earlier student handbooks and yearbooks. In offering this essay, I do not pretend to be objective, as I admired Father Owens very much and am indebted to him for his personal support and friendship, and most especially indebted to him for the legacy which I describe in the chapter. I am also indebted to Mr. Baker who succeeded him, and my own colleagues who served under him, most especially Ellen Davis, Robert Grab, Dave and Betty Barr, Eddie Hoyer, and Chick Meehan. I got a strong sense from them, in my early years especially, of what it was like to work for Father Owens and what he cared about and stood for.

enemy fire. With utter disregard for his personal safety, Captain Owens went out in an engineer launch, and rescued every man that he could locate. Later, when engineers reported that six men were stranded on a sand bar, Captain Owens again went out in a launch, in the face of heavy hostile fire, and, traveling approximately 400 yards downstream, brought the men to safety. After the bulk of his company had crossed the river, Captain Owens reorganized it and led his men in taking the town of Willmich, and the sheer cliff and castle behind it, without a casualty.

On 7 April 1945 near Thal, Germany when his company came under heavy enemy machine gun fire, Captain Owens aggressively moved to eliminate the hostile resistance. Promptly sending a messenger to the weapons platoon with directions for supporting fire, he personally moved across fifty yards of open terrain to the third platoon, whose position was most dangerous. Because of his personal direction and inspiring courage the third platoon was quickly removed from danger and the company combined its firepower to neutralize the enemy positions.[2]

THE ABOVE PASSAGES, THE first from John Owens's citation for the Silver Star, the second from his citation for the Bronze Star, describe two heroic and decisive actions by a twenty-six-year-old officer who personally turned the tide in two battles and saved many lives. What is worth noting as a footnote to these narratives is that this officer was extraordinarily tall (six feet, five inches), so a particularly good target for enemy fire. He crossed that river not once but twice to save his stranded men, and then moved across open terrain for fifty yards, again under enemy fire, to save his platoon. This was an extraordinarily brave and selfless young man.

Now, I did not know this young man. I did not meet him until he was seventy-three, and I was thirty-three. I had just come back to America from England and had just assumed the post of headmaster of Saint James School, and the greatly admired, even revered former headmaster of Saint James invited me to lunch. If I recall correctly, it was in Catonsville, where he had been visiting the All Saints Sisters, whom he served as Spiritual Director and Confessor.

He was still very tall, and he carried naturally, but also unassumingly, the habit of command, but he wore now a different uniform, the same one I did, the black suit, black shirt, and white collar of an Episcopal

---

2. Copies of these two citations hang on the wall of the Owens Library, Saint James School.

priest in the Anglo-Catholic tradition. Seeing him in person, I was awed, and I recognized immediately the "great Father Owens" I had heard so much about, "the legend" I would never be. And I think that I just proceeded to tell him all the problems I faced and all the challenges that confronted me, how impossible my job would be: The campus needed repair and rebuilding; the academic and social standards needed reasserting; the budget did not balance; there was debt on the new Field House; the endowment was too small; the alumni did not give; and so on. My list was a long one.

And he listened patiently; bought me lunch; completely understood, although he had been retired for eight years, and kept offering the same words of assurance: "Don't worry, Stuart; you're young." Frustrated that he offered no real solution, no hidden, generous donor or secret treasure hidden in the Bai Yuka,[3] I finally asked if he had any advice. And this was his answer: "When you make a decision, don't worry if it is popular or not; just worry if it is right or wrong." And I have now had twenty-six years to live into Father Owens's advice, and I think that I now better understand what he meant: not just "do the right thing" but be a *moral* and a *faithful* leader.

Father Owens was different from most headmasters in that he was an introvert and not an extrovert, so he did not enjoy giving speeches or "working the crowd." I remember when we were celebrating Dave Barr's retirement, and Father Owens agreed to elevate the gathering by returning to campus. When I asked if he wished to speak, he said no, but at the very end of the evening when we were gathered in the chapel after dinner, a hand went up at the back after everyone else had spoken.

"Father, may I just say something else?" "Of course." And the chapel fell silent as Father Owens walked to the front. "I would like to say something about Dave's wife, Betty, and the strength of their marriage." He then offered just a few words in praise of Betty because they should have been said, and then he sat down. With just three or four sentences and without intending to, he made the evening. This was the effect he—and only he—could have on the gathering.

I remember the same effect at an alumnus's funeral in the chapel. When he began the opening anthems from the back in his deep bass voice, "I am the resurrection and the life, saith the Lord . . . ," everyone

---

3. The Native American words for the "fountain rock" and pond in the center of campus.

turned around to see him. They were visibly moved and excited just to hear his voice.

Essentially shy and humble, Father Owens remained a very reluctant headmaster. He came to Saint James as chaplain in 1948 and served until 1950, when he left to serve a small parish on the Eastern Shore. Bishop Noble C. Powell then ordered him to return as headmaster in 1955, and he tried to return to a parish several times, but Bishop Powell would not let him. He served until he retired in 1984.

Father Owens's students called him "FO" (pronounced "Foh"), "Black Jack" because he was always in clericals, or "the Phantom" because they would look up from a football game and suddenly see him watching on the sidelines in his black raincoat, and then look up again, and he was gone. He was not the typical outgoing headmaster who loved to host gatherings, chair meetings, and be visible on campus. He brought with him from the army an officer's reserve and generally kept his distance from the students and most of the faculty as well.

Additionally, Father Owens was not vain, and let's face it, most great schools are built on the vanity of their heads, as we want our schools to reflect our "greatness." He was therefore not a very ambitious fundraiser. He was nevertheless an effective fundraiser and did much to improve the school. His record is remarkably impressive:

> During his years as headmaster, Father Owens' vision supported the school's continued improvement and success. Under his guidance, the faculty grew in number and improved in quality; enrollment increased from 110 to more than 150; coeducation was introduced; and, the endowment grew. He made many improvements to the campus.
>
> Campbell House was built in 1955 for use by the Selective Service. Just over a decade later, Hershey Hall was constructed, providing the Selective Service with additional space. In 1957, the Onderdonk residence was purchased and used as a dormitory for eight boys. It was nicknamed "Buckingham Palace" because two English exchange students roomed there—and "Buckingham" it remains to this day—though it now serves as faculty housing. Nelson House, next door to Buckingham, and named for long-time master, Russell Nelson, was built in l959.
>
> The Henry Evan Cotton Memorial Gymnasium, which greatly enhanced the school's athletic program, was completed in 1961. Two years later, the Powell Hall classroom building was completed. It was named for the Rt. Rev. Noble Powell, ninth

bishop of Maryland and a long-time friend of the school. Powell Hall stands on the site of the old Coit Gymnasium. The wing of Powell Hall facing "The Circle" housed the McIntyre Library, presented to the school by Mr. and Mrs. John Sharpless McIntyre, in honor of their two sons John Sharpless McIntrye, Jr. '58 and James Byrd McIntyre '61.

The Georgian brick Saint James chapel was consecrated in memory of Eleanor Blodgett Webster in 1965. Her husband, William Webster '61, provided the impetus for the chapel, and the establishment of an endowment fund.

Pipkin House, named in honor of Ruth and Benton Pipkin, and given by their sons John '53 and Ashmead '56, was built as a faculty residence in 1966. That same year, Bonner House was completed. This faculty residence was named for Mr. Kenneth Bonner, a trustee, former assistant headmaster, and a generous benefactor.

Under Father Owens' leadership, the school also bought two farms adjacent to the campus, primarily as a "buffer" against future development in the area: Sperow Farm, purchased in 1961, and Bloom Farm, purchased in l964. The school also purchased 20 acres of land to extend the baseball diamond and add playing fields for lacrosse, soccer, and field hockey. In 1980, the school bought the Old Orchard House. The 19th century structure serves as a faculty residence.[4]

Father Owens did not modernize or "grow" the school dramatically, as other American heads-of-school did in his time. The enrollment grew from 110 to 150 students, which was still relatively small. He did not really care if his teams won or where his graduates went to college; there was nothing "promotional" about him. He did care about the quality of the instruction, however, and the integrity of the school's discipline. He ran a tight budget, but he was quick to forgive the tuition when a family lost its income. He had a particular soft spot for mothers in distress, often intervening personally to help and support them.

Most notably, perhaps, he retained the faculty he inherited from Dr. Kellett, whom he had known during his brief stint as chaplain. In doing so, he continued to empower the faculty to run the school academically and to retain a great deal of administrative control. The consequence for Saint James was an older faculty of gifted teachers and "great characters" who were sometimes challenging to manage and did not always

---

4. *Brief History of Saint James School*, ix–x.

get along.[5] Many of these teachers are still very much remembered by alumni as powerful, transformative, and often challenging figures: George Belden (Spanish and French), George Hill (Athletics, Mechanical Drawing, and Math), George Hopkins (Science and Math), Russell Nelson (Lower School), Charles Roberts (Spanish, Latin, and Math), and Steve Webster (English). Significantly, they stayed in place through the early years of Father Owens's headmastership: Mr. Belden and Mr. Hill retired in 1964; Mr. Hopkins in 1965; Mr. Webster in 1968; Mr. Nelson in 1970; and Mr. Roberts died in 1979.

Thus the academic culture remained faculty led and largely untouched through the first half of Father Owens's headmastership. He also did not have complete authority over them, as they predated him and were difficult to control; this was sometimes on view in the refectory where they would pull "practical jokes" on each other in full view of the school.

Gradually, Father Owens did develop his own faculty, and the second half of his headmastership gained its own cast of dedicated and "larger than life" teachers: Larry Hoyer (Science) and Aleda James (Remedial Reading) in 1958, Eddie Hoyer (Math and Economics) and the returning Dave Barr (Athletics, History, and Math) in 1959, Frank Russell (French) and Al Watson (English) in 1964, Ted Eagles and Don (History) and Mary (Art) Woodruff in 1967, Rusty Allen (Science) and Chick Meehan (Athletics and Math) in 1969, and Frank Carden (Latin) in 1982. Interestingly, all but Larry Hoyer (1966), Ted Eagles (1977), and Frank Russell (1971) stayed with Father Owens for the rest of his headmastership, and the only one who retired with him was Mrs. James.

This was generously done on their part, as all the faculty in Father Owens's time carried multiple responsibilities and worked very hard. Also, faculty salaries and benefits did not rise with the market or indeed inflation, and housing, for dorm faculty especially, remained relatively cramped and challenging. The faculty continued to run the academic curriculum, which was initially the purview of the senior master and the registrar, but as the school transitioned into the sixties and seventies, teachers began to assume other named responsibilities as well. Mr. Hill and then Mr. Barr served as athletic directors; and Mr. Barr as "School Disciplinarian." Mr. Watson and then Rusty Allen assumed responsibility for College Placement. Don Woodruff assumed responsibility for

---

5. As told me by Eddie Hoyer, '52.

Admissions and Development, and Frank Carden became the academic dean. But in all these cases, these duties were assumed in addition to teaching.

The culture of the school therefore remained remarkably "old fashioned" with a fair, but severe system of discipline, administered by a largely older faculty not well positioned to respond to the social crises of the 1970s and early 1980s, most notably the general adolescent rebellion against adult authority and the "recreational" use of illegal drugs.

Saint James therefore was much the same when he left it as it had been when he arrived. There was still required chapel, three sit-down meals, afternoon sports, and evening study hall six days a week. The boys (and now a few girls) still wore their blazers, and the masters still worked for very little money and some still lived in two-room apartments. Father Owens himself was not highly paid and lived in Rich Cottage, a small single-story house in the center of campus, which was in no sense the typical "headmaster's residence."[6]

Father Owens was very optimistic about other people and was therefore in some ways quite innocent, almost naïve in his expectations. He always assumed that parents and alumni would want to give out of gratitude, so they should not need to be asked. He was especially disappointed that the many students who received financial aid during his time as headmaster did not feel more inspired to give to the school after they graduated. He also did not believe, as he once told me, in "spying on the boys," and he expected the faculty to act appropriately and to do their jobs. He therefore tended to be reactive rather than proactive when it came to faculty misbehavior and student discipline, and he reacted very much like an officer in the army, especially concerned to be fair and to "follow the rules."

As the 1960s and 1970s progressed and "the Greatest Generation" gave way to "Baby Boomers," the system Father Owens had inherited did not always deliver the best results. This was true of course at every school, but the challenge for Father Owens at Saint James was that his good reputation was essential to the reputation of the school, so there was a strong desire in every key constituency of the school for him to stay at the helm. This he dutifully and selflessly did, although he did take a seven-month

---

6. I lived in this house for the first ten years of my headmastership, and it was a delightful home for a traditional priest, with a beautiful view, but it was too small to host guests or to entertain more than ten people

sabbatical in 1970 when he sailed on a freighter around the world and taught the Asian sailors English.

Interestingly and typically, Father Owens was actually quite self-critical about the length of his tenure, which most view as a great achievement. In fact, when I knew him in his retirement, he would often say that "I stayed too long." This reflected, on his part I think, a humble awareness that he did not always adapt or respond to the changes around him as effectively as he could have.

Father Owens was more a priest than a headmaster. He was also a very prayerful priest who did not like to preach. He preferred to preach by example. He would say mass every morning before school, and the alumni who served him at the altar when they were students remember coming very early at the appointed time, only to find him already there fully vested, preparing to celebrate, lost in prayer. He would not notice their arrival (a stunning surprise to teenagers), and he was visibly moved with emotion.[7]

He cared deeply about the religion of the school and strengthened the Anglo-Catholic heritage of Saint James. He was initially supported in this by Bishops Powell and Leighton of Maryland, who were both high churchmen and very committed and active bishop presidents of the Board of Trustees, but as the diocese developed in a more modernizing and liberal direction, Saint James remained more "traditional." Bishop Eastman, Father Owens's last bishop as headmaster, was less involved in the running of the school than Bishop Powell and Bishop Leighton had been.

His Philosophy of a Church School

Father Owens articulated his own philosophy of a church school in an address on "Church Schools" to the diocese of Easton (1968).

> I believe that there are at least five reasons, most of them interrelated, for having Church schools. Dr. Kerfoot, the first headmaster of Saint James School, had a three-point philosophy when he came to the school as headmaster in 1842. The three points were sound learning, good manners, and deep religious convictions. At the Episcopal Schools Convention which met in Washington two years ago, Dr. Crocker, the former headmaster of Groton, outlined a somewhat similar list. I have combined these ideas

---

7. As told me by Jay Stein, '59.

of both Dr. Kerfoot and Dr. Crocker as a "platform" for Church schools. They are:

1. To bear witness to the fact that God is the source of all knowledge and acknowledgement of Him and a proper response to Him as revealed in Jesus Christ are basic to the understanding of life and to the formation of character.
2. To hold on to that which is good, which is eternal in our ever-changing world.
3. To maintain standards of excellence.
4. To use Christian standards as points of reference and departure as a basis for living.
5. To bear witness to the fact that the whole of life is God's concern.

Father Owens developed these five reasons into a "Philosophy of Saint James School."

> Saint James is a college preparatory Church school. As a Church school, it believes that God is the source of all knowledge and acknowledgment of Him and a proper response to Him as revealed in Jesus Christ are basic to the understanding of life and the foundation and formation of character. Since the whole of life is God's concern, the School endeavors to help each student build a solid foundation of body, mind and spirit and so prepares the student to complete higher education successfully and then to go on to a life of constructive service to mankind. To do this the School attempts to give each student a sound knowledge of academic subjects in an atmosphere conducive to learning and to provide the opportunity to develop special talents and abilities.
>
> A well planned and directed athletic program is carried on throughout the year in which all boys must participate in order to learn basic skills and good sportsmanship. The School strives to develop character by fostering the growth of integrity, a sense of personal and group responsibility, and a high standard of honor.
>
> All of this is done in an ordered and disciplined life within the structure of the faith and practice of the Church.[8]

Note here the progression that Father Owens uses to describe the purpose and character of Saint James School. He begins with the church and the church's faith in God revealed in Jesus Christ. This is "basic to

---

8. A copy of this text is in the school archives, Saint James School; see Owens, *Philosophy of Saint James School*, 3–4.

the understanding of life and the foundation and formation of character." The school then, because it is a church school, "endeavors to help each student build a solid foundation of body, mind and spirit." This means it "attempts to give each student a sound knowledge of academic subjects in an atmosphere conducive to learning and to provide the opportunity to develop special talents and abilities." This leads to a "well planned and directed athletic program . . . in order to learn basic skills and good sportsmanship." Similarly, as an ordered community, the school "strives to develop character by fostering the growth of integrity, a sense of personal and group responsibility, and a high standard of honor." And notice where Father Owens ends: right where he began. "All of this is done in an ordered and disciplined life within the structure of the faith and practice of the Church."

For those who know Saint James now and how we stand apart from other very selective college preparatory and even Episcopal schools, all of this sounds familiar, and this is, I would argue, Father Owens's most lasting achievement and his enduring mark on the school. At a time when most Episcopal schools were doing their utmost to flee their religious foundations by abandoning chapel and secularizing their missions, he starts and ends his printed philosophy with the church and then specifically the church's faith in God revealed in Jesus Christ. The work of Saint James is for him entirely faithful, even theological: to do the work of God, to inspire and equip the young to serve Christ in "the constructive service of mankind."

In reading this philosophy, we can only be impressed by the humility of its expression. Typically, Father Owens attributes his own ideas to Dr. Kerfoot and Dr. Crocker, whom he considers to be more distinguished headmasters than he. This is a recurring theme in his writing, as he rarely presents an important idea as his own. Also, unlike most headmasters of a school competing for fee-paying students, he does not seek to promote his school; neither does he boast of the quality of his school's programs. He seeks rather to explain what Saint James does and why: to form the character of its students.

Father Owens also does not seek to justify the Christian faith in relationship to "the market," but presents the faith as a given, which is the faith of the School and therefore not for any generation of students or indeed the headmaster to remove or alter. He writes: "As a Church school, *it* believes," which is to say, Saint James School believes, and this is the source and the purpose of its work.

So this is, in the end, the great work that Father Owens achieved by staying for so many years: He stayed true to the vision of Bishop Whittingham, Dr. Muhlenberg, and Dr. Kerfoot, and to his own understanding of what it means to serve God. He kept Saint James a church school. Such a school is not interested in the achievements of its students alone but also—and even more so—in their goodness, or to use the terms David Brooks uses in his recent book *The Road to Virtue*, in their "eulogy virtues" and not just their "résumé virtues."[9]

Father Owens also understood teenagers. Here is a passage on the subject from the source quoted above:

> In the 13–18 year old group we find rebellion against authority, suspicion of anything that smacks of uplift, and intense dislike of indoctrination, and a fear of being different from the group. Only a teacher who cares enough to be a sounding board to all sorts of confused thinking, who is prepared to absorb rebellion, resistance and even temporary hatred—only that kind can win a child to God.
>
> Canon Martin of St. Albans School[10] expressed this well when he said, "In relations with young people, we must hold them to standards that are right, not with softness, but with the firmness that is in love. But do so with understanding and with the full knowledge that we cannot mold or shape them into the way we believe right. But God, working in and through teachers and parents can shape people that are good, even in the confusion of today. If our young people trust us and know we understand them, those of our values which are worthy and abiding will speak to them with compelling force and give them strength and stability to live as usefully and as well as their elders, perhaps better.
>
> Young people ask essentially the same questions but in different ways and in varying degrees and depths of understanding. Throughout their life, underlying everything, as it is for us, is their search for meaning in life.[11]

Here we see how Father Owens's understanding of teenagers as young adults who are essentially good but resistant to authority, and his personal humility in relationship to God, informed his more reserved

---

9. Brooks, *Road to Character*.

10. Here again he quotes a "respected colleague."

11. Owens, *Philosophy of Saint James School*, 10–11. Interestingly, Canon Martin was my headmaster at St. Albans.

approach to raising them. The adult needs to "absorb rebellion, resistance and even temporary hatred" and "hold them to standards that are right" to "win a child to God."

The relationship between teacher and student then is essentially and vitally hierarchical; it is a heroic, even sacrificial role. The teacher does not seek to win students' affection or gain popularity, but sets the right example and relates to his students from a position of authority with sympathy and understanding. Surely, we see here how Father Owens is still in many ways Captain Owens, training his men and leading them into battle with his own heroic example.

Because it was so hierarchical, Father Owens's understanding of his role as headmaster would be greatly tested in the late sixties and seventies by his students and some faculty, who were increasingly less willing to trust and follow the authority he represented and exercised. The fact that he was reserved by nature and kept his distance from all but the most senior faculty made him even more misunderstood and feared,[12] although he was rigorous in his adherence to process and fairness, and personally very compassionate. Still, because he served as the ultimate authority in a system of discipline largely administered by the faculty, he was often reacting to misbehaviors on the part of students and also sometimes on the part of younger faculty without much personal involvement or engagement ahead of time. This sometimes caused strong personal resentment, and he was not universally loved, but again, he accepted this, and considered it his duty to be at times and by some disliked.

Certainly, any headmaster, most especially in the sixties and seventies, can be faulted in retrospect for decisions he made both in relationship to individuals and to the school as an institution, and Father Owens was often in retirement the first to criticize some of his own decisions. But what makes his tenure and gift to Saint James so remarkable was the integrity of his priesthood and the faith he defended for the school and modeled for his students. This is why he is still so admired, and why the school's identity remained so steadfast in the storms that swirled around him.

Perhaps the most famous story about Father Owens which reflects his compassionate nature is his intensely personal care of a student, Eric Mohn, '65, who was paralyzed in a car accident during the summer

---

12. I once spoke to an alumnus who called to report the misbehavior of a teacher during Father Owens's tenure. When I asked if Father Owens knew about this, the alumnus was shocked and said that it was this former teacher's greatest fear that Father Owens would find out.

before his sixth-form year. Eric was away from school for a year, and it was difficult to see how he could return, as he had become a quadriplegic, but Father Owens took him and his roommate George Brown into his house, bathed and dressed him every day, and pushed him up the hill to school in his wheelchair. Eric's mother often joined them, and Father Owens later married Eric to his wife.[13]

Eric became a famous artist who painted intricate watercolor landscapes by holding the brush in his mouth. He never forgot what Father Owens had done for him, and he gave many of his best paintings to Saint James to be sold for the scholarship fund.

When the Senior Master, Chick Meehan, also class of 1965, spoke to the students at lunch to give them something of a sense of who Father Owens was, he spoke about his war service and about his twenty-nine years as headmaster, and he pointed out that Father Owens essentially ran the school with a bookkeeper and a secretary.

But then Chick got to the point of his talk and tried to express how important Father Owens was to him, as he knew Father Owens not just as his "boss" when he started teaching at Saint James, but as a student when he came to Saint James as a boy of thirteen in the second form. He said that Father Owens was really his second father and the man he admired the most in his life, and then he stopped speaking very abruptly because he had lost his voice to emotion.

Because he had been headmaster for twenty-nine years and had run Saint James in such a traditional and personal way, Father Owens was almost impossible to replace. The task fell to a board that had relied upon him to run the school on his own authority for twenty-nine years, gathering for meetings only two or three times a year, with a "final collection" at the last meeting to cover the usual deficit. His successor, the Reverend Richard Baker, was also a priest, a former Rhodes Scholar, and an experienced school master, but he had a more informal manner and a more secular sense of his office and the school, more typical of the other Episcopal schools in his time. For instance, he preferred to be called "Mr. Baker," which came as a shock to many in the immediate and wider community of the school. He did however honor the more Catholic liturgy and traditions of the chapel, appointing the Reverend John Merchant chaplain in 1985, who was always addressed as "Father Merchant."

---

13. From conversations with Eric, his parents, and George Brown's widow.

The real challenge that Mr. Baker faced when he arrived on campus was how to "modernize" the school with limited resources. The school had a very small endowment compared to other schools, a lower tuition, a less developed annual fund, and a much smaller alumni body to support it. The "market" had also become increasingly challenging for boarding schools, and the salary, load, and housing expectations for faculty were much higher than Saint James could provide. This presented the new headmaster with the classic chicken-and-egg conundrum: How can you increase the staff and improve their packages without the resources to pay for it? In response to these challenges, he added a full-time business manager, academic dean, director of admission, and director of development, and he built on Father Owens's tentative first steps towards coeducation. He also built Alumni Hall in support of the athletic program. But after seven years of increasing financial challenges, he left in the spring of 1991, and Chick Meehan stepped in to serve as interim.

I came on July 5, 1992, as the third headmaster in three years to a school in financial distress and a community divided. Happily, Mr. Baker had made many of the hard decisions for me, but I needed Father Owens's help to regain momentum and to save Saint James.[14] I particularly needed him to come to my first Alumni Weekend as there was a brewing coup attempt on the part of a teacher I had not renewed. At first, Father Owens said no, but then he called the night before to say that he would join me at the Alumni dinner and serve as deacon at the Alumni Eucharist on Sunday. When I asked if he would preach, he said: "No. They will want to hear you."

He had not been back for several years, so his return was hugely symbolic. Immediately, the talk changed from "the new headmaster is too young and ambitious" to "Father Owens is coming back." I have never seen the alumni more excited or more moved. When he entered the main hall before dinner, they turned as one to greet him and parted reverently to make way for him as he walked through the crowd, and they cried when he spoke to them, each by name. I remember thinking that he was like Moses with the Hebrews.

At dinner, true to form, he gave a very short speech, passing the school to me. He said that he was pleased that I was headmaster because of my academic qualifications, but especially because I was in his words

---

14. Here I would just like to acknowledge my debt to both of my immediate predecessors, as they both reached out to me when I was appointed and were consistently kind to me and very supportive.

a "faithful priest" who would pray for his people and bring them to the altar of God. I will never forget his ending: "I have told Father Dunnan that my boys will support him." And with these words, Moses sat down, and I became his Joshua.

Father Owens enjoyed a long and happy retirement, most of it with his friend Bishop Montgomery, retired of Chicago. They prayed the office and said mass together every day, and traveled back and forth between their respective homes in Alexandria and Chicago. Bishop Montgomery was very generous to the school in his will, endowing both the Owens Scholarship and the Owens Chair in Religion. His retirement was exactly as long as his headmastership: twenty-nine years. As a priest, he still celebrated his students' marriages, baptized their children, corresponded with many of them, and prayed for them every day. He never stopped loving them, although still at a distance, and many of them realized this. Indeed, as they grew older and gained more wisdom with experience in life, they came to admire him even more.

In the last few weeks of Father Owens's life, Mike Lieberman, '58, one of his own boys, whom Father Owens had personally rushed to the hospital when his appendix burst and stayed with in his hospital room, was his doctor. He was the one who called to tell me that Father Owens was dying and then said that he was on his way to see him so that he could "give him a kiss goodbye."

When we released word of his illness, the letters flowed in: loving and grateful and fearful at his parting. That was the first thing out of his mouth when I went to see him: he was so grateful and moved by what his students had written and that they remembered him so fondly. I remember being very moved to see that his experience and relationships at the school remained so important to him almost three decades after he had retired and when he was now at the end of his life. I also noticed that his reserve was gone; he was much more openly grateful and loving.

This then may be Father Owens's most important gift to Saint James school: he was a truly great headmaster. Again, I am not claiming that he was perfect or that he always made the right decisions, but he was distinctive and remarkable, and he created, or rather recreated by the strength of his personality and his longevity as headmaster, a truly distinct and remarkable school.

I will always remember a visit I received from Byron Forbush, the very distinguished Head of Baltimore Friends School, at the beginning of my first year as headmaster. He drove out to Saint James to welcome me to the Baltimore Senate, the historic association of the original private schools in Baltimore. He told me that he made the trip rather than call me because he had admired Father Owens so much and therefore greatly admired Saint James.

The Senate has an annual dinner to which retired heads are also invited, and those who served in Father Owens's time always made a point of telling me how much they admired him. I know that my own headmaster at St. Albans, Canon Martin, admired him greatly, and I was very aware of his legacy and the continuing benefit of his coattails when I was inducted into the Headmasters Association in 2004.

The truth is that Father Owens significantly developed Saint James in ways that continue today. He made major improvements to the campus, began the school's endowment, and began the strategy of purchasing adjacent farmland to preserve the school's rural setting. He was also able to adapt as times changed and to expand the school's mission in ways that now define us: he decided to admit girls in 1976;[15] admitted the first students of color (both Native American and African American),[16] and he began to enroll international students (initially from Great Britain, Germany, and Japan) to preserve the peace he fought so heroically to restore in the Second World War.

But what made Father Owens *great* were the ways in which he kept Saint James different from other schools. Specifically, he kept Saint James smaller and humbler than the other established boarding schools (some of which are our children), and the newer, increasingly selective day schools in Baltimore and Washington. By maintaining a higher standard of honor and manners through the sixties, seventies, and halfway through the eighties, he preserved a culture of responsibility and civility, which is increasingly "countercultural" in American education. As a result, we still have an honor code, seated meals, a dress code, and a prefect council, which are aspects of boarding school life long since abandoned

---

15. Betty Barr always told the story that Father Owens asked her, "What do girls eat?" just before they arrived.

16. On the Board of Trustees, there was some resistance to admitting the first African American. Bishop Powell strongly and decisively supported Father Owens. In his Address to the Diocese of Easton, Father Owens declared: "The major problem of our day is that of race relations. We are judged by our young people not so much by what we say but by the example we set—our actions, whether these are of the individual or of the group. Certainly no Church school should do less than have an open policy concerning members of all races."

or greatly diminished at other schools for reasons of modernity, liability, or just "niche in the market."

He also restored the Tractarian (later described as Anglo-Catholic) spirituality of the school's foundation, both in the liturgy of the chapel and in the wider life of the school, refusing to build a cult of the school as an all-consuming idol and focusing instead on what was best for his students as young people "growing up in an unsteady and confusing world."[17] True to the values of the Oxford Movement, he remained committed to the Benedictine discipline of life in community, a life of common prayer and work, with an emphasis on servant leadership, mutual accountability and support, and moral and spiritual growth. This means that he never embraced the shift to "résumé values" so prevalent at other independent schools promising the "product" of "success" in college placement.[18] Rather, he remained committed to "eulogy values" as more important and central to the education of the whole person, and thus to the mission and work of the school.

So, even as we have improved and strive to improve academically, athletically, artistically, and musically, and as we seek to build and improve our buildings and facilities to support these programs, we are not "like the others." We are rather as other educators often refer to us at conferences "that High Church School" or that "very traditional school." But when I hear this, I smile inwardly because Saint James is just as lively, often more hilarious and joyous, certainly just as achieving, and usually much more diverse than the schools those educators serve.

But they are right, of course. We are not like the others; we are more religious, so more concerned about spirituality and morality, and more of a community, so more concerned about manners and honor, and we are smaller and less idolatrous, so more concerned that our students learn to lead, contribute, and serve. In these ways especially, we are still Father Owens's school.

---

17. *Book of Common Prayer*, 829.
18. Brooks, *Road to Character*.

7

Dunnan of Saint James

1992–2017

W. L. PREHN

THE 2004 BIENNIAL CONFERENCE of the National Association of Episcopal Schools met in a lovely hotel in the nation's capital. Perhaps a hundred persons gathered in a large room to hear the last reading of a new statement on the Episcopal identity of member schools. When the chair was prepared to declare the draft a final document, she asked if there were any other questions. A priest of the church rose midway down the room and asked a question. With the greatest courtesy for madame chairman, the drafting committee, and, indeed, all present, the priest gently asked whether two words might be added to the statement on Episcopal identity. "What words do you mean?" asked the chair. The priest replied, "I believe the document should include reference to *Jesus Christ* by name." After complete silence for a few moments, the chair and others on the committee nodded and agreed that the two words would go into the document.

The story illustrates the kind of man the Board of Trustees appointed rector and headmaster of Saint James School in 1992. If the Reverend Stuart Dunnan began his first headship when he was but thirty-two years old, he had great school experience already and proved to be wise for his age. As the school celebrated one hundred and seventy-five years, Father Dunnan entered his twenty-sixth year as headmaster. It is proverbial wisdom that institutions tend to improve slowly. In the case of Saint James, significant changes occurred immediately and have occurred year after year, but the old wisdom holds true. If the world looks on and admires, Father Dunnan knows better than anyone how much is yet to be done.

Dunnan commenced his work at Saint James with excellent credentials. First, and most importantly, he had been prepared at the St. Albans of Canon Martin.[1] As a schoolboy he was appreciated and mentored by that great priest of the church and successful headmaster. He was a chorister there, and the discipline and habits instilled in him by way of that excellent program have never left him. He wrote lines about Canon Martin which are echoed in Fountain Rock today when persons speak of Dunnan. "My own headmaster was steady in purpose, so predictable in his morality, so gracious in his charity. And he preached a very simple Gospel, well-chosen and well directed to the young: choose the hard right over the easy wrong."[2]

Dunnan had also done a lot for his years. When the trustees appointed him, he was serving as chaplain and junior fellow of Lincoln College, Oxford. Matriculating into the University of Oxford from Christ Church College, he successfully defended his DPhil thesis in historical theology. He earned both bachelor's and master's degrees from Harvard in four years (European History). Other achievements gave the trustees confidence in such a young man. Dunnan had already been a librarian of Pusey House, Oxford, and served the Harvard School in Los Angeles as history teacher, college counselor, and chaplain. While in Oxford, Dunnan was shaped into a pastoral academic leader by Father Philip Ursell, Principal of Pusey House.

Why did a man with these credentials want to come to a small boarding school in Western Maryland, a school which did not show particularly well on the first visit to the campus? With credentials such as his,

---

1. The Reverend Canon Charles Martin, DD (1907–97), was Headmaster of St. Albans from 1949 to 1977. The reader can see Father Dunnan in the following lines written by an alumnus about Martin at the time of his death in 1997: "Canon Martin's Episcopal faith was deep and powerful. He saw himself as a parish priest to what he always called "the school family," which gradually grew to encompass thousands of people—whose children he baptized, whose weddings he celebrated, whose parents' sickbeds he attended. His preaching was simple and guileless, without religiosity or false moralizing" (Ignatius, "Canon Martin").

2. Dunnan, *From the Pulpit*, 1:8.

Dunnan surely had some thoughts of becoming an Oxford don or an Ivy League professor or a cardinal rector or a bishop. And Dunnan speaks to these early ambitions.

> I had been happy at Oxford and comfortable as a college chaplain. Saint James was my chance to do something brave. I was impressed with the kids from the start, and I'll never forget the way one student asked me if I would even *want* to come and be headmaster at Saint James. That impressed me deeply . . . Quite simply, I felt called.[3]

Priest and Headmaster

Every now and then it is remarked that Father Dunnan is "a priest first and a headmaster second." While the headmaster heartily agrees that his duty to the church as a priest is a God-given command, he is quick to point out that the gifts and skills of a priest make him an even better head of school than would be the case otherwise. The most effective heads are neither Wall Street managers nor college professors. They are good shepherds of the flock, and a dedicated priest will naturally be a dedicated shepherd of the school flock. In fact, the good shepherd "lays down his life for the sheep." It is the hireling who shirks the duties of the shepherd.[4] This is one of the most important reasons for Father Dunnan's success as a head: his deep commitment to the standards and concerns of the ministerial priesthood.

Father Dunnan does not want the school to get too large because, in his philosophy, a great school is a fold wherein the shepherd really knows his sheep. Likewise, the ever-widening network of Saint James supporters has been solidified in part by Father's pastoral work among all constituencies. We should never be tempted to think that the performance of baptisms, weddings, funerals, and anniversary speeches, are incidental to the advancement of Saint James School over the last twenty-six years.

If the combination of priest *and* headmaster is rare in the United States today, it was not always so.[5] For centuries most of the great schools on both sides of the Atlantic were founded and run by priests of the

---

3. Dunnan, Tape-recorded conversation with the editor, September 3, 2016.

4. John 10:11–13.

5. In a most influential study, Rob Evans insists that the most effective school leaders must have some of the qualities of successful parish clergy. See Evans, *School Change*.

church. A survey of the history of boarding schools over the last several hundred years, and especially the really good ones, would establish that most of the schools were directed by a clergyman. In the United States, the fact applies to not only Saint James and the schools founded from Saint James—for instance, St. Paul's, Concord; Racine College in Wisconsin; and St. Mark's, Southborough—but to Groton, St. George's, Kent, and many others.[6]

The reason for priest-headmasters is not hard to find. If the ultimate aim of a school is deeper and higher than selective college admission or skills development for the working world, then the person at the top of the school must know what is actually required to attain the ultimate purpose. Not every talented educator knows what it takes to educate the *inner* person, which has been the objective of the traditional liberal education of Western civilization.[7] Moreover, teenage boys have a mystical side they seldom show and never discuss.[8] Adolescents aspire to more and higher things than we give them credit for, and the priest-headmaster ought to be and usually is better attuned to these hidden aspirations and can help a young man or woman own his or her spiritual nature. Though this fact of the deeper idealism of teenagers is seldom mentioned when persons converse about Father Dunnan as a headmaster, it is a central feature of his success in the role. Dunnan is a priest to his bones and God is not far away as he does his work and makes his rounds. If it is appropriate, a

---

6. There is even the case of Roxbury Latin School, where the late Reverend Dr. F. Washington Jarvis, an Episcopal priest of the Anglo-Catholic discipline, presided as Headmaster for thirty-two years. He was a priest in that non-sectarian school every day and all day, wearing his clerical habit and praying for and with the boys and masters.

7. In this chapter and certainly in Father Dunnan's perspective, "liberal education" is synonymous with the *comprehensive* education, the type of schooling designed to educate *every* part of human nature and not just the mind or the body.

8. When he was headmaster of Repton from 1910 to 1914, Archbishop William Temple (1881–1944) discovered that the religious, even mystical, side of boys is very real, though boys dare not show it to each other. Temple was educated by his father at Rugby School at a time when Rugby Chapel was still the center of campus life. While the younger Temple was quite the athlete, we know that he was developing a profound spirituality. He proceeded to Balliol College, Oxford, where the Master, Edward Caird (1835–1908), was an important mentor. Temple was Archbishop of Canterbury from 1942 to his untimely death in 1944. His volume of *Repton School Sermons* (1913) shows that Temple knew boys very well indeed. Temple's biography of Bishop John Percival (1834–18), the founding headmaster of Clifton College (1862) and later headmaster of Rugby (1887–95), abounds in headmasterly wisdom Father Dunnan also possesses.

student or a teacher might even hear a solid Christian doctrine set forth in a manner which resists gainsaying.

Dunnan's religion is convincing. He is a sincere and orthodox Christian believer who subscribes to the theology of the Creed and practices his faith without ostentation. And there is nothing precarious about Father Dunnan's religion. The Gospel is true. Jesus Christ is the Son of God and the model of school ideals. The church is Christ's body. The school is that body in its scholastic mode. The body has many different sorts of members and parts. It is our duty to give ourselves to Christ in worship. We must serve him with alacrity in all that we do and say. Hence religion is by no means a private affair for Father Dunnan; far from it. "In our secularized modern culture, religion must always be private and therefore invisible, and religious difference can only be controversial and awkward, and therefore must be avoided."[9] But Father Dunnan will not avoid religion and was determined from the beginning that Saint James will not reflect modern culture in this negligent way.

As mentioned above, in Father Dunnan's mind, the school *is* the church in its scholastic function; so the church is central to Dunnan's philosophy of education. The church is the body mystical of Christ. The benefits of membership in that body are infinite. Here are lines Dunnan preached in Oxford only a few months before his appointment as Headmaster of Saint James:

> The things of the Church are holy: her order, her discipline, her sacraments, her teaching, her wisdom—these are all things which have come to us in our generation from the generations which have gone before us, not as curiosities to be studied and observed, or as antiquities to be catalogued and forgotten, but as priceless treasures of the Faith, great gifts of Grace, precious vehicles for holiness.[10]

Dunnan urged in the same sermon that, "if you say your prayers, then others will join you; if you attend to the love of God in His sacraments, then the love of God will keep, strengthen, and sustain you." Stuart Dunnan has had a profound influence on the religion of many generations of Jacobites.

---

9. Dunnan, *From the Pulpit*, 2:157 (from a Holy Week homily at Roxbury Latin School, Massachusetts, in 2007).

10. Dunnan, "Sermon Preached at the Pusey House," 1992.

The headmaster was confirmed in the Episcopal Church when he was in the first form at St. Albans. His father Weaver Dunnan was a Presbyterian from the Midwest. His mother Diana is from a long line of New Jersey Methodists. But, her family attended St. Peter's-by-the-Sea in Cape Neddick, Maine. St. Peter's people had a marked influence on Stuart Dunnan, and all of the summer vicars of St. Peter's became good friends of the family.[11]

Dunnan was most influenced religiously by the clergy of St. Albans. And it must be noted that eight years in the National Cathedral Choir was going to have a profound influence on an intelligent boy. Practicing three hours a day, Dunnan rehearsed the great doctrines of the church as set to the most beautiful music in the world.[12] Becoming an Episcopalian when he came of age was only natural for Dunnan. It is not surprising that increased experience with the Episcopal Church and Anglican

---

11. Diana Baldwin Dunnan (born 1930) grew up in South Orange, NJ, and has spent much time in Maine and South Carolina. She is the daughter of Donald and Winifred Baldwin. Father Dunnan's great-grandfather Arthur Baldwin (1864–1939) and brother Leonard (1861–1933), partners in the practice of the law and many other concerns, established and endowed the liberal arts college at Drew Seminary in Madison, NJ. The institution became Drew University when the "Brothers College" was created. A Baldwin or Baldwin descendant has served the Drew University Board of Trustees ever since. From 1997, Father Dunnan has carried on the family tradition at Drew. The Baldwin brothers were definitely entrepreneurial. They used their shipping network to import reindeer to the Klondike to feed the miners. Finding the country club wait-list (for Yankees) tedious in Charleston, they bought Yeamans Hall, a plantation established by the colonial governor of that name in 1674, and created one of the best golf courses in the world. Observing Father Dunnan's approach to life, we see the Baldwin "can-do" ethic descended. From his father, the Headmaster learned how to make the very careful, air-tight case before any big decision or change is made at Saint James. Mr. Weaver W. Dunnan (1923–2010) was an eminent Washington attorney. His third son believes he was one of the most brilliant minds he's ever known. Weaver Dunnan was editor of the Harvard Law Review then clerked for Learned Hand and Felix Frankfurter. Judge Hand introduced Weaver Dunnan to the Episcopal Church. Dunnan possessed the goods to achieve in the law what he did achieve. Weaver Dunnan's four-greats grandfather was the Reverend John McMillan (1752–1833), a leader of the Scots-Irish in western Pennsylvania and founder of Washington and Jefferson College (1781), among several other academic initiatives in which he was involved. Father Dunnan's siblings are Bruce Baldwin Dunnan, Douglas Morgan Dunnan, Winifred Dunnan Faust, and John McMillan Dunnan. Father Dunnan has twelve nieces and nephews.

12. Dunnan was one of only two choristers asked to remain in the choir after his voice changed. The other was Drew Minter who became a famous counter-tenor.

Christianity generally led him to a further refinement of his religious practice: Anglo-Catholicism.[13]

Dunnan does not believe in "Christianity and water."[14] Christianity is about being a true disciple of Jesus Christ. In his first year as head, Dunnan said to the parishioners of St. John's Church, Olney, Maryland, that Americans must resist the pressure to make Christianity a private choice and thus reduce it to a commodity. In such a situation, "each of us is left to pick our faith much as we might pick a dandruff shampoo . . . If we insist upon approaching the Faith as a commodity, we will never be real Christians; we will only be users, not followers, of the Gospel."[15] The headmaster was and is determined that, at Saint James, there will be no wink-and-grin approach to the Christian religion.

To "love one another" is the crucial ethic of Saint James School. As for the evangelism which a headmaster might do in a school, the Spirit listeth where it will. Dunnan's approach is to "preach the Gospel always; use words if necessary."[16] What matters is to live the life. If and when the headmaster perceives that God has planted the seed in a student or a teacher, he is prepared to act with dispatch and with the most solicitous pastoral care and intelligent mentoring. This approach works very well at Saint James.

Another reason Father Dunnan has been effective as a school administrator and leader of the faculty is that transcendence and idealism are natural for ordained persons and good for schools. A colleague asks if a weakness of a clergy headmaster is the tendency to "retain a student longer than some of the rest of us recommend." But this colleague

---

13. It may be said with accuracy that Anglo-Catholicism was one of the great attractive energies in worldwide Anglican Christianity from the time of the Oxford Movement (1833–45) through the *Prayer Book* revisions of the 1970s. The Anglo-Catholics certainly met their match in the growing Evangelical, Charismatic, and Liberal-Revisionist parties emergent in the Episcopal Church after 1960. In the 1970s, a fault-line developed between Anglo-Catholics dedicated to the traditional liturgy (more or less Tridentine) and those leading "Rite II" reforms reflecting the Second Vatican Council in the Roman Catholic Church. As an organized movement within the Church of England and Episcopal Church, we might use the 1979 *Book of Common Prayer* to mark the high-tide of Anglo-Catholicism in the United States. In fact, the publication of that resource symbolized the victory of not a few of the principles of the church revival in Anglicanism. But, for most Anglo-Catholics, things began to change quickly thereafter.

14. Lewis, *Mere Christianity*, 26.

15. Dunnan, *From the Pulpit*, 1:9.

16. A saying attributed to St. Francis of Assisi.

answers his own question by remarking that Father Dunnan "believes in the student and wants to make it work."[17]

Chapel life at the school is reasonable, inviting, and Anglo-Catholic without the baroque.[18] The student Sacristans set the tone, take great pride in and are appreciated for their service. One senior Sacristan remembers that Father Dunnan never scolded the Sacristans for a mistake or misstep but was adamant that their daily leadership be a solemn duty and honor. "Solemn" denotes sober and serious but neither sad nor somber. The chapel preaching is always of a high standard, whether it is the headmaster or the chaplain doing it. Father does not long endure a chaplain who cannot deliver effectively in the pulpit, and a poor guest preacher will have been invited once. The headmaster is keen that the students will hear good, practical, and thoughtful sermons and homilies.

Stuart Dunnan's own preaching is the best example of his ideal. His sermons in the chapel are Christ-centered, seasonally apt, and relevant to the members of the community. The current senior master notes that the sermons "meet a crisis or are appropriate for the time and place . . . Some of his best sermons are lost forever, because they were written on a scratch of paper and are hidden in a Prayer Book somewhere in the Chapel."[19]

Not only in the pulpit but in any venue Father Dunnan sells Saint James with great skill and convincing earnestness. Dunnan's effectiveness in attracting persons to the mission goes much deeper than mere boosterism. A former chaplain notes that the secret is Dunnan's "willingness to be present and open and vulnerable in the midst of the community, to share the love he has with those he wishes to share in that love."[20] When the two were considering a tense situation with some wayward students who were separated from the school, Dunnan told this former chaplain, "If it ever comes up, tell them how much I love them."

Dunnan has a way with parents. His winsome, attractive manner cannot be taught. It is a gift from above, and Dunnan acknowledges that being able to give it is also from above. When he is introducing Saint

---

17. Theodore Camp (Senior Master and History Department Chairman, Saint James School, St. James, Maryland). Tape-recorded by the editor on August 9, 2017.

18. If there is another self-identifying Anglo-Catholic boarding or Episcopal school in the United States, the writer is unaware of it.

19. Theodore Camp (Senior Master and History Department Chairman, Saint James School, St. James, Maryland). Tape-recorded by the editor on August 9, 2017.

20. Arthur A. Callaham, the Reverend Canon (Vicar of Christ Church Cathedral, Houston, Texas). Note to the editor.

James to new parents, he has them eating out of the palm of his hand in five minutes. What explains this? For one thing, he understands that his students typically arrive in the second and third forms when they are still "children" journeying into adulthood. He also says routinely, "Saint James is filled with children whose parents want them at home, not in boarding school." Mothers who wonder why in the world they are permitting their children to go away to school love this remark. Parents know that Father Dunnan understands childhood and will celebrate and protect it with his life's blood. The headmaster also knows that the parents who choose Saint James want their sons and daughters to grow up while spending their days around other nice teenagers. When push comes to shove, the headmaster wants the nice boy or girl over the star athlete or impressive test-taker. Darn it all if Saint James is not filled with teenagers who are at once nice kids, star athletes, and academically impressive. If the headmaster has the impression that a prospect is too self-absorbed to give him- or herself to the demanding and robust community life of the school, where all have daily and weekly duties, the parents are not encouraged to enroll the student. Dunnan knows without any doubt what all great headmasters know: that the student with deficits and lots of growing up to do can be matured only if the majority of the school community is strong, sound, and eagerly pursuing the school's ideals.

Knowing he has the trust of most parents, the headmaster will ask them hard questions and challenge them. Just a bit over a month after the destruction of the World Trade Center in 2001, Dunnan offered a sermon to Saint James parents that reminded them why they have their sons and daughters at Fountain Rock.

> Times of challenge and of hardship require moral absolutes. Let me state a few: It is good to offer oneself, even one's own life, to help or indeed save another. It is good to defend the weak, to serve justice, and to preserve peace. To save oneself at the expense of another, or worse, to refuse to suffer hardship at the expense of another, is morally weak and cowardly. To hate for any reason, to be animated by hate, lost to hate, to seek revenge or to wish to brutalize because of hate can only be understood as evil.[21]

It is central to the headmaster's philosophy that teenagers belong to God and not to their parents alone. God has a plan for each. Parents are

---

21. Dunnan, *From the Pulpit*, 1:160.

the loving and wise guardians of young persons who must be prepared for the purposes of their creator.

> For what good are we for Christ if we remain hidden, fearful, and selfish, in our homes, driving our cars from known place to known place, guarding ourselves from strangers? And what good are our children if we protect them from a world which could harm them? Yes, it could harm them; in fact, it will harm them, but it will challenge them too. It will challenge them to grow up, and thus to grow into their remarkable promise as God's children and not just ours, as brothers and sisters of Christ. Surely this is the work of the Church's schools, the work of Saint James as much today—maybe more today—than it was 165 years ago: just to get the process started, to be a place for young people of promise where they can take that brave first step into the darkness, that step into the world and into new company to learn for themselves who they are and what it is that God wants them to do.[22]

One former Chaplain remembers a favorite quip of Father Dunnan's: "Parents need to quit raising little Buddhas." Dunnan "means we cannot raise healthy adults if they continue to believe the lie that they are the center of the universe. Adam and Eve tried that and got kicked off the team."[23] The same former colleague notes that Father Dunnan makes sure that Saint James "plugs into an abiding, pressing need of all teenagers: ritual." Ordained headmasters know about ritual, and they know that the people most likely to threaten a mutiny if you change their rituals and traditions, are the teenaged students.

> Every parent knows that, while their adolescent children rail against routine, they actually crave it. Due to its historic and unapologetic Benedictine regimen, Saint James offers high-school students what they crave, whether they are remotely religious or not.[24]

Father Dunnan is quick to praise the extraordinary group of chaplains who have served Saint James during his headship. In the transition

---

22. Dunnan, Sermon for Evensong, St. Luke's Episcopal Church, San Antonio, Texas, March 2007.

23. Gahan, W. Patrick, III, the Reverend Dr. (Rector of Christ Church, San Antonio, Texas). Note to the editor.

24. Gahan, W. Patrick, III, the Reverend Dr. (Rector of Christ Church, San Antonio, Texas). Note to the editor.

from Father Owens to Father Baker, the Reverend John Merchant served as both chaplain and assistant headmaster and kept the Anglo-Catholic tradition and practice alive at Saint James in enlightened ways. Since upon his arrival Dunnan restored both daily chapel and the Sunday Eucharist, the role of school chaplain became suddenly more crucial. Father Jim Sprague was a very popular and enthusiastic chaplain, then Fathers Callaham, Gahan, FitzGerald, Sam Keyes, and Brandt Montgomery have been especially strong chaplains. One brilliant theologue who served Saint James as a kind of chaplain even as a layman was Mark Michael, who has since been ordained to the priesthood. Senior Master Chick Meehan was always a good churchman, and Jennifer Sherman and Ted Camp are strong leaders of the established religious life of the school.

When you watch Father Dunnan in action, for instance as he makes his rounds late at night with Charlie, his cairn terrier, you see that this is a father addressing and looking after his children. Hence, Father Dunnan is actually more than a "good shepherd." He is a loving father. As we observe his work and assess the performance of this very successful head of school, we may well ask what it is about our modern or post-modern culture—what fear, what compulsion?—turns father and motherly heads-of-school into executive directors of corporations? So much do we expect the latter that the former looks strange to us. The good news is that Saint James School is getting the real thing.

Diversity

Diversity is not the very purpose of a church school; but, diversity is indisputable evidence that an institution is part of the one, holy, catholic, and apostolic church, wherein social catholicity characterizes that school. This is because the catholic church in the real world is filled with many different sorts of human beings. Mere pluralism in a community should not be confused with social catholicity or diversity. Throwing disparate peoples and cultures together in a large school where each people and culture is allowed to go on with its own business without much regard for other groups does not create the desired social catholicity or diversity a church school should manifest. "Our diversity," remarks the headmaster, "has happened naturally. The church identity has been a great reason for our diversity. Anglicans from Africa and Muslims from Washington

County like our faith-based approach to community, education, and morality."[25]

In 2002, when Stuart Dunnan had been Headmaster of Saint James for almost ten years, he addressed the alumni in chapel.

> This then is what God requires of us, all of us, Christian, Jew, Muslim, Buddhist, Hindu, Catholic, Protestant, European, African, American, black, brown, white, rich, poor, northern, southern, city, country, however we can be different. We must lose our labels to live in love as friends, and this we must do, for we are, all of us, branches of the same vine, rooted in the same soil, and called to bear the same good fruit, reflecting the good purpose of the Creator of us all.[26]

In a scholastic world struggling to be at once faithful and welcoming of the teeming diversity of our age, Saint James School has achieved to an impressive extent the social catholicity of the worldwide church. The crucial step toward this happy (instead of tense) diversity is a leader at the top who possesses deep and confident faith that the Gospel is true, that the church is indestructible, and that Christians need not fear the other. A second requirement is that the school must not be so large that particular groups can avoid the wider fellowship. When diverse cultures and peoples are thrown together in a smallish scholastic community requiring full participation through the course of the academic session, the wide world of the twenty-first century becomes more intimate. Citizens begin to communicate on a deep level and greater understanding and sympathy develop. Bona fide friendships are created.

Father Dunnan could double the size of Saint James in a few days by admitting all the international students who wish to come. He believes the level of international students should be roughly twenty-five percent and no more. In this way, both the foreign students and their native fellows gain the full benefits of their association. They become friends instead of discrete nations keeping their distance and pretending to be united. This policy is part and parcel of the painstaking attention to maintaining the rich communitarian experience of the school. The international students are both blessed and a wonderful blessing in this scenario. They are truly integrated into the fellowship. They feel the liberty and the confidence to be themselves. The world is diverse, and

---

25. Private conversation with the editor, September 2018.
26. Dunnan, *From the Pulpit*, 1:170–71.

the school is diverse. This makes the students grow. Race, socio-economic power, religious and ethnic differences: They are secondary facts at Saint James School, where the reality of the world is modeled every day. The headmaster is aware that there is still room for improvement in this important feature of a great school; however, Dunnan believes that "we have shown that the commitment to diversity and the Church's identity can go together."

Understanding Teenagers

Father Dunnan's college roommate, also an Episcopal priest, once told Dunnan that he was "nuts" to spend his life with teenagers.[27] But the headmaster knows he has a knack for such work, and the gift is very rare. Since Father is good at many things, it is easy to overlook his foundational gift of being able to work effectively with adolescents. To help young persons combat selfishness and develop into adults who can do good in the world is Stuart Dunnan's life's work. Dunnan speaks of "the magical transformation" of teenagers which makes them fun to watch and even fun to be with. The interesting change has to do with "their transition from being recipients of love to being agents of love."[28]

In pondering the reasons for Father Dunnan's success, we must first consider his traditional approach. While he realizes that the surrounding culture can keep teenagers from maturing properly, he does not believe that they should grow up too fast. Human beings are not hothouse plants which can be finessed into mature and early-producing organisms in response to market demand. Time, patience, and painstaking carefulness are required to do it the right way. In a famous article of 2003, Dunnan articulated his strong disagreement with the tendency of most boarding schools in America to prematurely offer the liberties and enticements of higher education. Today's parents too easily accept the lack of authentic community in our schools. The antidote to the widespread loss of nurturing scholastic fellowship in America is to resist it instead of accepting it as inevitable. This is how Saint James is a truly countercultural community: Bona fide scholastic fellowship is believed in and maintained at all costs.[29]

---

27. Dunnan, *From the Pulpit*, 1:115 (the 1999 Baccalaureate Sermon at Washington and Jefferson College).

28. Dunnan, *From the Pulpit*, 1:115.

29. Dunnan, *From the Pulpit*, 2:38–40 ("The Ozymandias Syndrome").

The "arms race" among boarding schools which means raising millions of dollars to add facilities and buildings in order to make boarding schools more like colleges ruins the engendering community life adolescents need. We may well ask to what extent this frenetic campus building makes the conditions for the scandalous boarding-school behaviors and adult misconduct now revealed by the national media?

Many parents today are quite okay with the peer-driven culture by which their children are pushed along, and the electronic media enabling it, because they don't want their children to be left behind. But the purpose of secondary education is to *prepare* children for college rather than to be college already.

Dunnan's skill as a headmaster can be seen in many different episodes of his headship. The following remark betrays one of his secrets. "One of my favorite strategies as a headmaster is to listen to the aggrieved parents' opening diatribe and to find some aspect of what they are saying with which I can agree. 'You know, you are right; we should have informed you earlier,' or 'the teacher should not have said what he said so bluntly, but your child does have this problem, and we would like to help.'"[30]

A Mission to Advance

Since taking over as rector and headmaster in 1992, Stuart Dunnan and the trustees have raised almost $75 million and added seventy-five thousand square feet of new or renovated space. The fundraising, plant improvements, increasing endowment, and new square footage have not come at the expense of generous financial aid and scholarships. Tuition grants have steadily grown since 1993 both in the total budgeted amount and the size of individual grants. John Mattingly, '58, Vice-Chairman of the Trustees for some years, disclosed recently that there is a riddle associated with Father Dunnan. "How do you know when Father Dunnan is beginning a new capital campaign?" The correct answer is: "Because another capital campaign is just ending."

When Stuart Dunnan took over the school, budgeted enrollment was 145 students but only 112 students matriculated. The budget was only $1.7 million. It is $12.5 million now. The headmaster remembers with a particular vividness what he found upon arrival.

---

30. Dunnan, *From the Pulpit*, 2:68 (Sermon at the Cathedral Church of SS. Luke and Paul, Charleston, SC).

The budget was very small. The endowment was somewhere between three and four million. We had a debt of five hundred thousand on the field house, that had never been paid, and we had a projected deficit in our operating budget of about four hundred fifty thousand. We had tremendous deferred maintenance. The top of Laidlaw Infirmary was unusable. Kemp Hall had snakes in the ceilings. None of the buildings had screens or air-conditioning. Claggett had furniture bought, I think, in the sixties. It looked really, really run down—the whole campus . . . The School was horribly disproportionate just to look at. There was this huge gym, and no library to speak of. But the Chapel was beautiful. Father Owens had built the Chapel and Powell Hall. Charles Nes was the architect, and they were and are beautiful Georgian buildings.[31]

Dunnan's first project "to show evidence of life" was the renovation of Cotton Gymnasium into the fine and performing arts center. In a much appreciated article published in a national journal in the 1990s, Dunnan wrote, "Beware of the grand and glorious campus. The consequence of such benefaction may destroy the boarding school society you remember with such gratitude."[32] The headmaster has been very thoughtful, even circumspect about campus expansion. He has always avoided what he calls "the arms race" in boarding school building projects, each one giving the anxious school more to take care of and, more importantly, distract students from their common life. "When the fine arts center and athletic centers are completed," he said to the trustees in June 2018, "we will be competitive without being over-built."

When Father Dunnan arrived, the annual fund goal was $40,000. He decided to set a good example by pledging the whole amount himself and asking the Board of Trustees to match his pledge. The plan worked. Not only trustees but parents were inspired and the school raised $150,000 that first year. Dunnan sets the pace every year with his own personal financial commitment and many other forms of giving.

Adna and Barbara Fulton and John and Peggy Waltersdorf stepped forward immediately with generous giving that primed the pump. In Dunnan's first summer, he got word while in Maine that John Ferguson left a charitable remainder trust of $2.2 million for an endowment to improve faculty salaries. It was a great windfall for the young school head who was

---

31. Dunnan, Tape-recording with the editor, September 2016.
32. Dunnan, *From the Pulpit*, 2:38–49.

about to make significant changes and shake things up. He was able to raise salaries immediately and significantly. Dick McCleary, a builder who lived across the road at Bai Yuka house, was very generous to the school. Jeremy Biggs, who became President of the Trustees when Admiral Holloway retired, was determined to be generous from the very beginning. John Mattingly, an alumnus and trustee, supported every campaign with a leadership gift. Mattingly ensured that Mattingly Hall became a reality. Bob Lee was an effective fund-raiser in the early days of Dunnan's headship, and generous local support of the school has increased continuously since 1994. Key donors such as Jim and Toni Turner and Geoff and Anne Kline Pohanka were inspired by the commitment and generosity of the early donors. Steady generosity has come from Dona and Roland Young, Stuart Teach, and Ann and John Davis, who are past parents, and from alumni such as Henry Davenport and Mayo Boddie. Many alumni and friends have been eager to share their resources with the school.

Several years into Dunnan's tenure, the first capital campaign of $5 million was much easier to complete than expected. It brought about the Quadrangle, which was the first renovation of Kemp, the Owens Library, and Coors Hall. Dunnan felt strongly that more had to be done to attract new students to the School. Practically on the tails of the Quadrangle project, the second initiative was to borrow $5 million in bonds to build a second girls' dorm, named to honor Admiral Holloway and in memory of his son James L. Holloway IV, Class of 1963. The new Kerfoot Refectory, the tennis courts, and the fitness center were built at this time. About the same time, $2 million was raised for the endowment, bringing it to $10 million. Meanwhile, "we were ratcheting up the annual fund." Today, the permanent endowment is $25 million and the Annual Fund is over a million dollars a year. The third capital campaign raised almost $25 million. The Fulton Building was added to the Powell Building, and the old part of the latter was renovated. This work greatly increased the academic space. Dunnan has steadily guaranteed that all built spaces on the campus are in good taste and have small adornments to finish them off. Colorful Persian rugs in the academic halls, beautiful appointments in the chapel, and fine furniture in the offices of Claggett subliminally remind every member of the school and visitors that the institution is aiming high.

From the beginning, Father Dunnan has wanted to deliver to the trustees not only a balanced budget but a surplus. This admirable goal has been met in twenty-five of his twenty-six years. Business managers will often effect a "pessimistic" budget in order to ensure that it is balanced. This is common practice in the interest of caution, but such a practice means that the extra money is not made available in the current year budget to advance the mission of the school in a given fiscal year. With the help of his long-serving business manager Bill Wivell, Father Dunnan has been able to establish a substantial cash reserve, which protects the school in hard times and finances unexpected expenses. There is currently an annual "give" of several hundred thousand dollars. With such "little" surpluses, Dunnan has each year been able to accomplish a great many projects such as replacing the roofs, refurbishing dorm rooms, purchasing new furniture, and enhancing the quality of appointments and details throughout the plant, campus, and facilities. Of great strategic importance has been the purchase of 400 additional acres of land, which gives the school a permanent buffer against the numerous residential development projects in the area.

And yet Dunnan does not believe he is a particularly successful fundraiser. He has done his duty but does not seem to be aware how successful a fundraiser he is. He is proud of what the generous support of patrons has made possible at Fountain Rock. Like Father Owens before him, Father Dunnan assumes that good people will give. "I may not be aggressive enough," says the headmaster. He notes that there were potential major donors who did not give because their children were dismissed from the school. Never shirking his responsibility to the students, Dunnan learned quickly that the advancement of an institution is a multi-layered phenomenon. He makes the tough decisions precisely because he is thinking of the advancement of the school in the long run instead of the short. "I think I let some people off the hook, in the way that a more secular head, who is not also their priest, would not . . . If I were the sort of head who keeps the kid in the school then goes back for the third ask, or who takes that gift as a sort of bribe, I think I could have raised another twenty to twenty-five million by now. But I can't do that. And Saint James isn't like that."[33]

---

33. Dunnan, Tape-recording with the editor, September 2016.

Taking Command

When Dunnan arrived in 1992, he faced as a young, first-time head a divided faculty and staff. He would approach four discernible groups with his new plans for the school.

> There were the frustrated reformers who saw the potential of a small school with a caring culture, and they were all relatively new. Then there were the loyalists—Chick Meehan, Dave Barr, Eddie Hoyer, and a few others. They loved Saint James School and wanted to save it but they needed a plan. I brought these two groups together. The other two groups were the prima-donnas and the slackers. I didn't renew the slackers and the prima-donnas quit. The big factor in bringing the loyalists and the reformers together was when we gave Dave Barr a sabbatical year and then he retired after that. It was a great way to honor him. He was just an extraordinary man.
>
> In 1992, the School was not diverse. There were perhaps four or five African American students, one or two boys from China, and a local Indo-Asian boy. The School was very white, very male, very Southern. There was a real hazing problem that I had to address and I threw several students out. At the most, there were twenty girls. Boarding for girls had only just recently begun with one floor in Hershey (now Mattingly) Hall.[34]

Dunnan recounts that he began to feel he had command of the ship after the third year. He began to feel his strengths. From his fourth year, momentum only increased. He also began to see that the culture of the School had improved; that being small was a virtue and not a weakness. He came to realize an all-important principle of Saint James: Fulfillment of the mission demands a smaller school.

Many things had been accomplished as year four began. A key to the good working of the school was the reform of the prefects. When the command was handed over to Dunnan, the prefects had keys to every boy's room. This ended quickly. He also got rid of scary teachers. "I did not want lazy teachers. I did not want any sort of culture of hazing." "Walter Bergen, who was the Headmaster of Mercersburg, gave me very good advice. He said, 'Clean house, but do it now.' He said that he had failed to do it at Mercersburg and he always regretted it, because the [recalcitrant faculty] subverted him from then on. Bob Hallett who was the head of St. Paul's, Brooklandville, told me the same thing."

---

34. Dunnan, Tape-recording with the editor, September 2016.

Father Owens came out to Alumni Weekend in Dunnan's first year and told his boys to support Dunnan, and they did. Al Watson and Ted Eagles helped. A great good fortune for Dunnan was that the board chair, Admiral James Holloway, '39, mentored him in the ways and means of command.[35] "He was very direct, very take charge, and a real father figure to me," says Dunnan. "He knew that we needed to make tough decisions, and he was very comfortable with that . . . I worried what he, a navy man, would think about my crackdown on hazing, but he backed me. He hated it."

Dunnan restored daily chapel, enforced the rules, honored hardworking faculty, and protected younger faculty from taking on too much. He shut down the weekend parties because they were distracting and endangering the students. Early in the 1994–95 session, Dunnan made a decision that nearly broke him. He shut down the annual bonfire. It appears that this tradition had become an excuse for drinking and smoking, marijuana included. The headmaster remembers, "I had to fire most of the prefects and then write a letter to the parents apologizing for my own mistakes in the episode. That was a tough year. It made me wonder if I was too young to do this job."[36] Several years later, Dunnan banned cars. "As a consequence, we've never lost a student."[37]

Dunnan's third year was as tough as years one and two, but the faculty as a whole were now enforcing the rules. The transition was occurring but not without pain to those—masters no less than students—who had come in under a different regimen. Some parents too were concerned that the headmaster was removing all the fun. Dunnan saw that Chick Meehan, the interim headmaster for the 1991–92 session, was devoted to the school and had great influence in the faculty. Meehan was the athletic director, an alumnus, and a beloved long-time teacher and coach. He was a great "school man" upon whom Dunnan could implicitly rely. He also

---

35. The reader may find on the world wide web great quantities of information about Admiral James L. Holloway III, one of the most distinguished of twentieth-century naval officers, who died in his ninety-seventh year in 2019. Born in 1922 in Charleston, SC, Holloway hailed from a Navy family, and his father also attained the rank of admiral. The younger Holloway was an aviator and ended his career serving the United States as Chief of Naval Operations. A champion wrestler at Saint James, and never pinned while a Midshipman in Annapolis, Holloway's military career is the stuff of legend. He was firmly committed to his alma mater and served as President of the Board of Trustees for some years.

36. Dunnan, Tape-recording with the editor, September 2016.

37. Dunnan, Tape-recording with the editor, September 2016.

relied on Sandra Pollock, whom he made academic dean to help him reform the curriculum and strengthen the faculty. Chris Hughes (now of Garrison Forest School) had a real impact as a young but gifted college counselor and dean of students.

Coeducation is important to Dunnan. He has built both of the girls dorms and encouraged the growth of girls' athletics. When he promoted Sandra Pollock to the post of academic dean, she was the only woman on the faculty. In Dunnan's tenth year, Pollock was made assistant head of school. "With Sandra it was a partnership," says Dunnan. "It was great for the school."

"After the third year," Dunnan reflects, "I believe it was generally accepted that I was not ruining the school. Enrollment was growing. The SAT scores and college placement had improved. Families began to look upon us as a real choice among boarding schools. Of course, we still had a lot of work to do. But we were going in the right direction."[38]

Because of his lifelong commitment to the fine and performing arts, Dunnan has surprised some patrons of the school with his strong advocacy of athletics. But this is not out of character, since Dunnan's objective is to ensure that Saint James is a school where students grow in every aspect of human nature. Most of the beautiful playing fields on the campus have come or were improved since 1992. These years have seen many team champions in girls' and boys' sports. The varsity basketball team became dominant in the entire region, and half a dozen Jacobites now play Division I basketball. An uncommonly large number of Saint James athletes have gone on to play sports in elite liberal-arts colleges such as Davidson, Sewanee, and Kenyon.

These improvements were achieved while the fine and performing arts were equally nurtured. Dunnan has ensured that Saint James has two dance studios, a working auditorium, stage and backstage apparatus, music rooms, and studio arts spaces. The Pohanka Fine Arts Center is the *coup de gras* of an intentional plan going back to Dunnan's early years at Fountain Rock.

---

38. The SAT mean has increased by three hundred points (old calculation) since 1995. In the spring of his third year, Father Dunnan was approached by one of the most illustrious of American schools to enter the search process for head of school. He prayed about it and gave it serious thought. "It was very tempting!" he remembers. But he never sent credentials and has not done so for any search since. He finds "running" for jobs distasteful.

If he has ensured that splendid athletic facilities—including two weather-turf fields—have been built, Father Dunnan is equally committed to building state-of-the-art facilities for the studio and performing arts.[39] The Pohanka Fine & Performing Arts Center was finished in 2020. The Turner Athletic Center will complete a master plan giving Saint James School every facility it needs to fulfill its mission into the future. The headmaster, faculty, and staff of Saint James are committed to the two-sport requirement. The reason for the requirement is moral and spiritual, even if it contradicts the American trend of specialization in sports and everything else. "Students develop character by doing what they are *not* good at," comments Dunnan. "They should strive and grow in those areas in which they are not particularly gifted."[40]

Chick Meehan, Marty Collin, and Sandra Pollock all retired with the highest praise in June 2017. Their contribution to the school and to the lives of generations of Jacobites is immense. Collin was a brilliant English teacher and the backbone of the performing arts program. "St. George and the Dragon" became a coveted tradition under his direction, he enhanced the annual Mummers frivolity, and he directed other successful dramatic events. In 2017, Dunnan began to realize that the group known to students as "the Old Guard" was really the *new* guard he hired: Even with the retirements of the Great Trio of Meehan, Pollock, and Collin, a worthy corps of committed senior faculty remain: Beth Flowers is a superlative teacher and successfully runs Holloway Hall. Jennifer Sherman continues to teach Spanish while serving as dean of faculty. Ted Camp succeeded Mr. Meehan as senior master. Marc Batson is assistant head of school for academics. Karl Yergey has significant seniority and remains a beloved history teacher, coach, and mentor. These now long-serving persons have almost two hundred years combined tenure at Saint James School.

Before passing to the closing section of this chapter, we must remark on the headmaster's "style" as an executive director of a complex organization. It cannot be doubted that Father Dunnan has been strong and not weak. He has faced enormous challenges since becoming the skipper in 1992. In the beginning, he faced limited financial resources, a complicated staff situation, unreasonable parent expectations, and students who preferred to do things their way. In the face of these challenges, Father

---

39. A four-lane rubber track and a new baseball field and stadium have also been built since 1992.

40. Dunnan, Private conversation with the editor, September 2018.

Dunnan was more than willing to take charge of the school. He has always assumed and still assumes that the head of school must have full authority to cultivate the mission ideals and pursue the strategic goals established by the trustees. Dunnan believes that strong authority at the top is a *sine qua non* of any great institution fulfilling its purpose. Every now and then a person concerned with the school—perhaps a parent or an alumnus—will suggest that Father Dunnan assumes *too much* control of Saint James. There are parents in every generation who believe that the students are not given enough liberty; that the cell-phone and social media policies are too rigid; that the curfews are too early for older students; and that the headmaster has been too unbending when he has decided to expel a student.

Given these questions, it is noteworthy that the headmaster recently said that "perhaps I have been too forgiving at times and in some cases could have acted more quickly for the sake of the School as a whole."[41] Dunnan is hopeful about and believes in his students. Most observers believe that his willingness to be the strong and decisive commander-in-chief is a key to the current strength of Saint James. Many parents in today's boarding-school market are attracted to Saint James precisely because they want for their children what Dunnan and his colleagues are doing at Fountain Rock. While the headmaster believes firmly in the rule of law, he more firmly believes that a well-functioning school holding up the highest standards will have a lasting good effect on the moral development of human persons.[42]

The Art of a Schoolmaster

It should be obvious by now that Stuart Dunnan is an effective and successful head of school. In 1992, he and the trustees set goals and they have achieved them. Dunnan has been very concerned that Saint James

---

41. Dunnan, Private conversation with the editor, December 2018.

42. Dunnan believes that the great schools are "constitutional monarchies." While such schools are not democracies, neither are they run by heads with absolute power. Dunnan knows that the head of school is accountable not only to his conscience and to handbook protocols and standards of behavior; he or she is accountable to the Board of Trustees. It is very clear that Stuart Dunnan believes that the buck stops with him and that, if things go wrong, he is the responsible party. He has no confusion about the responsibility to serve the school as its "quality-control engineer." Such a leader will have opinions about everything and a plan ready to go.

be successful in its niche as a small but superlative boarding school. To remain faithful to the Christian tradition as Saint James has received it since 1842; to welcome all; to have a program wherein the whole child is thoroughly educated; to ably and intelligently serve both male and female in a single school; to have the facilities to deliver the mission goals; to be financially secure; and to be better known around the nation, especially by Episcopalians and parents who care about faith-based education: Each of these goals has been met by Father Dunnan and his trustee and staff colleagues.

But just as there is more to greatness than meeting strategic goals, there is more to Father Dunnan's headship than being an effective administrator. Running Saint James School is not just a big and satisfying job; it is a godly calling. Dunnan's total and consuming devotion to Saint James has been from the beginning a beautiful thing. Such committed and focused love is the crucial factor in the current greatness, ethos, and attractiveness of the school. Inspired by the apostolic witness of St. Paul and other admired saints, Dunnan early felt the vocation to celibacy. Dunnan recently remarked on a most solemn occasion,

> The real gift of celibacy is a gift of availability and time, the chance to do two jobs instead of one and to be available to help in many other ways as well . . . There is an emotional vulnerability to celibacy, a personal aloneness which allows the celibate to connect emotionally to more people and to connect more deeply. Like Mary when she hears the greeting of the Archangel Gabriel and accepts her unexpected and terrifying role as the Mother of the Son of God . . . we are called as Christians to offer ourselves with courage and humility to the loving and transforming purposes of God, to be like Christ, children of the Father to be used, broken, given by the Holy Spirit.[43]

Saint James School is the beneficiary of Dunnan's sacrifice. The School is the family he cherishes and for which he lays down his life. He is qualified for many other professions. He could easily be a scholar and professional historian. He could run a college or a university without difficulty. He could serve quite ably and wisely as a bishop, and would make a large impact in the Episcopal Church today. He would fully enjoy and doubtless be a sensational parish rector. But it would be a shame if Dunnan were doing any of these other jobs; for he has in twenty-six years

---

43. Dunnan, Homily for the Requiem for the Reverend Doctor F. Washington Jarvis.

made St. James a "light set upon the hill." Today Saint James is a model for others who are doing school in the twenty-first century.[44]

Throughout the years, Dunnan has maintained his strong sense of humor. He promised from the pulpit once that a good head of school will have "a robust ego, an open heart, a critical mind, and a ready smile."[45] The ready smile indicates an all-important virtue for a headmaster: a sense of humor.

Dunnan is able to see his failures and speak of them candidly. In the fall of 2016, he said to a trustee, "I had a lot to learn when I came to Saint James. And I sometimes think I haven't moved at times as quickly as someone else might have done. Someone else might've been able to raise money for the endowment more aggressively than I have done. But I am working on increasing the endowment now, and when I retire I hope we'll see an endowment of at least forty million, and we'll have the Fine Arts Center and the Athletic Center."

Father Dunnan almost died in the year 2000 due to an acute diverticulitis attack caused in some measure by overwork. The ever-faithful physician and trustee George Newman took care of Dunnan for four months. Says Dunnan of this ordeal, "I think that it was my most anchoring moment in relationship to the community of the School, and I shall always be grateful for it." It deepened the bond between the headmaster and the community he loved so well.

The Finishing Touch

Stuart Dunnan reports that "serving for many years in the same school is like living in the land of the becoming."[46] The one hundred and seventy-fifth year was the headmaster's twenty-sixth; he is now serving his twenty-ninth. Since 1992, Saint James School has moved from a barely known regional boarding school to the first choice of many families coming to Fountain Rock from far and near. It is commonplace to say that Father

---

44. The four oldest Episcopal boarding schools in the United States are the Episcopal High School in Alexandria, VA (1839), Saint James School and St. Mary's School in Raleigh, NC (1842), and Stuart Hall in Staunton, VA (1844).

45. The Installation of Robert Graves as Headmaster of Holland Hall, Tulsa, OK. Dunnan, *From the Pulpit*, 1:80.

46. The quotations are from the following sources in order: Dunnan, *From the Pulpit*, 2:182; Dunnan, *From the Pulpit*, 2:49; and Dunnan, *From the Pulpit*, 1:18 (1993 Letter to Parents on the Bonfire).

Dunnan has been most dedicated to Saint James. In fact, his utter devotion to the school and his manifest job-well-done reminds us of those great headmasters in American history, not the least, of Muhlenberg, Kerfoot, and their scholastic heirs in New England and elsewhere. Dunnan's intelligent dedication to the institution over nearly three decades is no less than inspiring. But, through all these years, it is the headmaster's dedication *to each student* that is most impressive. He firmly believes it his duty to ensure that each boy and each girl gains the opportunity to embody in his or her life the mission imperative of the School: to be "leaders for good in the world." For Dunnan, the mission ideals of Saint James are practical and beneficial to every student. Hence his paternal and personal touch as a head of school is of infinitely more value than what might be learned as a technique for successful businessmen. Father Dunnan's approach to headmastering has been a happy burden and has everything to do with the success of both the students and the institution.

Since 2017, the trustees have been working on a comprehensive strategic plan.[47] The objective is to ensure that Saint James is all it can be according to its historic mission ideals. The trustees want the school to be competitive in the market of the small boarding school. During the strategic planning, the subject of "the succession" has been broached. Father Dunnan is exemplary in his already-thoughtful planning for the transition to his successor a few years down the road. Dunnan intends to guarantee that the next head of Saint James and the school in general will gain the benefit of a flawless and happy transition when the time comes for his retirement from active duty. To Father Dunnan's great honor and credit, the trustees affirmed in June 2018 that the next headmaster of Saint James ought to be a priest of the church, if a qualified ordained person can be found. The trustees realize that a priest-headmaster brings gifts and graces critical to the identity and mission of Saint James School, but they also know that the day-to-day operation and administration of the school have benefitted enormously by this priest who is the headmaster.

It is a tradition at Saint James that, just before they make the procession to the steps of Claggett Hall, the senior class meets for one last time in the chapel. The headmaster uses the opportunity to address his beloved students in that well-used sacred space. The Class of 2018 heard the following thoughtful words:

---

47. The consultant for this work is Rob Hershey of Heads Up Educational Consulting. Hershey was for some years the celebrated head of the Episcopal High School, Alexandria. He is most impressed with what Saint James has become in its market.

The world you are entering is not exactly like Saint James, but that does not mean that Saint James has not prepared you. . . . You have learned, I hope, how to love here, how to be grateful, loyal, generous, and honest, and how to meet your challenges bravely and with success. So, always remember what we have taught you in this chapel; that you are only truly happy and truly blessed when you live a giving life and become yourself the gift that God intends.

For the opportunity to work very hard on behalf of the school for nearly three decades, Father Dunnan has one word: "Gratitude." He has given exemplary attention to the often tedious details of boarding school administration. He has been constant in prayer. He has provided indefatigable personal leadership, traveling all over the world to advance the school and extend a friendly hand to new prospects and alumni. He has an unending love for students, staff, parents, past-parents, grandparents, trustees, and many other friends in the large Saint James family of which he is the admired father. Faith, love, grace, hard work, and gratitude have enabled the Reverend Dr. D. Stuart Dunnan to make Saint James School one of the best in America.

Bibliography

Editor's Note

ALL SOURCES USED BY chapter authors, whether primary or secondary, are listed in the respective bibliographies of each. We heartily thank Mrs. Mary Klein, Archivist of the Maryland Diocesan Archives (MDA), Baltimore, for her expert help. Personnel at the Maryland Center for History and Culture, Baltimore, were more than generous. We also thank Mr. Ted Camp, Senior Master, History Chair, and Archivist of Saint James School, for his thoughtful advice and generosity to all concerned. The David K.M. Prehn Collection at Saint James School is a growing resource for any person interested in researching the national church school movement.

Correspondence and Recordings

Arthur A. Callaham
D. Stuart Dunnan
F. Washington Jarvis
Patrick Gahan
Theodore Camp
Todd FitzGerald

Chapter 1 Bibliography

Ahlstrom, Sydney E. *A Religious History of the American People.* New Haven: Yale University Press, 1972.
Bonomi, Patricia. *Under the Cope of Heaven.* New York: Oxford University Press, 1986.
Brewer, Clifton Hartwell. *A History of Religious Education in the Episcopal Church to 1835.* New Haven: Yale University Press, 1924.

Butler, Diana Hochstedt. *Standing Against the Whirlwind: Evangelical Episcopalians in Nineteenth-Century America*. New York: Oxford University Press, 1995.

Collini, Stefan. *Public Moralists: Political Thought and Intellectual Life in Britain 1850–1930*. Oxford: Clarendon, 1993.

Conkin, Paul Keith. *Cane Ridge: America's Pentecost*. Madison: University of Wisconsin Press, 1991.

Cross, Whitney. *The Burned-Over District: The Social and Intellectual History of Enthusiastic Religion in Western New York, 1800–1850*. Ithaca: Cornell University Press, 1950.

Dayton, Donald. *Discovering an Evangelical Heritage*. Peabody, MA: Hendrickson, 1976.

Finke, Roger, and Rodney Stark. *The Churching of America, 1776–1990*. New Brunswick, NJ: Rutgers University Press, 1992.

Hambrick-Stowe, Charles. *Charles G. Finney and the Spirit of American Evangelicalism*. Grand Rapids, MI: Eerdmans, 1996.

Harrison, Hall. *The Life of the Right Reverend John Barrett Kerfoot, D.D., LL.D., First Bishop of Pittsburgh*. 2 vols. New York: Pott, 1886.

Hein, David. "The High Church Origins of the American Boarding School." *Journal of Ecclesiastical History* 42 (1991) 577–95.

Hein, David, ed. *Religion and Politics in Maryland on the Eve of the Civil War: The Letters of W. Wilkins Davis*. 1988. Rev. ed. Eugene, OR: Wipf & Stock, 2009.

Hein, David, and Gardiner H. Shattuck. *The Episcopalians*. New York: Church Publishing, 2005.

Hill, Samuel S., et al., eds. *Encyclopedia of Religion in the South*. Macon, GA: Mercer University Press, 2005.

Holmes, David L. *A Brief History of the Episcopal Church*. Valley Forge, PA: Trinity Press International, 1993.

Isaac, Rhys. *The Transformation of Virginia, 1740–790*. Chapel Hill: University of North Carolina Press, 1999.

Mann, Arthur. *Yankee Reformers in the Urban Age*. Cambridge: Belknap, 1954.

Manross, William Wilson. *A History of the American Episcopal Church*. New York: Morehouse-Gorham, 1950.

McLachlan, James. *American Boarding Schools: A Historical Study*. New York: Scribner's, 1971.

McVicar, John, and Walter Farquhar Hook. *The Early Life and Professional Years of Bishop Hobart*. Oxford: Talboys, 1838.

Mullin, R. Bruce. *Episcopal Vision / American Reality: High Church Theology and Social Thought in Evangelical America*. New Haven: Yale University Press, 1986.

Noll, Mark A. *A History of Christianity in the United States and Canada*. Grand Rapids, MI: Eerdmans, 1992.

Noll, Mark A., et al., eds. *Evangelicalism: Comparative Studies of Popular Protestantism in North America, the British Isles, and Beyond, 1700–1990*. New York: Oxford University Press, 1994.

Perry, William Stevens. *History of the American Episcopal Church, 1587–1883*. 2 vols. New York: Osgood, 1885.

Prehn, W. L. "Episcopal Schools: History and Mission." In *The Praeger Handbook of Faith-Based Schools in the United States*, edited by Thomas C. Hunt and James C. Carper, 1:76–90. Santa Barbara: Praeger/CLIO, 2012.

Reid, Daniel G., et al., eds. *Dictionary of Christianity in America*. Downers Grove, IL: InterVarsity, 1990.

Shrimpton, Paul. *A Catholic Eton? Newman's Oratory School*. Warminster: Gracewing, 2005.

———. *'The Making of Men': The Idea and Reality of Newman's University in Oxford and Dublin*. Warminster: Gracewing, 2014.

Smith, Timothy L. *Revivalism and Social Reform: American Protestantism on the Eve of the Civil War*. New York: Harper, 1957.

Tiffany, Charles C. *A History of the Protestant Episcopal Church in the United States of America*. New York: Scribner's, 1903.

Wood, Gordon. *The Radicalism of the American Revolution*. New York: Vintage, 1993.

Chapter 2 Bibliography

Arnold, Matthew. "Emerson." In *Discourses in America*, 138–226. 1885. London: Macmillan, 1912.

———. "Preface." In *Culture and Anarchy*, vi–xxxvii. London: Smith, Elder, 1869.

Ayres, Anne. *The Life and Work of William Augustus Muhlenberg, D.D.* New York: Harper, 1881.

Brand, William Francis. *Life of William Rollinson Whittingham, Fourth Bishop of Maryland*. 2 vols. New York: E. & J. B. Young, 1886.

Church, Richard William. *The Oxford Movement: Twelve Years, 1833–1845*. London: Macmillan, 1891.

Coit, Henry Augustus. "An American Boys' School—What It Should Be." *The Forum*, September 1891.

Coit, Joseph Howland. "Recollections of Bishop Kerfoot's Life and Work at St. James's." In *The Life of the Right Reverend John Barrett Kerfoot, D.D., LL.D., First Bishop of Pittsburgh*, by Hall Harrison, vol. 1:319–70. New York: Pott, 1886. Also filed in the Owens Library Archives, Saint James School, Maryland.

Collini, Stefan. *Public Moralists: Political Thought and Intellectual Life in Britain 1850–1930*. Oxford: Clarendon, 1993

"Columba, St." In *The Oxford Dictionary of the Christian Church*, edited by F. L. Cross and E. A. Livingstone, 379–80. 3rd ed. Oxford: Oxford University Press, 1997.

Cross, F. L., and Elizabeth A. Livingstone, eds. *The Oxford Dictionary of the Christian Church*. 3rd rev. ed. Oxford: Oxford University Press, 2005.

DeLaura, David. *Hebrew and Hellene in Victorian England: Newman, Arnold, and Pater*. Austin: University of Texas Press, 1969.

Douglas, Ann. *The Feminization of American Culture*. New York: Knopf, 1977.

Harrison, Hall. *The Life of the Right Reverend John Barrett Kerfoot, D.D., LL.D., First Bishop of Pittsburgh*. 2 vols. New York: Pott, 1886.

Hein, David. *Religion and Politics on the Eve of the Civil War: The Letters of W. Wilkins Davis*. Eugene, OR: Wipf & Stock, 2009.

Honey, J. R. de S. *Tom Brown's Universe*. Chicago: Quadrangle, 1977.

Hopkins, John Henry. *Memoir of the Reverend Milo Mahan. D.D.* New York: Pott, Young, 1875. anglicanhistory.org/usa/mahan/memoir.html.

Johnson, Allen, and Dumas Malone. *Dictionary of American Biography*. Vol. 10. New York: Scribner's, 1943.

Kaestle, Carl F., ed. *Joseph Lancaster and the Monitorial School System: A Documentary History*. New York: Teachers College Press, 1973.

Bibliography

Kerfoot, John B. *An Address to the Parents and Guardians of the Pupils in St. James's Hall, Washington County, Maryland.* New York: Sparks, 1843. Pamphlet File, MDA.

———. "Education Catholic: Part 1." *The True Catholic* (June 1, 1843) 60–65. Baltimore, MD, 1843. Bound Journals, Maryland Diocesan Archives.

———. "Education Catholic: Part 2." *The True Catholic* (August 1, 1843) 156–61. Baltimore, MD, 1843. Bound Journals, Maryland Diocesan Archives.

———. *The Faithful Parent.* Baltimore: Jos. Robinson, 1850. Pamphlet File, MDA.

———. "Prospectus for St. James's Hall [1841]." Pamphlet File, MDA.

———. *A Statement of the Studies, Discipline, Order, &c., of St. James's Hall, Near Hagers-Town, MD, December 1842.* Pamphlet File, MDA.

———. *Three Addresses from the Commencements of the College of St. James.* Washington County, MD: Fountain Rock, 1848. Pamphlet File, MDA.

Muhlenberg, William A. *The Application of Christianity to Education. Being the Principles and Plan of Education to be Adopted in the Institute of Flushing, L.I.* Jamaica, L.I., New York: Sleight & George, 1828.

———. *Christian Education: An Address by Wm. Augustus Muhlenberg Delivered after a Public Examination of the Students of the Institute at Flushing, L.I. and an Essay on the Study of the Classics on Christian Principles, by Samuel Seabury.* New York: Protestant Episcopal, 1831.

Newman, John Henry. *Fifteen Sermons Preached Before the University of Oxford.* London: Rivingtons, 1871.

———. *Parochial and Plain Sermons.* 8 vols. Edited by William J. Copeland. London: Rivingtons, 1876 (volume 1 first published in 1839).

Newton, William Wilberforce. *Dr. Muhlenberg.* American Religious Leaders. Boston: Houghton Mifflin, 1891.

Parker, Eric, ed. *Floreat: An Eton Anthology.* London: Nisbet, 1923.

Prichard, Robert W. *A History of the Episcopal Church.* 2nd ed. Harrisburg:Morehouse, 1999.

———. *The Nature of Salvation: Theological Consensus in the Episcopal Church, 1801–1873.* Champaign, IL: University of Illinois Press, 1997.

Register of the College of St. James, and the Grammar School; Washington County, Maryland, for the Tenth Session, 1851–52. Fountain Rock, MD: College of St. James, 1852. (Printed in Baltimore by Joseph Robinson.)

Rudolph, Frederick. *The American College & University: A History* [1962]. Athens: University of Georgia Press, 1990.

———. *Curriculum: A History of the American Undergraduate Course of Study since 1636.* San Francisco: Jossey-Bass, 1977.

Skardon, Alvin. *William Augustus Muhlenberg: Church Leader in the Cities.* Philadelphia: University of Pennsylvania Press, 1971.

Whewell, William. *On the Principles of English University Education.* London: Parker, 1837.

Whittingham, William R. "Bishop's Address." *Journal of the Proceedings of the Council of the Episcopal Diocese of Maryland, 1864.* Baltimore: Robinson, 1865.

———. "Bishop's Address." *Journal of the Proceedings of the Council of the Episcopal Diocese of Maryland, 1841.* Baltimore: Robinson, 1842.

———. Whittingham Papers, MDA, Baltimore, Maryland.

Chapter 3 Bibliography

Alexander, Ted. "'A Regular Slave Hunt': The Army of Northern Virginia and Black Civilians in the Gettysburg Campaign." *North & South* 4.7 (September 2001) 85–88.

Amt, Emilie. "Down From the Balcony: African Americans and Episcopal Congregations in Washington County, Maryland, 1800–1864." *Anglican and Episcopal History* 86.1 (March 2017) 1–42.

Bates, Samuel P. *History of Pennsylvania Volunteers, 1861–1865*. Vol. 5. Harrisburg, PA: Singerly, 1871.

Bingham, Charles. "A Little Boy in Maryland during the Civil War." In *Crossroads of War: Washington County, Maryland in the Civil War*, edited by S. Roger Keller, 36–55. Shippensburg, Pennsylvania: Burd Street Press, 1997.

Brand, William Francis. *Life of William Rollinson Whittingham, Fourth Bishop of Maryland*. 2 vols. New York: E & J. B. Young, 1883.

Bunting, Jay. "Did You Know? Oxford Cadet Accepted Truce at Appomattox." *The Oxford Historian* (newsletter). Oxford, MD: Oxford Museum, 2008.

Census Data, National Archives and Records Administration, 1820–1860. Digital images at Ancestry.com. *1860 Census, Montgomery County, MD, First District, Slave Schedule p. 7*, NARA (National Archives and Records Administration) M653. All census citations are from digital images at Ancestry.com and refer to population schedules for Washington County, MD, unless otherwise noted.

Centennial Portrait and Biographical Record of the City of Dayton and of Montgomery County, Ohio, containing Biographical Sketches of Prominent and Representative Citizens. Edited by Frank Conover. Dayton: Bowen, 1897.

Coit, Joseph Howland. *Hall Harrison, 1837–1900*. Concord, NH: Privately printed, n.d.

Creighton, Margaret S. "Living on the Fault Line: African American Civilians and the Gettysburg Campaign." In *The War Was You and Me: Civilians in the American Civil War*, edited by Joan E. Cashin, 209–36. Princeton: Princeton University Press, 2002.

Cuthbert, Samuel S. "Naked in the Midst of Armies: The College of St. James, 1861–1864" (unpublished MS., 1994). Hagerstown, MD: Western Maryland Room, vertical file: "St. James College."

Davis, Angela Kirkham. "War Remembrances." In *Crossroads of War: Washington County, Maryland, in the Civil War*, edited by S. Roger Keller, 3–35. Shippensburg, Pennsylvania: White Mane, 1997.

Douglas, Henry Kyd. *I Rode with Stonewall: The War Experiences of the Youngest Member of Jackson's Staff*. Chapel Hill: University of North Carolina Press, 1968.

Duncan, Richard R. "The College of St. James and the Civil War: A Casualty of War." *Historical Magazine of the Protestant Episcopal Church* 39 (Sept 1970) 265–86.

"Family-Papers-Warfield-Allen-Doleman." http://archives.dolemanblackheritagemuseum.org/documents/Family-Papers-Warfield-Allen-Dolemam.pdf.

Grivno, Max. *Gleanings of Freedom: Free and Slave Labor along the Mason-Dixon Line, 1790–1860*. Urbana: University of Illinois Press, 2011.

Hait, Michael. *The Civil War Draft in Maryland: Lists of Drafted Men, 1862–1865*. Washington, DC: Hait Family History Research Services, 2010.

Harrison, Hall. *Life of the Right Reverend John Barrett Kerfoot, D.D., LL.D., First Bishop of Pittsburgh*. Vol. 1. New York: Pott, 1886.

Harvey, Frank J. "The College of St. James During the Civil War: 'It Will Stand.'" *St. James School Review* (Winter 1995) 10–12; (Spring/Summer 1995) 14–16.

Heckscher, August. *St. Paul's: The Life of a New England School*. New York: Scribner's, 1980.

Hein, David. *Religion and Politics in Maryland on the Eve of the Civil War: The Letters of W. Wilkins Davis*. Eugene, OR: Wipf & Stock, 2009.

Henry, Thomas W. *From Slavery to Salvation: The Autobiography of the Rev. Thomas W. Henry of the A.M.E. Church*. Edited by Jean Libby. Jackson: University Press of Mississippi, 1994.

The Herald of Freedom & Torch Light. Hagerstown, MD, 1853–1864.

Journals of the Annual Conventions of the Diocese of Maryland. https://catalog.hathitrust.org/Record/008634664.

Keller, S. Roger. *Events of the Civil War in Washington County, Maryland*. Shippensburg, PA: Burd Street, 1995.

Kerfoot, John B. Letters to Bishop William R. Whittingham and Others. Maryland Diocesan Archives, Baltimore, MD.

Landrum, J. B. O. *History of Spartanburg County*. Atlanta: Franklin, 1900.

Litwack, Leon F. *Been in the Storm So Long: The Aftermath of Slavery*. New York: Vintage, 1980.

Manning, Chandra. *What This Cruel War Was Over: Soldiers, Slavery, and the Civil War*. New York: Vintage, 2008.

McLachlan, James, ed. "The Civil War Diary of Joseph H. Coit." *Maryland Historical Magazine* 60.3 (September 1965).

Miles, G. H. *"Grandma," Or, the Life of Mrs. Eliza Miles*. Carthage, NC: Privately printed, n.d. (Western Maryland Room, Hagerstown, Maryland).

Mitchell, Charles W., ed. *Maryland Voices of the Civil War*. Baltimore: Johns Hopkins University Press, 2007.

Munson, E. B., ed. *North Carolina Civil War Obituaries*. Jefferson, NC: McFarland, 2015.

National Archives and Records Administration and/or Census. *Carded Records Showing Military Service of Soldiers Who Fought in Confederate Organizations*.

———. *Civil War Records and Basic Research Sources*. https://www.archives.gov/research/military/civil-war/resources.

———. *Index to Compiled Service Records of Volunteer Union Soldiers Who Served in Organizations from the State of Pennsylvania* (1965), M554. https://www.fold3.com/title/793/civil-war-service-index-union-pennsylvania/description.

———. *U.S. Census Records*. Digital images at Ancestry.com.

———. *Civil War Data*. https://www.archives.gov.

National Park Service. *U.S. Civil War Soldiers, 1861–1865* (online); Register, 1854.

"The Negro Regiment Bill before Congress." *The American and Commercial Advertiser* (Baltimore), Jan. 31, 1863, 2.

Nelson, Russell. *Reminiscences*. Privately printed, 1973.

Nesbitt, Otho. Diary entries in *Windmills of Time*, edited by David E. Wiles. Clear Spring, Maryland: Clear Spring Alumni Association, 1981.

New York, Civil War Muster Roll Abstracts, 1861–1900. https://www.ancestry.com/search/collections/1965/.

Onderdonk, Adrian Holmes. *Memoirs* [1952]. Edited by Stevenson W. Webster. St. James, MD: Privately printed, 1974.

Phillips, David. *Maps of the Civil War: The Roads They Took*. New York: MetroBooks, 1998.
Pipkin, A. P. "The (Almost) Battle of St. James College," *St. James School Review* (Fall 2009) 27–29; (Winter 2010) 24–25; (Spring 2010) 38–39.
Register of the College of St. James and the Grammar School. Several Volumes for the Years 1843 to 1863. Maryland Historical Society, Baltimore, MD.
Sharpe, John. *Growing Up with Raleigh: Smedes York: Memoirs and Reflections of a Native Son*. Raleigh, NC: Privately published, 2014.
Smith, James Ripley. Diary in *Hancock, 1776–1976*. Edited by Emily Leatherman. Privately printed, 1976.
St. Mark's Parish Register (various volumes). Boonsboro, MD: St. Mark's Parish (Lappans).
Washington County Circuit Court (Land Records) 1858–1859, IN 13, 298–99, MSA CE 18-18 (online).
Wilder, Craig Steven. *Ebony and Ivory: Race, Slavery, and the Troubled History of America's Universities*. New York: Bloomsbury, 2013.

Chapter 4 Bibliography

Adams, Henry. *The Education of Henry Adams: An Autobiography* [1907]. Cambridge: The Riverside Press for the Massachusetts Historical Society, 1918.
Alford, Terry. *Fortune's Fool: The Life of John Wilkes Booth*. New York: Oxford University Press, 2014.
"At Saint James Dies Mrs. Onderdonk at Age of 80 Years." *Hagerstown Daily Mail*, May 28, 1916.
Callcott, George H. *A History of the University of Maryland*. Baltimore: Maryland Historical Society, 1966.
Dawley, Powel Mills. *The Story of the General Theological Seminary: A Sesquicentennial History, 1817–1967*. New York: Oxford University Press, 1969.
Duncan, Richard R. "The Impact of the Civil War on Education in Maryland." *Maryland Historical Magazine*, March 1966.
"Henry Onderdonk." https://c1.staticflickr.com/7/6034/6258589333_e430f62f49_b.jpg.
Diocese of Maryland. "Journal of the Ninety-Fourth Annual Convention." https://babel.hathitrust.org/cgi/pt?id=nyp.33433070793744&view=1up&seq=11.
———. "Journal of the Ninety-Fifth Annual Convention." https://babel.hathitrust.org/cgi/pt?id=nyp.33433070793744&view=1up&seq=11.
———. "Journal of the Ninety-Seventh Annual Convention." https://babel.hathitrust.org/cgi/pt?id=nyp.33433070793744&view=1up&seq=11.
———. "Journal of the One Hundredth Annual Convention." https://babel.hathitrust.org/cgi/pt?id=nyp.33433070793736&view=1up&seq=11.
———. "Journal of the One Hundred Fourth Annual Convention." https://babel.hathitrust.org/cgi/pt?id=nyp.33433070793710&view=1up&seq=11.
Lawrence, John E. "The Episcopate of Benjamin Tredwell Onderdonk, IV Bishop of New York." http://anglicanhistory.org/usa/btonderdonk/lawrence1970.pdf.
"Mary Onderdonk."https://www.myheritage.com/names/mary_onderdonk;
McCalla, John Moore. Diary.

McCoy, Stephen. "Frederick W. Brune (1776–1860)." https://www.immigrant entrepreneurship.org/entry.php?rec=113.

Minaya, Mariana. "Divided by War." *The Diamondback*, September 14, 2005.

Norris, Heather. "Catonsville's Connection to Lincoln Assassin John Wilkes Booth." *Catonsville Times*, April 14, 2015. http://www.baltimoresun.com/news/maryland/baltimore-county/catonsville/ph-ca-booth-student-0408-20150414-story.html.

Onderdonk, Adrian Holmes. *Memoirs of Adrian Holmes Onderdonk*. Edited by Stevenson W. Webster. St. James, Maryland: Privately printed, 1974 (Saint James School Archives).

Onderdonk, Henry. *A History of Maryland Upon the Basis of McSherry, For the Use of Schools*. Baltimore: John Murphy, 1868.

———. *Sources by and about Henry Onderdonk*. Maryland Diocesan Archives, Episcopal Diocese of Maryland, Baltimore, MD.

———. "St. James Commencement." *Hagerstown Herald and Torch Light*, June 25, 1885.

Perry, William Stevens. *The Bishops of the American Church, Past and Present*. New York: Christian Literature, 1897.

Prehn, W. L. "Saint James School at 175." https://www.scribd.com/document/376018493/WL-Prehn-Saint-James-School-at-175.

"Presidents of the Baltimore and Ohio." http://borail.net/Presidents.html.

Rudolph, William, and A. Kate Sheerin. *Julian Onderdonk: American Impressionist*. Dallas: Dallas Museum of Art, 2008.

Saint James School Archives, Hagerstown, MD. Document produced for "The 125th Anniversary of Saint James School." 1967.

"Samuel Gerish Wyman." https://www.findagrave.com/memorial/48918685/samuel-gerish-wyman.

Steven. "A College Divided: University of MD (Maryland Agricultural College) During the Civil War." *Civil War Washington, D.C.* (blog), September 7, 2011. http://civilwarwashingtondc1861-1865.blogspot.com/2011/09/college-divided-university-of-md.html.

Waldonia. "A Life of Honor and Piety: Mary Latrobe Onderdonk." *Photographicus Baltimorensis* (blog), January 6, 2013. https://19thcenturybaltimore.wordpress.com/2013/01/06/a-life-of-honor-and-piety-mary-latrobe-onderdonk/.

"War of the Rebellion." https://ehistory.osu.edu/books/official-records/114/0670.

Wyatt-Brown, Bertram. *The House of Percy: Honor, Melancholy, and Imagination in a Southern Family*. New York: Oxford University Press, 1994.

Chapter 5 Bibliography

"Charles Hartwell." https://en.wikipedia.org/wiki/Charles_Hartwell.

Garraty, John A., and Mark C. Carnes. *American National Biography*. 24 vols. New York: Oxford University Press, 1999.

Hein, David. "Henry St. George Tucker." In *American National Biography*, edited by John A. Garraty and Mark C. Carnes, 21:895–96. 24 vols. New York: Oxford University Press, 1999.

Sargent, Porter E. *Handbook of the Best Private Schools in the United States and Canada*. Boston: Sargent, 1920.

Chapter 6 Bibliography

The Book of Common Prayer and Administration of the Sacraments and Other Rites and Ceremonies of the Church, Together with The Psalter or Psalms of David, According to the use of The Episcopal Church. New York: Oxford University Press, 2007.
A Brief History of Saint James School. Owens Library Archives.
Brooks, David. *The Road to Character.* New York: RandomHouse, 2015.
Owens, John. *Address to the Episcopal Diocese of Easton, Maryland, April 5, 1968.* Easton: Diocesan Journal, 1959.
———. *Philosophy of Saint James School.* Fountain Rock, MD: Saint James School, 1958.

Chapter 7 Bibliography

Callaham, Arthur A. Dean of Christ Church Cathedral, Houston. Note to the editor.
Camp, Theodore A. Senior Master, History Chair, and Archivist, Saint James School. Recorded conversation with the editor.
Dunnan, D. Stuart. *From the Pulpit of Saint James.* Vol. 1, *Collected Thoughts of a Priest Headmaster.* Canton, MA: Watson, 2002.
———. *From the Pulpit of Saint James,* Vol. 2, *Further Thoughts of a Priest Headmaster.* Canton, MA: Watson, 2009.
———. Headmaster of Saint James School. Recorded conversations.
———. *A Homily for the Requiem for the Reverend Doctor F. Washington Jarvis, Saturday 13 October 2018, All Saints Church Ashmont, Dorchester, Massachusetts.* Manuscript. Saint James School Archives.
———. "Sermon Preached at the Pusey House, Oxford (October 1992)." *The Journal of the Friends of Pusey House* (Fall 1992).
Evans, Rob. *The Human Side of School Change: Reform, Resistance, and the Real-Life Problems of Innovation.* San Francisco: Josey-Bass, 1996.
Gahan, W. Patrick, III. Rector of Christ Church, San Antonio. Note to the editor.
Ignatius, David. "Canon Martin." *The Washington Post,* May 5, 1997.
Jarvis, F. Washington. Late Headmaster of Roxbury Latin School. Conversations with the editor.
Journal of the Friends of Pusey House. Oxford: Pusey. Published semi-annually.
Lewis, C. S. *Mere Christianity.* London: Macmillan, 1952.
Temple, William. *Repton School Sermons: Studies in the religion of the Incarnation: Being the sermons preached in Repton School Chapel between September 1910 and July 1912.* London: Macmillan, 1914.
"William Temple." In *The Oxford Dictionary of the Christian Church,* edited by F. L. Cross and E. A. Livingstone, 1986. 3rd ed. Oxford: Oxford University Press, 1997.

Index of Names

Adams, Henry, 99
Adley, Mary, 54
Aisquith, Henry, 75
Allen, Rusty, 142
Anselm of Canterbury, St., 44
Arnold, Samuel, 90
Arnold, Thomas, 20, 41, 122
Arnold, Matthew, 30
Arthur, Chester A., 97
Ayres, Anne, 19

Badger, Richard C., 82
Baker, Richard H., Jr., 139, 149
Bankard, Jacob J., 73
Barnam, Isaac, 120
Barr, David, 142, 171
Barr, Betty, 152
Baxter, L., 115
Beldon, George, 142
Belt, Edward, 66
Bergen, Walter, 172
Biggs, Jeremy, 169
Black, Ernest, 127
Blackiston, William Thomas, 79
Boddie, Mayo, 169
Bonner, Kenneth, 141
Booth, John Wilkes, 90
Bowie, Robert, 99
Boyd, Hunter, 83
Boteler, Silas, 73
Bowman, Samuel, 49
Boyle, Francis Atherton, 74
Breathed, John W. 57, 82
Breck, James Lloyd, 18
Brooks, Kitty, 55, 56

Brown, Arthur George, 64
Brown, George (mayor), 94
Brown, George (Owens era student), 149
Brune, Frederick W (second), 94
Bull, George, 36
Burke, Edmund, 43
Burt, Nathaniel, 129
Butler, Joseph, 46

Callaham, Arthur A., 161
Calvert, George Lord Baltimore, 2
Camp, Theodore, xi, 161
Campbell, Mason, 94
Campbell, John G., 122, 127, 136
Campbell, Thomas, 118, 122
Carden, Frank, 142
Carter, Bernard, 117
Carter, Shirley, 99
Carter, Julian, 99
Cicero, Marcus Tullius, 46
Chase (Latin master), 115
Chase, Philander, 9
Chase, William Merritt, 96
Chesley, James Belt, 80
Coit, Joseph 46, 48, 51, 72–73
Coit, Henry Augustus, 45
Coleridge, Samuel Taylor, 43
Clarkson, M.C. 55
Collin, Marty, 174
Collins (waiter), 54
Columba of Iona, St., 19
Conkin, Paul 5
Conyngham, John Redmond, 61
Coster, Robert, 69, 79, 84

Index of Names

Cotton, Henry Edward, 140
Coxe, Arthur Cleveland, 94
Crawford, Jane, 129
Crocker, John, 144

Dashiell, Julius, 53
Davenport, Henry, 169
Davis, Ann, 169
Davis, Ellen, 139
Davis, John, 169
Davis, W. Wilkins, 23, 31, 34, 35, 51
Dean, Edward Jefferson, 59
Diggs, Jerningham, 119
Diggs, Letitia, 84, 121
Dinsmore, Robert, 127, 129
Dorsey, Ellen, 54
Douglas, Henry Kyd, 82
Duckett, Joseph Gabby, 63
Dunham, J.A. (of Boys' Latin), 114
Dunnan, Bruce B., 159
Dunnan, Charlie, 164
Dunnan, Diana Baldwin, 159
Dunnan, Douglas M., 159
Dunnan, Donald, 159
Dunnan, D. Stuart, xi, 154ff.
Dunnan, John McMillan, 159
Dunnan, Weaver W., 159

Eagles, Ted, 142, 172
Early, Jubal, 83, 91
Earp, Samuel, 80
Eastman, Bishop Theodore, 144
Edmundson, Thomas G., 72

Falk, Bertha, 78
Falk, Alexander, 53, 84
Faust, Winifred Dunnan, 159
Febri, George, 53
Ferguson, John, 168
Finney, Charles Grandison, 4
FitzGerald, Todd, 164
Forbush, Byron, 151
Frankfurter, Felix, 159
Fulton Adna, 168
Fulton, Barbara, 168

Gahan, W. Patrick III, 163
Giles, John Redmon, 81

Giles, William (senior), 81
Giles, William B., 81
Giles, Clayton, 81
Gormley, George Aston, 68
Grab, Robert, 139
Graves, Robert, 177
Griswold, Alexander Viets, 6
Griswold, B.B., 87

Hand, Learned, 159
Harrison, Charley, 78
Harrison, James H., 116, 117
Harrison, Hall, 76, 78, 85, 99
Harrison, William G., 58, 94
Hartman, Paul, 53
Hartwell, Charles, 122, 123
Hayden, George, 79
Haywood, Duncan C., 65
Haywood, Graham, 66
Heighe, J.C., 73
Hein, David, 44, 45
Hershey, Rob, 178
Hill, George, 142
Hobart, John Henry, 6
Holloway, Admiral James L. III, 169, 172
Hollyday, Henry, 75
Hooper, Henry C., 76
Hopkins, George 142
Howard, Alfred, 57
Howe, Charles Avery, 68
Hoyer, Eddie, 139, 142, 171
Hoyer, Larry, 142
Hughes, Chris, 173
Hughes, Walton, 75
Hunt, Robert, 1

Ives, Levi Silliman, 56

James, Aleda, 142
Jarvis, F. Washington, 176
Jefferson, Thomas, 3
Johnson, Bradley, 91
Jones, Sophia, 54

Keating, Henry W., 117, 118, 126
Kellett, Vernon B., 141
Kemp, James, 89
Kemper, Jackson, 9, 19

Index of Names

Kerfoot, Abel, 53, 66
Kerfoot, Annie, 53, 66
Kerfoot, Catherine, 53
Kerfoot Helen, 53
Kerfoot, Eliza Anderson, 47, 53
Kerfoot, John Barrett, 12, 51, 87, 146, 147
Keyes, Samuel, 164
Klein, Mary, xi

Laidlaw, Elliott, 133, 134
Langford, "Zig," 126
Langford, A.M., 123, 124, 125
Latrobe, Benjamin H., 16, 96
Latrobe, Benjamin, H., Jr., 96
Latrobe, Osman, 75
Latrobe, Richard S., 73
Lee, Fitzhugh, 90
Lee, John Boykin, 59
Lee, Robert E., 66, 90
Leighton, Bishop David K., 144
Lieberman, Mike, 151
Lincoln, Abraham, 51, 71, 83
Locke, John, 42
Longstreet, James, 74, 75
Lyman, Theodore Benedict, 17, 18

Mahan, Milo, 19, 22
Marsh, Elisha, M.D., 68
Martin, Canon Charles, 152, 155
Mattingly, John, 167, 169
McCleary, Dick, 169
McDowell, William G., 118, 121
McIntyre, James Byrd, 141
McIntyre, John Sharpless, 141
McIntyre, John Sharpless, Jr., 141
McLachlan, James, x, 47
McMillan, John, 159
McSherry, James, 91
Meade, William Creighton, 80
Meade, George (general)
Meade, William (bishop), 22
Mealey, Edward W., 80
Meehan, Charles "Chick," 139, 142, 149, 150, 171, 172, 174
Merchant, John, 149, 164
Minter, Drew, 159
Mohn, Eric, 148

Montgomery, Brandt, 164
Montgomery, Bishop James Winchester, 151
Moore, Richard Channing, 8
Muhlenberg, William Augustus, 9, 16ff., 90, 147
Murray, Bishop John Gardner, 130, 131, 133

Nes, Charles, 168
Nelson, Russell, 127, 142
Newman, George, M.D., 177
Newman, John Henry, St., 11, 36
Nicholson, John Joseph, 75
Norris, Carlyle, 69

O'Loughlin, Michael, 90
Onderdonk, Adrian (headmaster), xi, 97, 98
Onderdonk, Adrian (headmaster Adrian's son), 136
Onderdonk, Andrew (headmaster Henry's son), 96
Onderdonk, Bishop Benjamin T., 87, 88, 89, 94, 107
Onderdonk, Evelynne Richardson, 126
Onderdonk, Harriette Henry, 96, 107
Onderdonk, Henry (headmaster), xi, 88
Onderdonk, Henry U. II, "Harry" (headmaster Henry's son), 96
Onderdonk, Bishop Henry U., 88, 107
Onderdonk, Henry II (headmaster Adrian's son), 136
Onderdonk, Julian (headmaster Henry's grandson), 96
Onderdonk, Latrobe (headmaster Henry's son), 97
Onderdonk, Mary Elizabeth Latrobe, 96, 107
Onderdonk, Richardson (headmaster Adrian's son), 136
Onderdonk, Robert Jenkins (headmaster Henry's son), 96, 107
Onderdonk, William, 107
Otey, James Hervey, 19
Owens, John E., 139ff.

Paret, Bishop William, 117
Passmore, John, 53, 65
Passmore, Joseph, 94
Passmore, Susan, 53
Peabody, Endicott, 35
Pearce, Ellen, 54
Pearce, Sally, 54
Peeker, Catharine, 57
Percival, Bishop John 157
Pipkin, Ashmead, 141
Pipkin, Benton, 141
Pipkin, Rush, 141
Pitts, Charles H., 73, 77
Pitts, Thomas D., 73, 80
Pohanka, Anne Kline, 169
Pohanka, Geoffry, 169
Pollock, Sandra, 173, 174
Porter, Eliza, 47, 53
Porter, Fitz-John, 53
Powell, Bishop Noble C., 140

Ramseur, Dodson, 82
Reichard, John, 55
Rich, Ernest, 99, 115, 121
Richardson, William C., 126
Ridgely, John, 134
Ringer, John, 55
Ringgold, Samuel, 17, 33
Roberts, Charles, 142
Robison, Eliza, 56
Russell, Frank, 142

Sargent, Porter E., 119
Schley, Frederick, 70
Scott, Walter, 37
Scull, Charles O., 130, 131
Shakespeare, William, 97
Shattuck, George Cheyne, 79, 81
Slingluff, Harry, 99
Smith, Captain John, 1
Snodgrass, Isaac B., 74
Sparks, Jared, 49
Stark, Coach, 127
Stein, Jay, 144
Strout, Charles W., 127, 132
Stuart, King Charles, 1
Stuyvesant, Peter G., 89
Swope, Cornelius, 58

Taylor, Jeremy, 36
Teach, Stuart, 169
Temple, Archbishop William, 157
Thomas, Edwin, 75
Thompson, Ellen, 57
Trevett, Russell, 39, 55
Tucker, Bishop Henry St. George, 118
Turner, Jim, 169
Turner, Toni, 169

Ursell, Philip, 155

Van Bokkelen, Libertus, 19, 90, 107, 108
Van Horn, Ellen, 54
Vergil (Virgil), 23

Waddell, Lucien P., 53, 69
Waltersdorf, John, 168
Waltersdorf, Peggy, 168
Watson, Al, 142, 171
Webster, Eleanor Blodgett, 141
Webster, Stevenson W., 108, 126, 142
Webster, William, 141
Weddell, John Archibald, 73
Weisel, Daniel, 80
Westcott, Brooke Foss, 23
Whewell, William, 31
Whittingham, William Rollinson, 11, 15ff., 47, 55, 89, 94, 95
Williams, A.S., 61
Wilson, Thomas, 356
Winsor, Frederick, 115
Wivell, Bill, 170
Wood, Gordon, 2
Woodruff, Don, 142
Woodruff, Mary, 142
Wykeham, Bishop William of, 27
Wyman, Samuel, 94

Violet (a servant), 55

Xenophon, 23

Yergey, Karl, 174
Yonge, Charlotte, 37
Young, Dona, 169
Young, Roland, 169

www.ingramcontent.com/pod-product-compliance
Lightning Source LLC
Chambersburg PA
CBHW051736230426
43670CB00012B/2051